Trading Women's Health and Rights?

Trade Liberalization and Reproductive Health in Developing Economies

edited by Caren Grown, Elissa Braunstein and Anju Malhotra

Z

ZED BOOKS
London & New York

Trading Women's Health and Rights? Trade Liberalization and Reproductive Health in Developing Economies was first published in 2006 by Zed Books Ltd., 7 Cynthia Street, London N1 9 and Room 400, 175 Fifth Avenue, New York, NY 10 www.zedbooks.co.uk

Cover designed by Andrew Corbett

Photo credit:
© 1997 Deborah S. Doyle, Courtesy of Photoshare

Caption: A woman in Cairo, Egypt

Disclaimer: Photoshare images used in this material are
for illustrative purposes only. They do not imply any
particular health status, attitudes, behaviors, or actions on
the part of any person who appears in the photograph.

Typeset by Exeter Premedia Services Private Ltd., Chennai, India
Printed and bound in the UK by Biddles Ltd., King's Lynn

Distributed in the USA exclusively by Palgrave Macmillan,
a division of St. Martin's Press, LLC, 175 Fifth Avenue,
New York, NY 10010

A catalogue record for this book is available from the British Library
US CIP data is available from the Library of Congress

ISBN 1 84277 774 2 (Hb)
ISBN 1 84277 775 0 (Pb)

ISBN 978 1 84277 774 9 (Hb)
ISBN 978 1 84277 775 6 (Pb)

Contents

CONTENTS

CONTENTS

CONTENTS

List of Tables

List of Figures

List of Abbreviations

ACWF	All China Women's Federation
AIDS	acquired immune deficiency syndrome
ARV	antiretroviral
ASEAN	Association for Southeast Asian Nations
BIP	Border Industrialization Program
CAFTA	Central America Free Trade Agreement
CHMT	community health management team
CIPR	Commission on Intellectual Property Rights
CIS	Commonwealth Independent States
COSATU	Congress of South African Trade Unions
DAS	district administrative secretary
DED	district executive director
DfID	Department for International Development
DoH	Department of Health
DPE	domestic private enterprise
DPO	district planning officer
ECJ	European Court of Justice
EIU	Economist Intelligence Unit
EPZ	export processing zone
EU	European Union
FDA	Food and Drug Administration
FDI	foreign direct investment
FGD	focus group discussion
FGM	female genital mutilation
FIE	foreign-invested enterprise
FIRST	Full Impact Review and Screening of Trade
FPASL	Family Planning Association of Sri Lanka
FTZ	free trade zone
GATS	General Agreement on Trade in Services
GDP	gross domestic product
GEP	gender-specific environmental parameter
GNP	gross national product

GTAC	Global Treatment Action Campaign
HAART	highly active antiretroviral therapy
HIV	human immunodeficiency virus
ICM	International Confederation of Midwives
ICPD	International Conference on Population and Development
ICRW	International Center for Research on Women
IIPI	International Intellectual Property Institute
ILO	International Labour Organization
IMF	International Monetary Fund
IMSS	Mexican Institute of Social Security
IoM	Institute of Medicine
IPR	intellectual property rights
IUD	intrauterine device
LDC	least developed countries
MCH	maternal and child health
MDG	Millennium Development Goals
MERCOSUR	Southern (America) Common Market
MFA	Multi-Fibre Agreement
MFN	most-favoured nation
MMR	maternal mortality ratio
MoH	Ministry of Health
MSF	Médecins Sans Frontières
NAFTA	North American Free Trade Agreement
NGO	non-governmental organization
OECD	Organization for Economic Co-operation and Development
PAHO	Pan American Health Organization
PAI	Population Action International
PBS	Pharmaceutical Benefits Scheme
PC	provisioning capacity
PhRMA	Pharmaceutical Research and Manufacturers of America
PMA	Pharmaceutical Manufacturers' Association of South Africa
POST	Parliamentary Office of Science and Technology
PRS	poverty reduction strategy
RH	reproductive health
RMB	Renminbi
RTI	reproductive tract infection

SA 8000	Social Accountability 8000
SBA	skilled birth attendant
SOE	state-owned enterprise
STD	sexually transmitted disease
TAC	Treatment Action Campaign
TBA	traditional birth attendant
TDHS	Tanzania Demographic and Health Survey
TIR	Trade Impact Review
TJM	Trade Justice Movement
TL	trade liberalization
TRIPS	Trade-Related Intellectual Property Rights
UCE	urban collective enterprise
UNCTAD	United Nations Conference on Trade and Development
UNDP	United Nations Development Programme
WHO	World Health Organization
WIDE	Women in Development Europe
WTO	World Trade Organization
ZDV	zidovudine

Preface

This book has been in the making since 2002, when the Ford Foundation generously gave a grant to the International Center for Research on Women (ICRW) for a project to explore the linkages between trade liberalization, women's employment, and reproductive health and rights at the macro- and micro-levels.

ICRW organized a series of exploratory meetings in 2002 and 2003 with experts from around the world to understand the issues in the different regions and to develop a framework that could be useful to both scholars and activists for understanding the pathways by which the liberalization of trade affects the provision of and women's access to reproductive health care services. Following these meetings, ICRW identified a set of authors to write the chapters that are included in the present volume. These chapters have been vetted at seminars at ICRW and reviewed by experts in public health, sociology, anthropology and economics. The authors and editors are grateful for the constructive feedback that was received through these channels.

ICRW nourished the project from its inception to completion and provided a supportive home for the research. Geeta Rao Gupta, ICRW's President, offered intellectual stimulation and constructive feedback throughout the project. Suzan Atwood and Elizabeth Nicoletti provided logistical support to the project with unflagging enthusiasm and good humour. Keera Allendorf and Kerry Macquarrie undertook research for two ICRW working papers prepared in 2002–03 that form the basis for Chapter 1.

Special thanks are due to Sarah Costa, Program Officer at the Ford Foundation, who provided the inspiration for the project and attended the working meetings. In addition, the editors would like to acknowledge the contributions of the following individuals: Maitreyi Das and Guadalupe Duron each co-authored a working paper with Caren Grown on the indirect and direct pathways linking trade liberalization and reproductive health. Their ideas influenced several chapters in this volume and Chapter 1 draws extensively on this joint work. The project could not have been launched without their assistance. Ruth Dixon-Mueller attended the project's first exploratory meeting and helped to define the framework that is described in Chapter 1. We would also like to thank Jessica Dixon of the Levy Economics Institute at Bard College for her careful editing and help with final production. Finally, the editors are grateful to Anna Hardman, Commissioning Editor at Zed Books, for her support and commitment to this book.

This volume is dedicated to advocates of gender equality and women's rights.

Caren Grown
Elissa Braunstein
Anju Malhotra

INTRODUCTION

Reproductive Health, Trade Liberalization and Development

Elissa Braunstein and Caren Grown

This volume explores the connections between the liberalization of international trade and reproductive health and rights. The exploration of these themes is timely: negotiations of core trade agreements to conclude the Doha Development Round are in flux, and there are large disagreements among countries over further liberalization in services and agriculture and the rules governing non-agriculture market access and intellectual property rights. Countries have also recently concluded the five-year review of progress towards the Millennium Development Goals and reaffirmed the commitments they made in Cairo in 1994 to advance reproductive health and rights.[1] The international climate thus presents important opportunities to raise awareness about the interdependence of economic and social development and reproductive health and rights.

The purpose of this collection is to synthesize the most current, cutting-edge information on specific aspects of the linkages between trade liberalization and women's health and to stimulate further research and policy development. It is intended for an interdisciplinary audience of economists, public health professionals, demographers, sociologists, anthropologists and women's studies specialists. It will also be of interest to academic and non-academic readers, including policy-makers and representatives of civil society organizations working on health, economic justice and employment issues.

This introduction is organized as follows. First, we explain how most chapters in this volume define the key concepts of trade liberalization and reproductive health. We then outline the framework used to organize the volume, briefly describe the chapters and close with some reflections for additional work on this topic.

Definitions

Trade liberalization

Trade liberalization refers to the increasingly free flow of goods and services in international markets, and the institutions that govern these flows. One way to assess these flows is by considering their increase over time. Tables I.1 and I.2 detail the increasing importance of trade in various groupings of economies since the 1970s. As a percentage of GDP (Table I.1), trade has increased for all the country groupings, especially for low- and middle-income countries, as well as for East Asia and the Pacific and Southeast Europe and the Commonwealth Independent States. Table I.2 illustrates the rising significance of trade in these flows (where total trade is the sum of goods and services trade). Although services trade is growing in all country groupings, the leader in terms of total trade is South Asia, reflecting the popularity of India as a services exporter.

Table I.1   Trade as a percentage of GDP

	1970	1980	1990	2002
Low-income countries	20.8	34.6	36.3	50.4
Middle-income countries	23.0	33.7	36.9	59.9
High-income countries	27.9	39.8	38.1	44.4
East Asia and Pacific	18.8	35.0	49.5	78.0
Latin America and Caribbean	18.3	24.9	26.1	39.8
Middle East and North Africa	60.3	69.3	63.4	63.4
South Asia	12.4	21.4	20.9	35.1
Sub-Saharan Africa	47.8	63.0	52.8	67.1
High-income OECD	18.9	33.8	30.1	34.6
Southeast Europe and CIS	16.6	14.4	50.1	75.8
World	27.0	38.8	38.3	47.2

Source: Authors' calculations based on the World Development Indicators Database except for data on Southeast Europe and the Commonwealth of Independent States (CIS), which are based on authors' calculations of the UNCTAD Statistics Handbook.

Note: East Asia and the Pacific includes Japan, which is also included in the OECD grouping, as are some countries in the Southeast Europe and CIS category.

Investment liberalization is often associated with trade liberalization, because capital movements can be treated as either complements to or substitutes for exports and imports. Tables I.3 and I.4 detail the recent history of foreign direct investment (FDI) flows and stocks. FDI refers to capital flows where the investing country has a controlling stake in the host country investment, typically defined as 10 per cent

Table I.2 Commercial services trade as a percentage of total trade

	1975	1980	1990	2002
Low-income countries	4.6	12.0	16.2	17.5
Middle-income countries	4.3	10.6	12.3	14.3
High-income countries	14.5	16.0	18.7	19.9
East Asia and Pacific	4.1	7.1	13.6	14.3
Latin America and Caribbean	8.3	19.6	18.3	13.6
Middle East and North Africa	3.8	15.7	17.0	10.9
South Asia	9.0	19.0	20.4	24.0
Sub-Saharan Africa	8.6	16.2	18.5	10.1
High-income OECD	15.4	17.0	19.9	20.7
Southeast Europe and CIS	–	6.0	7.8	18.3
World	12.1	15.0	17.6	18.6

Source and Notes: See Table I.1; commercial services trade includes all trade except for government services.

Table I.3 Net FDI inflows as a percentage of GDP

	1970	1980	1990	2000
Low-income countries	0.2	0.1	0.4	0.6
Middle-income countries	0.7	0.4	0.9	3.1
High-income countries	0.05	0.6	1.0	5.4
East Asia and Pacific	–	–	1.6	2.8
Latin America and Caribbean	0.7	0.9	0.7	3.9
Middle East and North Africa	0.7	−0.6	0.6	0.4
South Asia	0.1	0.1	0.1	0.6
Sub-Saharan Africa	0.3			1.8
High-income OECD	0.5	0.6	1.0	4.2
Southeast Europe and CIS	–	–	–	2.2
World	0.5	0.5	1.0	4.9

Source and Note: See Table I.1.

Inward stock of FDI by region/economy (percentage of world

	1980	1985	1990	2000	2002
Developed economies	56.0	58.4	71.6	68.0	64.5
Western Europe	33.3	29.3	40.7	40.4	39.0
United States	11.9	18.9	20.2	17.8	19.0
Developing economies	44.0	41.6	28.2	30.7	32.8
	4.6	3.5	2.6	2.6	2.4
Latin America and the Caribbean	7.2	8.2	6.0	6.7	10.7
	32.2	29.9	19.6	21.4	19.7
	1.1	3.9	2.1	1.7	1.0
Central Asia	–	–	–	0.1	0.4
South, East and Southeast Asia	30.9	26.0	17.4	19.4	18.3
	0.2	0.1	0.1	0.1	0.1
Central and Eastern Europe	–	0.0	0.1	1.3	2.6

World Investment Report 1999 and 2003, Annex table B.3.

or more of an entity's total stock. Although FDI flows have grown substantially in recent years, it is still much less important than trade, as illustrated by FDI as a percentage of GDP in Table I.3. Still, the 1990s saw a tremendous upsurge in FDI, with world FDI inflows increasing per cent of GDP in 1990 to 4.9 per cent in 2002. Table I.4 shows the distribution of FDI stocks (which are accumulated flows) over a similar time period. The first thing to note is that the majority of FDI is located within developed economies, which as a group claimed about 65 per cent of world FDI stocks in 2002. Among developing countries, the stocks of FDI are also highly concentrated, with East, South and Southeast Asia hosting about 56 per cent of world FDI 2002, and Latin America and the Caribbean hosting another per cent of these stocks.

Labour is the absent partner in this portrait of the rise in global capital and trade flows. Despite some rise in global labour flows, strong on global migration make services trade a more significant factor in trade liberalization than the flow of people.

Trade liberalization is not just about increases in actual flows, but institutions that govern them as well. The World Trade Organization established in 1995 to replace the General Agreement on Tariffs services, agriculture, intellectual property and investment. For developing countries, the International Monetary Fund (IMF) and the World Bank are also significant, in that their loans and aid programs often come with associated requirements to liberalize trade and investment.

In addition to these global institutions, a number of regional and bilateral trade agreements also liberalize trade rules. Bilateral agreements are the most numerous, but better known are regional agreements or unions, such as the North American Free Trade Agreement (between Canada, Mexico and the US), ASEAN (the Association for Southeast Asian Nations), the European Union and MERCOSUR (the Southern [South American] Common Market). Liberalizing investment agreements are also quite numerous at the bilateral level. The total number of bilateral investment agreements increased from 446 in 1990 to 2,181 in 2002 (UNCTAD BIT database). In terms of regions, developed economies averaged forty-five agreements per economy in 2002, with developing countries averaging twelve (ibid.).

As discussed in more detail in the following chapters, national institutions also play a critical role in trade liberalization. National governments operationalize international agreements by ensuring that a wide array of national policies conform to and are in compliance with the agreements' rules. Such policies include capital controls, exchange rate policies, monetary and fiscal management and public sector reforms – including health sector reform. The contributions to this book cover many of these issues, as global institutions are merely abstract rules until they are implemented at the national level.

Reproductive health and rights

The second major focus of this volume is reproductive health. The definition of reproductive health has evolved considerably over the past decade. The chapters in this volume adapt to varying degrees the definition of reproductive health agreed upon by governments at the International Conference on Population and Development (ICPD) held in Cairo, Egypt, in 1994:

> Reproductive health is a state of complete physical, mental and social well-being and not merely the absence of disease or infirmity, in all matters relating to the reproductive system and to its functions and processes. Reproductive health therefore implies that people are able to have a satisfying and safe sex life and that they have the capability to reproduce and the freedom to decide if, when and how often to do so. Implicit in this last condition are the right of men and women to be informed and to have

access to safe, effective, affordable and acceptable methods of family planning of their choice, as well as other methods of their choice for the regulation of fertility which are not against the law, and the right of access to appropriate health care services that will enable women to go safely through pregnancy and childbirth and provide couples with the best chance of having a healthy infant. (ICPD Programme of Action, Paragraph 7.2)

Thus, reproductive health is multifaceted, with biomedical, sociopolitical, demographic and human rights dimensions. Because it is not one 'thing', it is important to distinguish those aspects of reproductive health that are mostly likely to be affected by the liberalization of trade. Several chapters focus on reproductive health problems or conditions, such as birth defects or infertility caused by workplace toxins, and the needs of women for health services within a given population, such as needs for family planning or maternal health services (Chapters 5–7). Others focus on the nature and distribution of reproductive health services, such as the supply of health workers (Chapters 2 and 10). Some chapters also consider how liberalization affects reproductive rights (Chapters 11 and 12).

Pathways between the Liberalization of Trade and Reproductive Health

It is now accepted that the achievement of reproductive health depends upon an enabling macroeconomic environment. In the words of Rosalind Petchesky (2003: 14), 'how can women take advantage of health services if they lack the financial resources to pay or transportation to get to them, if their workplace is contaminated by pollutants that have an adverse effect on their pregnancy?' In order for reproductive health, or health more generally, to be fully attained, economic policies (finance, trade, fiscal policy and sector-specific policy) and health and rights regimes can no longer be conducted in separate realms (Petchesky 2003: 18).

Chapter 1 by Grown presents a useful conceptual framework for understanding the pathways through which the liberalization of trade affects women's reproductive health problems and provision of services. She identifies an *indirect pathway* through which trade policies and flows affect women's demand for services indirectly through changes in their labour force participation. Trade-related changes in female labour force participation influence women's reproductive needs and capacities, so trade-related work is an intermediate variable between trade liberalization and reproductive health. Grown also identifies a *direct pathway* through which trade policies affect the supply, for example, the quality, quantity and cost, of reproductive health services. Several chapters in the volume illustrate the nature of these pathways.

Trade liberalization, employment and reproductive health

The chapters by Amin, Denman, Hewamanne and Tan et al. in Part II all exemplify the indirect pathway. These chapters discuss trade-induced changes in women's employment in factories that produce for export in Bangladesh, Egypt, Vietnam, Mexico, Sri Lanka and China, and the implications for women's reproductive and occupational health (e.g. marriage timing, fertility, sexual debut, risks of sexually transmitted infections, pregnancy). Although this employment is 'formal' in that the factories are registered and nominally comply with the country's labour laws, the conditions of work are far from ideal. Women have lower pay, experience higher turnover and are more likely than men to be passed over for promotion. The factories they work in have poor ventilation and lighting and hazardous equipment, and workers are exposed to toxic substances and ergonomic stress associated with repetitive assembly-line motions and body positions.

However, what this employment means for women's social welfare and reproductive health is heavily context-dependent, as Basu notes. For instance, Amin points out that new factory jobs for women in Bangladesh have had the positive effect of delaying marriage, increasing women's economic and household autonomy and improving overall demographic outcomes. In Mexico, Denman finds that *maquiladora* employment grants women relief from domestic burdens, access to health care services, the ability to improve their living conditions and send their children to school, and escape abusive, neglectful or non-supportive spouses or partners. In China, Tan et al. show that the development of non-state-owned enterprises has enabled many rural women, especially young women, to move into non-farm work. Their urban experiences promote improved health relative to their fellow rural villagers because of higher incomes, lifestyle changes and increased access to services. But migration to work in private urban enterprises also has negative effects on the reproductive health of female migrant workers, emanating from the limits of official reproductive health services, the pressure exerted by family planning administrations, the sometimes unsafe working and living conditions in private enterprises, and the increased likelihood that these women will engage in unprotected sex. In Egypt and Vietnam, the trade-related decline in job security and the push into more stringent and unpleasant factory work has meant a loss of status and autonomy for women who were formerly employed in the public sector.

In all countries, these new sites of employment have given rise to new 'cultures' of health and sexuality. In Mexico, Denman contends that the networks and options available formed a common 'culture of health' for the women who work in the export factories. Within this culture, women sought desirable physicians, found treatment for certain complaints, accepted or rejected physician recommendations, negotiated domestic roles and leveraged their status as expectant mothers at work and at home. In Sri Lanka, garment factory workers in the Katunayake Free Trade Zone developed new knowledge and attitudes about sexuality and reproductive health, which they acquired from schools, tabloid magazines, mainstream newspapers and NGO workshops. Hewamanne notes that with this knowledge they actively engaged in a transgressive subculture, which centred on fashion, language and the creation of new tastes in leisure activities.

The chapters in this part are rich in detail. They do not lead to one overarching conclusion, but rather show that the indirect pathway between trade liberalization and reproductive health must be contextualized in country, sector and even firm-specific analyses. Much more work is needed to identify the positive and negative effects of specific types of employment on women's reproductive health problems and access to services.

Direct effects of trade liberalization on reproductive health

The direct pathway between trade liberalization and reproductive health pertains to how trade agreements and their associated institutions affect the supply of reproductive health goods and services. At the most aggregate level are global economic institutions such as the WTO, the IMF and the World Bank. Beginning with the WTO and the various trade agreements under its purview, it is perhaps obvious to note that liberalizing trade rules may raise the global supply of reproductive health services and products by lowering barriers to trade.

Lipson takes up this point from the perspective of the WTO General Agreement on Trade in Services (GATS). In addition to providing a conceptual framework for tracing the routes and mechanisms by which trade liberalization affects health care systems generally, Lipson examines how GATS rules and specific commitments in the health sector may influence reproductive health services and rights. She identifies the potential for some unintended consequences as well, such as service sector commitments that might constrain government health policy options.

Gerein and Green emphasize the services trade aspect of these issues in their chapter on the global migration of nurses and midwives. There is increasing concern in national health systems and international agencies over the growing shortage of midwives and nurses in many countries, a shortage that is compounded for the global South by active recruitment from high-income countries in the global North. It is likely that any increase in global labour migration, as envisioned by GATS, will worsen this crisis for Southern countries unable to compete with the higher salaries and better working conditions proffered in the North. Gerein and Green assess these trends from the perspective of protecting women's health in low- and middle-income countries, and discuss what sorts of national and international policies will enable countries to manage these trends better.

In addition to GATS, the WTO agreement on Trade-Related Intellectual Property Rights (TRIPS) is also of potential importance for women's reproductive health by affecting the supply and price of reproductive health medicines. Maharaj and Roberts use a gender perspective to analyse how TRIPS affects the supply of antiretrovirals to treat the HIV/AIDS epidemic in South Africa. South Africa has played a leading role in shaping the global debate on access to affordable essential medicines for developing countries within the parameters of the TRIPS Agreement. Maharaj and Roberts also emphasize, however, the significance of national debates in potentially slowing down the benefits introduced by global policy shifts. Local civil society plays an important role at both the national and global levels, with the potential to ensure that governments can and do rise up to meet public health needs, instead of uncritically conforming to global economic rules.

These three chapters illustrate how trade agreements can shape the health sector and directly impact the capacity of governments to deliver health services through changes in global rules. But trade liberalization may also have more indirect effects on government capacities via the

revenue channel. Because developing country governments typically
derive a substantial proportion of their revenues from trade taxes (owing
to different taxation structures relative to more developed countries),
the lowering of tariffs required by trade agreements will have a direct
impact on government budgets, with potential consequences for health
sector funding and women's reproductive health. In her chapter on
trade liberalization and women's autonomy, Braunstein demonstrates
how the declining ability of governments to fund social welfare programmes limits the promise of trade-related employment to deliver
women from the binds of gender inequality. These constraints stem
not only from the impact of declining trade tariffs on government
budgets, but also on the increase in global capital mobility and competition from other potential production platforms – rendering firms less
willing (and sometimes less able) to support government programmes
through taxes.

Developing country government budgets are also under stress from
structural adjustment-type conditionalities, loan requirements imposed
by the IMF and World Bank that link debt repayment with export-
oriented growth and lowering government spending. Nanda considers
the effects of these policies in Tanzania, where its worsening terms of
trade, a decline in trade taxes and the retrenchment of public spending
as a result of structural adjustment have resulted in the institution of
user fees for health care. She considers the impact of user fees on
women's reproductive health in particular, and finds that women's
abilities to pay user fees are conditioned by gender inequity. For
instance, women face restricted mobility, limited economic autonomy
and choice of employment relative to men. These inequities are compounded by the fact that during their reproductive years, women have
greater reproductive and sexual health needs than men. As a result,
trade-induced public sector reforms can have inequitable effects on
women and men from a reproductive health perspective.

Mediating influences

The final chapters in the volume show how the impact of trade liberalization on reproductive health can be mediated by collective action
and advocacy. Although trade liberalization may be inevitable, White
identifies several entry points for advocacy that can influence the
decisions of policy-makers and perhaps shift negotiation outcomes.
While Basu and White agree that advocacy can focus on those facets

of trade agreements that lead to increased access to reproductive health services and enable women to secure high-quality health care, they diverge on the extent to which advocacy should be directed to the proximate versus ultimate determinants of reproductive health. White recommends several specific actions, including strengthening the use of various public health and human rights frameworks in trade policy decision-making, building bridges between reproductive rights and gender and trade activists, and developing national-level advocacy strategies targeted to health and trade ministers.

Basu argues that if we are interested in improving reproductive health, it makes more general sense to focus on the proximate determinants of reproductive health and on the influences on the proximate determinants of reproductive health, including the provision of health services and female employment that strengthens women's bargaining power. There is thus also a case for more direct interventions to improve work conditions (as Denman also notes) and transportation services that women need to enter the labour force, which can lessen the risk of sexual harassment and gender-based violence.

Conclusion and Organization of the Volume

As the work in this volume indicates, there are significant actual and potential linkages between reproductive health and trade liberalization. In this book we have tended to focus on the impact of trade liberalization on reproductive health – whether direct or indirect. Looking back on this work we feel it is important to emphasize that reproductive health is also a lens with which to understand better the social dynamics of trade liberalization. As trade liberalization increasingly dominates development policies designed to achieve poverty reduction, and with reproductive health being such a central component of well-being (a component that is also determined by poverty), changes in reproductive health outcomes are an important way to understand the impacts of trade liberalization on poverty and well-being. We hope that this volume is the first step of many to understand these linkages better.

The volume is organized into four parts. The first is conceptual, giving an overview of the direct and indirect linkages between reproductive health and trade liberalization. The second focuses on indirect linkages via the intermediary of women's employment, while the third looks at the direct relationship between trade liberalization and government capacity to deliver reproductive health services. The final part concludes by addressing policy and advocacy issues that arise for advocates of both reproductive health and rights and economic justice. Together, these chapters are a good vantage point from which to consider further research on this topic. As the global economy becomes increasingly important in determining development trajectories, advocates, scholars and policy-makers must also increasingly acknowledge and incorporate the linkages between trade liberalization and reproductive health in their efforts for positive change.

Note

1. Leaders of 189 countries met at the United Nations in New York in September 2005 to review progress towards the eight development goals to halve poverty and recommit to development, peace building, human rights, democracy and security.

Reference

Petchesky, R. (2003) *Global Prescriptions*, London and New York: Zed Books.

PART I

Conceptual Overviews: Direct and Indirect Linkages

I

Trade Liberalization and Reproductive Health: A Framework for Understanding the Linkages

Caren Grown

Introduction

A growing literature discusses the impact of the liberalization of international trade – the progressive reduction of barriers to imports and exports – on health worldwide. Few contributors to this literature, however, have examined the specific impacts of trade liberalization on reproductive health – 'the state of complete physical, mental and social well being in all matters relating to the reproductive system and to its functions and processes' (UN 1995, paragraph 7.2). Yet, such liberalization is likely to affect provision of and access to quality reproductive health services and commodities. Trade liberalization can possibly create new opportunities for improving reproductive health. For instance, a more liberalized health trading system can improve a country's competitive capacity, attract foreign investment, create employment for women, increase income levels, improve access to reproductive health technologies and ultimately raise the quality of health care delivery (UNCTAD/WHO 1998). On the other hand, trade liberalization can also make it more difficult to advance reproductive/sexual health and rights objectives in policies, programmes and services. There is concern about higher costs of services and supplies, concentration of services which may restrict the access of lower-income or remote populations, lower quality of services, and shortages of critical medical personnel (e.g. doctors, nurses and midwives) that result from migration both from the public to the private sector and from developing to developed countries, as health professionals opt for higher salaries and better opportunities for professional development.

To date, there is more heat than light about each of these effects, and the net impacts are not yet well documented. This chapter presents a conceptual framework for understanding the linkages between trade liberalization and reproductive health, and discusses the challenges in tracing the linkages at the national or subnational level. It reviews the theoretical and empirical evidence for the linkages and concludes with recommendations for future research and policy to advance women's reproductive health and rights in a more globalized world. The analysis in this chapter focuses largely on developing countries, although occasional reference will be made to industrialized countries.

Trade liberalization

The liberalization of international trade is now one of the most important global economic processes. The flows of goods and services that are exported across national borders have increased substantially in the post-war period. Since 1948, the volume of global trade has grown by an annual average of 6 per cent (WTO 2003). Exports from developing countries have grown faster than the world average since the early 1980s and now account for about one-third of world trade (UNCTAD 2004). Moreover, the share of imports and exports in the gross domestic product (GDP) of developing countries increased by 30 per cent between 1990 and 2000. The increase was most significant in Europe, Central and East Asia, and in the Pacific, where the increase was by more than 50 per cent.

Although much of this growth has been in the manufacturing sector, trade in services, including health services, has increased rapidly and is estimated as 20 per cent of all exports in 2003 (WTO 2004). The liberalization of health services often involves removing restrictions on entry by foreign health service providers and their terms of practice, changing ownership through privatization, and relaxing regulations (for instance, concerning accreditation and licensing requirements) and making regulations more 'pro-competitive' (Chanda 2001). Comprehensive and internationally comparable data are not available, but cross-border delivery of health services has increased worldwide through the movement of personnel and consumers and through cross-border trade in data processing and other activities (Chanda 2001). There has also been significant growth in foreign direct investment in the health sector. The continuing removal of some of the regulatory barriers to trade at the regional, multilateral and national levels means that trade in health services is likely to assume greater importance in the future (Chanda 2001).[1]

Reproductive health

Reproductive health is critical for national economic development and individual well-being. Yet, women's reproductive health is poor and their reproductive rights remain unrealized in many countries. Table 1.1 summarizes recent trends in some of the salient components of women's reproductive health status.[2] As shown in columns 2–4 of this table, the fertility rate declined in most parts of the world between 1990 and 2002. Maternal mortality rates remain high in many developing countries: maternal deaths per 100,000 live births are well over 1,000 in almost all sub-Saharan African countries.

The overall proportion of HIV-positive women has increased steadily since 1997 (UNAIDS 2004). The epidemic is most 'feminized' in sub-Saharan Africa, where 57 per cent of infected adults are women and 75 per cent of infected 15–24 year olds are women and girls (UNAIDS/WHO 2004). The prevalence of HIV-infected women also increased slightly in South and Southeast Asia, and somewhat more so in North America, Latin America and the Caribbean, Eastern Europe, and Central Asia.[3] These reproductive health problems all require technologies and services that are affected by the liberalization of trade.

Pathways between Trade Liberalization and Reproductive Health

The linkages between health and trade are both direct and indirect, and operate at multiple levels (household, country, international). Trade liberalization and reproductive health are multidimensional, and it is important to define them precisely in order to understand the linkages and impacts.[4] Figure 1.1 summarizes some of the most salient dimensions of trade liberalization that are likely to affect reproductive health and some of the key dimensions of reproductive health that are most likely to be affected by growing trade liberalization. This figure distinguishes between trade agreements, trade policies and trade flows on the left, and reproductive health services and reproductive health needs/problems on the right.

Table 1.1 Key reproductive health indicators for selected countries: 1990–2003

	Total fertility rate			Maternal deaths per 100,000 live births			Percentage of women among population (15–49 years) with HIV/AIDS	
	1990	1995	2002	1990	1995	2000	1997	2003
Afghanistan	6.90	6.90	6.80	1700	820	1900		
Albania	3.03	2.64	2.23	65	31	55		
Algeria	4.49	3.68	2.75	160	150	140		15.56
Angola	7.20	7.08	7.00	1500	1300	1700	52.00	59.09
Antigua and Barbuda	1.78	1.70	1.70					
Argentina	2.90	2.70	2.44	100	85	82	18.33	20.00
Armenia	2.62	1.63	1.15	50	29	55		36.00
Australia	1.91	1.82	1.75	9	6	8	5.00	7.14
Austria	1.45	1.40	1.31	10	11	4	18.67	22.00
Azerbaijan	2.74	2.29	2.07	22	37	94		
Bahamas	2.12	2.18	2.12	100	10	60	33.87	48.08
Bahrain	3.76	3.46	2.30	60	38	28		<83.33
Bangladesh	4.12	3.35	2.95	850	600	380	14.76	
Barbados	1.74	1.74	1.75	43	33	95	33.33	32.00
Belarus	1.91	1.39	1.25	37	33	35		
Belgium	1.62	1.57	1.62	10	8	10	36.11	35.00
Belize	4.39	3.72	2.95		140	140	24.76	37.14
Benin	6.62	6.15	5.30	990	880	850	50.00	56.45

Bhutan	4.85	5.79	5.10	1600	500	420	14.23	27.08
Bolivia	1.70	4.36	3.75	650	550	420		
Bosnia and Herzegovina		1.60	1.30		15	31		57.58
Botswana	5.07	4.55	3.82	250	480	100	48.95	36.92
Brazil	2.74	2.45	2.14	220	260	260	22.81	<100
Brunei Darussalam	3.20	2.92	2.47	60	22	37		
Bulgaria	1.81	1.23	1.25	27	23	32		
Burkina Faso	7.02	6.84	6.30	930	1400	1000	48.57	55.56
Burundi	6.80	6.49	5.77	1300	1900	1000	50.00	59.09
Cambodia	5.56	4.74	3.80	900	590	450	50.00	30.00
Cameroon	6.00	5.20	4.60	550	720	730	48.39	55.77
Canada	1.83	1.64	1.52	6	6	6	13.02	23.64
Cape Verde	5.50	4.12	3.46		190	150		
Central African Republic	5.46	5.06	4.60	700	1200	1100	50.00	54.17
Chad	7.06	6.75	6.20	1500	1500	1100	50.60	55.56
Channel Islands	1.71	1.75	1.75					
Chile	2.58	2.37	2.15	65	33	31	18.00	33.46
China	2.10	1.92	1.88	95	60	56	12.00	22.89
Colombia	3.07	2.82	2.48	100	120	130	15.28	34.44
Comoros	5.80	4.85	4.05	950	570	480		
Congo, Democratic Republic of	6.70	6.70	6.70	870	940	990	50.00	57.00
Congo, Republic of	6.29	6.29	6.29	890	1100	510	49.47	56.25
Costa Rica	3.20	2.78	2.30	55	35	43	26.00	33.33
Cote d'Ivoire	6.18	5.40	4.55	810	1200	690	49.25	56.60

Continued

Table 1.1 *Continued*

	Total fertility rate			Maternal deaths per 100,000 live births			Percentage of women among population (15–49 years) with HIV/AIDS	
	1990	1995	2002	1990	1995	2000	1997	2003
Croatia	1.63	1.58	1.45		18	8		
Cuba	1.69	1.48	1.58	95	24	33	32.14	33.33
Cyprus	2.42	2.13	1.90	5	0	47		
Czech Republic	1.89	1.28	1.20	15	14	9		32.00
Denmark	1.67	1.81	1.73	9	15	5	24.84	18.00
Djibouti	5.98	5.62	5.20	570	520	730	50.00	55.95
Dominica	2.70	2.14	1.90					
Dominican Republic	3.38	3.24	2.60	110	110	150	33.33	27.06
Ecuador	3.71	3.27	2.76	150	210	130	13.89	34.00
Egypt	3.97	3.63	3.05	170	170	84	10.49	13.33
El Salvador	3.85	3.58	2.90	300	180	150	24.44	34.29
Equatorial Guinea	5.89	5.89	5.51	820	1400	880	47.83	
Eritrea	6.50	5.97	4.80	1400	1100	630		56.36
Estonia	2.04	1.32	1.25	41	80	63		33.77
Ethiopia	6.91	6.23	5.60	1400	1800	850	48.00	55.00
Fiji	3.09	3.30	2.60	90	20	75	<38.46	33.33
Finland	1.78	1.81	1.73	11	6	6	20.00	<33.33
France	1.78	1.71	1.88	15	20	17		26.67

French Polynesia	3.25	2.93	2.50		20	20	50.00	57.78
Gabon	5.09	4.64	4.05	500	620	420	48.46	57.14
Gambia	5.90	5.52	4.80	1100	1100	540		33.33
Georgia	2.21	1.41	1.10	33	22	32	19.43	22.09
Germany	1.45	1.25	1.35	22	12	8	50.00	56.25
Ghana	5.50	4.55	4.11	740	590	540		20.00
Greece	1.40	1.32	1.32	10	2	9		
Guam	3.34	3.81	3.75		12	12		
Guatemala	5.33	5.10	4.30	200	270	240	24.81	41.89
Guinea	5.90	5.60	5.02	1600	1200	740	50.00	55.38
Guinea–Bissau	7.10	7.10	6.60	910	910	1100	51.82	
Guyana	2.61	2.49	2.31		150	170	33.00	55.45
Haiti	5.42	4.93	4.20	1000	1100	680	33.89	57.69
Honduras	5.16	4.79	4.00	220	220	110	24.39	55.93
Hong Kong, China	1.27	1.30	0.96	7	23	16	38.71	34.62
Hungary	1.84	1.57	1.30	30	16	16		
Iceland	2.31	2.08	1.95	0	16	0		<100
India	3.80	3.40	2.92	570	440	540	24.39	38.00
Indonesia	3.04	2.80	2.32	650	470	230	25.49	13.64
Iran	4.68	3.28	2.00	120	130	76		12.26
Iraq	5.88	5.10	4.05	310	370	250		
Ireland	2.12	1.87	1.90	10	9	5		30.77
Israel	2.82	2.90	2.70	7	8	17		
Italy	1.26	1.18	1.25	12	11	5	30.00	32.14
Jamaica	2.94	2.78	2.30	120	120	87	31.43	47.62

Continued

Table 1.1 Continued

	Total fertility rate			Maternal deaths per 100,000 live births			Percentage of women among population (15–49 years) with HIV/AIDS	
	1990	1995	2002	1990	1995	2000	1997	2003
Japan	1.54	1.42	1.33	18	12	10	5.59	24.17
Jordan	5.40	4.35	3.50	150	41	41		
Kazakhstan	2.72	2.26	1.80	80	80	210		33.54
Kenya	5.64	4.90	4.23	650	1300	1000	48.75	65.45
Korea, Democratic Republic of	2.39	2.15	2.07	70	35	67		
Korea, Republic of	1.77	1.75	1.45	130	20	20	12.90	10.84
Kuwait	3.44	2.97	2.52	29	25	5		
Kyrgyz Republic	3.69	3.31	2.40	110	80	110		<20.51
Laos	6.00	5.50	4.80	650	650	650	52.00	<29.41
Latvia	2.02	1.25	1.16	40	70	42		33.33
Lebanon	3.22	2.74	2.22	300	130	150		<17.85
Lesotho	5.08	4.85	4.30	610	530	550	50.00	56.67
Liberia	6.80	6.50	5.80	560	1000	760	50.00	56.25
Libya	4.72	3.92	3.32	220	120	97		
Lithuania	2.03	1.49	1.27	36	27	13		
Luxembourg	1.62	1.68	1.78	0	0	28	<33.33	<38.46
Macedonia	2.06	1.97	1.75		17	23		

Country								
Madagascar	6.22	5.88	5.20	490	580	550	50.00	58.46
Malawi	7.00	6.55	6.05	560	580	1800	49.25	56.79
Malaysia	3.77	3.40	2.85	80	39	41	19.70	16.67
Maldives	5.70	4.82	4.00		390	110		
Mali	6.86	6.68	6.40	1200	630	1200	50.00	59.17
Malta	2.05	1.83	1.81	0	0	21		
Mauritania	6.02	5.30	4.60	930	870	1000	49.15	57.30
Mauritius	2.25	2.14	2.00	120	45	24		
Mexico	3.31	2.90	2.40	110	65	83	11.67	33.13
Moldova				60	65	36		
Mongolia	4.03	3.13	2.43	65	65	110		<40
Morocco	4.01	3.42	2.75	610	390	220		
Mozambique	6.34	5.61	5.00	1500	980	1000	48.33	55.83
Myanmar	3.76	3.42	2.80	580	170	360	20.91	30.31
Namibia	5.39	5.28	4.80	370	370	300	50.00	55.00
Nepal	5.26	4.55	4.15	1500	830	740	40.00	26.67
Netherlands	1.62	1.53	1.70	12	10	16		20.00
New Zealand	2.18	2.01	1.90	25	15	7	14.62	<14.28
Nicaragua	4.80	3.87	3.44	160	250	230	24.39	33.87
Niger	7.64	7.47	7.10	1200	920	1600	50.82	56.25
Nigeria	6.04	5.72	5.07	1000	1100	800	50.00	57.58
Norway	1.93	1.87	1.75	6	9	16		<25
Occupied Palestinian Territory		5.82	4.90		120	100		
Oman	7.38	5.56	3.97	190	120	87		<38.46

Continued

Table 1.1 *Continued*

	Total fertility rate			Maternal deaths per 100,000 live births			Percentage of women among population (15–49 years) with HIV/AIDS	
	1990	1995	2002	1990	1995	2000	1997	2003
Pakistan	5.84	5.20	4.50	340	200	500	19.35	12.19
Panama	3.01	2.73	2.42	55	100	160	25.00	41.33
Papua New Guinea	5.55	4.76	4.30	930	390	300	50.00	30.00
Paraguay	4.60	4.33	3.84	160	170	170	17.74	26.00
Peru	3.68	3.39	2.64	280	240	410	15.49	33.75
Philippines	4.12	3.78	3.24	280	240	200	30.43	22.47
Poland	2.04	1.61	1.30	19	12	13		
Portugal	1.43	1.38	1.54	15	12	5	19.43	19.55
Puerto Rico	2.20	2.00	1.90		30	25		
Qatar	4.34	3.32	2.48		41	7		
Romania	1.84	1.34	1.32	130	60	49		
Russian Federation	1.89	1.34	1.28	75	75	67		33.72
Rwanda	7.15	6.51	5.70	1300	2300	1400	48.57	56.52
Samoa	4.76	4.54	4.00	35	15	130		
Saudi Arabia	6.56	5.98	5.30	130	23	23		
Senegal	6.20	5.67	4.90	1200	1200	690	50.00	56.10
Serbia and Montenegro	2.08	1.88	1.74		15	11		20.00
Seychelles	2.82	2.34	2.09					

Sierra Leone	6.50	6.24	5.59	1800	2100	2000	50.00	24.39
Singapore	1.87	1.71	1.37	10	9	30	19.68	
Slovakia	2.09	1.52	1.30		14	3		
Slovenia	1.46	1.29	1.15	13	17	17		
Solomon Islands	5.87	5.68	5.26		60	130		
Somalia	7.25	7.25	6.95	1600	1600	1100		
South Africa	3.32	3.08	2.80	230	340	230	50.00	56.86
Spain	1.33	1.18	1.28	7	8	4	20.83	20.77
Sri Lanka	2.53	2.28	2.10	140	60	92	29.85	17.14
Sudan	5.42	5.06	4.40	660	1500	590		57.89
Suriname	2.64	2.54	2.40		230	110	32.96	34.00
Swaziland	5.30	4.86	4.20	560	370	370	50.62	55.00
Sweden	2.13	1.73	1.64	7	8	2	24.33	25.71
Switzerland	1.59	1.47	1.50	6	8	7	34.17	30.00
Syria	5.34	4.20	3.40	180	200	160		<40
Tajikistan	5.05	3.70	2.87	130	120	100		
Tanzania	6.25	5.75	5.03	770	1100	1500	48.57	56.00
Thailand	2.27	2.02	1.80	200	44	44	37.66	35.71
Timor-Leste			6.50		850	660		
Togo	6.60	5.40	4.90	640	980	570	51.25	56.25
Tonga	4.16	4.18	3.40					
Trinidad and Tobago	2.36	1.89	1.75	90	65	160	32.84	50.00
Tunisia	3.50	2.67	2.08	170	70	120		<50
Turkey	3.00	2.65	2.23	180	55	70		56.25
Turkmenistan	4.17	3.75	2.70	55	65	31		

Continued

Table 1.1 *Continued*

	Total fertility rate			Maternal deaths per 100,000 live births			Percentage of women among population (15–49 years) with HIV/AIDS	
	1990	1995	2002	1990	1995	2000	1997	2003
Uganda	6.98	6.72	6.00	1200	1100	880	49.43	60.00
Ukraine	1.85	1.40	1.20	50	45	35		33.33
United Arab Emirates	4.12	3.62	3.00	26	30	54		
United Kingdom	1.83	1.71	1.66	9	10	13		29.79
United States	2.08	2.02	2.10	12	12	17	19.75	25.53
Uruguay	2.51	2.60	2.19	85	50	27	17.31	32.76
Uzbekistan	4.07	3.60	2.35	55	60	24		33.64
Vanuatu	5.54	4.94	4.26	280	32	130		
Venezuela	3.43	3.10	2.72	120	43	96	14.81	32.00
Vietnam	3.62	2.67	1.87	160	95	130	19.77	32.50
Yemen	7.53	6.48	6.00	1400	850	570		
Zambia	6.32	5.92	5.05	940	870	750	50.68	56.63
Zimbabwe	4.78	4.10	3.65	570	610	1100	51.43	58.13

Source: UN *Demographic Yearbook* (UN 2002), *World Development Indicators* (World Bank 2004) and UNAIDS *Report on the Global AIDS Epidemic* (UNAIDS 1998, 2004).

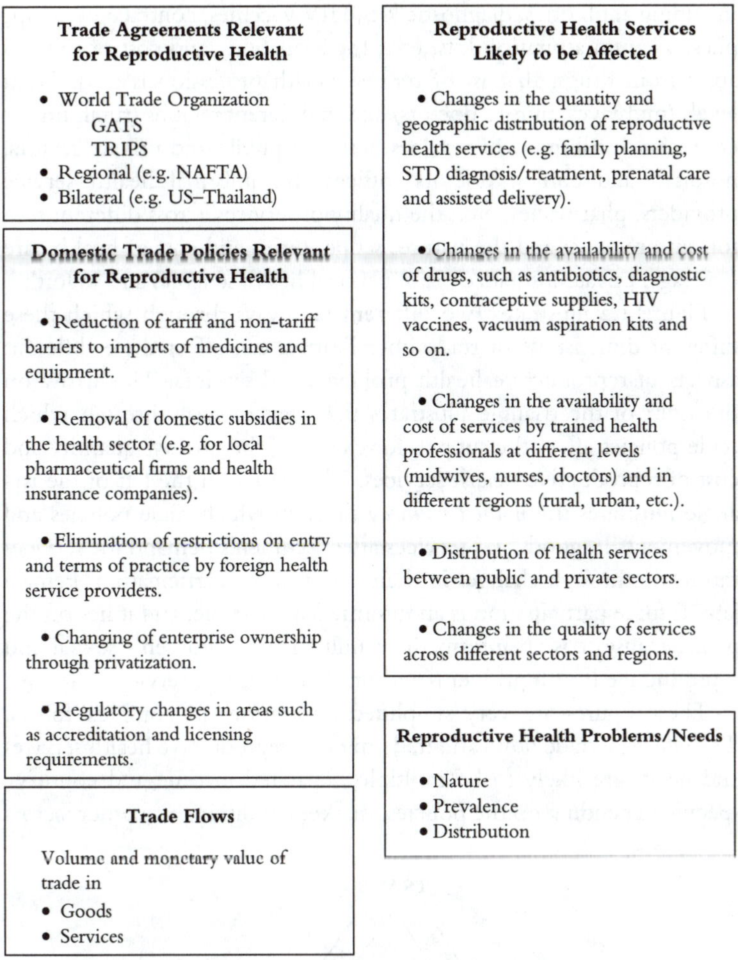

Trade Agreements Relevant for Reproductive Health	Reproductive Health Services Likely to be Affected
• World Trade Organization 　　GATS 　　TRIPS • Regional (e.g. NAFTA) • Bilateral (e.g. US–Thailand)	• Changes in the quantity and geographic distribution of reproductive health services (e.g. family planning, STD diagnosis/treatment, prenatal care and assisted delivery).

Domestic Trade Policies Relevant for Reproductive Health

• Reduction of tariff and non-tariff barriers to imports of medicines and equipment.

• Removal of domestic subsidies in the health sector (e.g. for local pharmaceutical firms and health insurance companies).

• Elimination of restrictions on entry and terms of practice by foreign health service providers.

• Changing of enterprise ownership through privatization.

• Regulatory changes in areas such as accreditation and licensing requirements.

Trade Flows

Volume and monetary value of trade in
• Goods
• Services

• Changes in the availability and cost of drugs, such as antibiotics, diagnostic kits, contraceptive supplies, HIV vaccines, vacuum aspiration kits and so on.

• Changes in the availability and cost of services by trained health professionals at different levels (midwives, nurses, doctors) and in different regions (rural, urban, etc.).

• Distribution of health services between public and private sectors.

• Changes in the quality of services across different sectors and regions.

Reproductive Health Problems/Needs

• Nature
• Prevalence
• Distribution

Figure 1.1 Dimensions of trade and reproductive health.

Certain trade policies such as the reduction of barriers to imports of medicines and equipment, the removal of domestic subsidies (e.g. for local pharmaceutical firms and health insurance companies), foreign direct investment in private medical facilities and changes in patent regulations can be expected to have direct effects on the quantity and geographic distribution of reproductive health services of various types (e.g. family planning, STD diagnosis and treatment, prenatal care, and assisted delivery); the availability and cost of drugs and lab procedures, including antibiotics, diagnostic kits, HIV vaccines, contraceptive supplies, vacuum aspiration kits, etc.; the availability and cost of services apart from drugs, that is, of trained health professionals at different levels (midwives, nurses, doctors) and in different regions (rural, urban, etc.); the distribution of services between public and private sectors, hospitals and clinics, doctors' offices and informal health service providers, pharmacies, etc.; the quality of services across different sectors and regions; and the nature, scope, terms and cost of health care coverage, private insurance plans, national health schemes and so forth.[5]

Figure 1.2 illustrates two different pathways through which these different dimensions of trade liberalization can affect these different aspects of reproductive health problems and services. The arrow on the right of the triangle illustrates the *direct pathway* through which trade policies affect the supply, for example, the quality, quantity and cost of reproductive health services. The arrow on the left of the triangle illustrates the *indirect pathway* through which trade policies and movements in goods and services affect women's demand for services indirectly through changes in their labour force participation. Female labour force participation is an intermediate variable, and it lies on the path because it is an intermediate influence on women's sexual and reproductive health problems and on their access to services.

These figures are very simplified illustrations of complex forces. The effects of trade flows and trade rules on reproductive health services and needs are likely to be multiple, separated in time and country-specific depending on the policies, market conditions and other factors

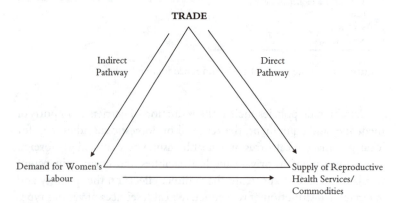

Figure 1.2 Pathways between trade, women's employment and reproductive health.

that prevail at any given time in a country. Furthermore, the framework in Figure 1.2 indicates that assigning causality may be complicated as the arrows go in multiple directions, for example, from trade policies to reproductive health and also from health outcomes and health services to trade flows. Well-designed prospective longitudinal studies that track the direction and order of magnitude of effects within countries and over time will be important for disentangling and understanding the causal linkages.

Direct Pathways: Trade Agreements and Provision of Reproductive Health Services

Two core World Trade Organization (WTO) agreements for reproductive health are the General Agreement on Trade in Services (GATS) and the Agreement on Trade-Related Aspects of Intellectual Property Rights (TRIPS).[6] This section reviews the potential impact of these agreements on the provision of reproductive health services, commodities and technologies.

General Agreement on Trade in Services

GATS, established in 1994, is the first multilateral agreement to provide a framework for countries to determine which service sectors of the economy they wish to open up to foreign suppliers and to competition, and what restrictions countries wish to implement to limit trade.[7] Lipson (see Chapter 2) describes the rules and commitments of GATS and their influence on reproductive health services. She notes that, to date, GATS rules and individual country commitments have had minimal direct or significant impact on national policies concerning reproductive health. However, as more countries schedule GATS commitments, and as for-profit actors gain ground in the delivery and financing of reproductive health services, GATS and the public regulation of providers will become more important. Thus, the potential impacts described below provide a guide to the issues that should be documented in future research.

Health services under GATS can be traded through four modes: (1) *cross-border supply*, defined as the provision of services from a practitioner in one country to a patient or practitioner in another country, predominantly through the Internet, satellite transmission of medical images, teleconference and international telephone calls; (2) *consumption abroad*, where patients travel from one country to another to obtain treatment; (3) *commercial presence*, when a foreign company invests in or opens a subsidiary office in another country to provide health services; (4) *the emigration of health professionals* (doctors, nurses, specialists, paramedics, midwives, technicians, consultants, trainers, health management personnel and other professionals) between different countries. Each of these modes may affect access to and provision of reproductive health services.

The provision of telemedicine across national borders may have several different effects on the availability and quality of reproductive health care for women in developing countries. Telemedicine can help rural women whose reproductive health needs tend to be underserved, owing to the lack of primary health clinics and medical personnel in more remote areas. The quality of reproductive care can be enhanced through exchange of knowledge between medical professionals across borders about the range of reproductive health issues, service provision and new technologies. Moreover, 'virtual' partnerships between hospitals in developing countries and medical research centres in the developed world can facilitate and speed up the transfer of technology and knowledge that increases the quality of health care delivery. The most obvious disadvantage of cross-border supply of health is that it is largely dependent on telecommunication infrastructure, which developing countries generally lack, particularly in rural areas. As a result, it is plausible that cross-border provision will serve a minority of the female population, predominantly from urban areas. This can further exacerbate the persistent inequalities that exist between rural women, who tend to be poorer and have less access to health centres, and urban women, who tend to be better off economically and have better access to quality health care. Moreover, although telemedicine is still in its infancy and is largely being explored through pilot projects on a non-commercial basis, its growth requires substantial investment, which could potentially divert funds from rural and primary health care for women towards specialized centres catering to the more affluent population in developing countries.

Mode 2 of GATS could have a positive benefit for reproductive health if countries invest in the education and training of medical and nursing personnel, medical technology and equipment at public health centres, and if they raise wages and make other improvements that make them desirable medical care destinations.[8] However, there is concern that consumption abroad can create a dual market system consisting of a high-quality expensive structure catering to wealthy nationals and foreigners, and a lower quality and resource constrained system for the poor (Chanda 2001). Thus, it can potentially compromise women's access to affordable and quality reproductive care at public hospitals and health clinics.

The third mode, commercial presence, can generate investment in health infrastructure and modern medical technology as well as strengthen health personnel's skills and knowledge about emerging reproductive health issues. Foreign investment may also increase women's employment opportunities in a variety of occupations in the health sector. Increased income may enable women to afford preventative care that can improve their overall health, influence their quality of life and increase their longevity (see the section on 'Indirect Pathways' below). Commercial presence also has the potential to stimulate competition in service delivery, potentially raising the quality of health care. Additionally, partnerships between local hospitals and medical facilities in industrialized countries can also help improve facilities in developing countries by introducing more modern and preventative technologies such as ovarian cancer screening exams.

On the other hand, corporate hospitals may be established, using public funds and subsidies, diverting resources away from the public health system, which can affect the availability of public services and the quality of care. Furthermore, commercial presence exacerbates the danger of a dual health care system, whereby corporate facilities tend to a minority of the population using the latest technologies and more skilled health professionals. Internal 'brain drain' can also result as better-trained nurses and doctors move from the public to the private sector, owing to better salaries and affiliation with a more modern and sophisticated hospital. The drain of medical personnel from the public health care system would affect women, especially poor women, more significantly than men due to their greater use of public health care (PAHO 2002). As the quality of public health care deteriorates, women's reproductive health may be compromised. They may face higher risks of infection and disease that could be prevented with adequate medical staffing and with properly equipped public health centres.

Although GATS does not force governments to privatize, it facilitates the commercialization of basic public services, especially when combined with the other pressures for privatization that developing countries face, whether through conditionality in multilateral loan

agreements or donor-financed sector-wide approaches, or because of
resource constraints. Critics caution that committing to foreign commercial presence in the health sector should be done only after careful
scrutiny, as the involvement of foreign companies in the health sector
requires national and regional health authorities to develop strong
regulatory, analytical and managerial capacity if local authorities are to
see the benefits of working with foreign companies (Hilary 2001). The
majority of the developing world does not have this framework in
place, and privatization of health care can potentially compromise the
quality of public health care. A final worry is that because the governments in many developing countries have made substantial commitments and accepted a higher share of full market access bindings under
Mode 2 (cross-border supply) and Mode 3 (commercial presence),
without implementation experience, they may have less latitude to
reverse course.[9]

To date, most GATS Mode 4 commitments have remained limited
in breadth and depth; evidence suggests that national policies provide
better access conditions for foreign health professionals than those
bound under GATS (WHO and WTO 2002). On the positive side,
this mode of trade may have two impacts for reproductive health.
First, knowledge may be transferred and cultural norms in the exporting country may change in ways that open up opportunities for better
reproductive health care. Second, remittances sent by medical professionals living abroad can supplement household incomes, paying for
expenses that women traditionally absorb, such as food security and
children's education. As a result, women may be able to afford reproductive care, or better quality care, than they were previously able to
access. On the other hand, there is overwhelming concern about the
effects of the brain drain of skilled medical professionals from developing to developed countries on health services in the exporting countries
(see Chapter 10).

Trade-Related Aspects of Intellectual Property Rights Agreement

The TRIPS Agreement, formally adopted by WTO member countries
in January 1995, requires signatory countries of WTO to recognize and
protect both process and product innovations in all technological
fields, including pharmaceuticals.[10] This agreement is likely to affect
research, production and distribution of pharmaceuticals, reproductive

technologies, supplies and vaccines, with implications for access, quality of care and informed choice. On the negative side, it can potentially increase drug prices and limit women's access to affordable and preventative reproductive health supplies. Indeed, a series of studies conducted on the impact of patents on drug prices in a set of developing countries showed that patents increase drug prices between 12 and 68 per cent (Scherer and Watal 2001).

On the other hand, the TRIPS Agreement can, in principle, increase access to more affordable generic drugs, which has important implications for price competition. For instance, generic drugs can enter the market more readily and become more accessible through TRIPS safeguards such as compulsory licensing, parallel imports and the Bolar provision.[11] Governments can reduce drug prices by granting compulsory licensing for the production and importation of cheaper generic drugs. However, since only a small group of developing countries have the manufacturing potential to produce generic drugs, the full potential of this safeguard is limited to them. Through parallel importation, poor countries can buy patented drugs at the lowest price offered in the world market by the patent holder. Finally, the Bolar provision would hasten the process of introducing generic drugs into the local market.

A case study of the impact of TRIPS on patented HIV/AIDS drugs in South Africa is provided in Chapter 9. Although the TRIPS provisions have not yet been fully implemented in many developing countries, the South African experience of securing access to antiretroviral treatment in response to the AIDS crisis shows the difficulty, in practice, in implementing these flexibilities.

Trade liberalization and financing reproductive health services

Beyond GATS and TRIPS, trade liberalization may affect financing for reproductive health systems. It is widely accepted that achieving quality and effective health and supply systems, including access to essential drugs and technologies, requires substantial domestic and international resources. Much has been made of the potential of export revenues to finance health and human development. However, one point often underemphasized in these discussions about the public finance implications of trade liberalization is that, at least in the short term, the liberalization of trade may create a fiscal squeeze in many countries, resulting from reductions in revenue from tariff and non-tariff duties (Rao 1999; Hilary 2001; UNDP 2004). Jordan, for instance, has seen international trade taxes decline from 48 per cent of total government revenue in 1980 to 23 per cent in 1997, and Botswana from 39 per cent to 12 per cent (World Bank 2000).

Few countries have managed to offset the negative effect of tariff reductions by a corresponding expansion in their total value of trade (Rao 1999; Hilary 2001). Moreover, in several developing countries, the transition from trade taxes to domestic taxes is not always feasible in the short term and other sources of revenue are necessary to fill the gap. In this context, increased attention should be given to alternatives such as increased donor donations, foreign assistance and the mobilization of domestic revenue through tax reform.

Indirect Pathways: Trade Liberalization, Women's Employment and Reproductive Health

One indirect pathway through which trade liberalization affects reproductive health is through gendered changes in labour markets.[12] Trade liberalization affects both employment demand and supply, but this chapter focuses on changes in labour demand brought about by the reduction of tariff and non-tariff barriers to trade, as well as associated flow of foreign investment (see Das and Grown 2002 for a more elaborate treatment of the indirect pathway).

Different components of trade will affect labour demand differentially. For instance, foreign direct investment may give rise to considerable labour mobility that is gender-differentiated, that is, to job shifts across and within sectors, to geographical mobility, and to transitions in and out of the labour force. The elimination of tariffs, quotas, subsidies and other instruments of trade policy can also affect labour demand according to the geographic location, worker characteristics (e.g. age, sex, marital status, education, skill level), economic sector (e.g. agriculture, manufacturing, services), type and size of economic enterprise (e.g. public, private or parastatal, formal and informal, family-based enterprises), type of employment (e.g. wage and salary, own-account, unpaid family labour), and conditions of work, including nature of employment contract, job security, seasonality, benefits and working hours. This section briefly reviews the empirical evidence on the impact of trade liberalization on selected dimensions of women's employment and women's reproductive health problems and access to services.

The effect of trade liberalization on women's employment

Both increased foreign direct investment and elimination of export taxes have increased the demand for female labour in manufacturing, services and some types of agricultural employment in many countries. Semi-industrialized economies that emphasize export manufacturing have experienced a rise in the female share of employment, especially in the early phases of industrialization, although the process of femi-nization of export employment may decline or even reverse as these economies mature.[13] In developing economies that rely heavily on service exports (such as informatics and tourism), women also constitute a large share of export workers (Davidson-O'Connell and Sanchez-Taylor 1999; UN 1999; Freeman 2000). An additional benefit of service-sector export labour (e.g. nurses or domestic workers) is the remittances that generate foreign exchange for the home economy (UN 1999).[14] Finally, in developing economies that have emphasized exports of agricultural crops as part of their liberalization strategy, women have increased job opportunities as seasonal or contract workers or as labourers on husbands' or relatives' land (Deere 2004).[15]

Import liberalization, on the other hand, has been associated with job losses, especially in manufacturing sectors that are import sensitive, in both developed and developing countries. Several studies have found that traditional or domestic industries where women predomi-nate may be displaced by the import of cheaper goods and services (Joekes 1995). In India, for instance, employment losses from trade liberalization were concentrated in the traditional textile industry. In industrialized countries, Kucera and Milberg (2000) find evidence of declines in females' share of manufacturing employment in industries sensitive to import competition.

As noted above, the importance of women's employment in the indirect path from trade to reproductive health and rights is primarily in its influence on girls' and women's sexual and reproductive health problems, on their access to services through their health insurance coverage, and their ability to pay for medical care.[16] Work-related health problems include: occupational health and safety issues (such as birth defects or infertility caused by chemicals), exhaustion, stress, sexual harassment on the job, forced pregnancy tests or a myriad of other problems and needs. Work-related health insurance coverage or the ability to pay for services can include the gain or loss of a variety of health benefits, private or public, such as eligibility for national health insurance paid by employer and employee contributions, or cash incomes to pay for services. Refusal to permit time off from work for health-related reasons, or a woman's concern about loss of income if she does take time off, can interfere with her access to services for herself and her family. The following sections review the evidence for trade-induced changes in women's employment and the implications for reproductive health problems and access to services.

Factory employment

Export-oriented factory employment can be both positive and negative for women's reproductive health and rights. The mixed nature of the effects is evident, for instance, in Bangladesh, where the recruitment of adolescent girls into the burgeoning garment industry has had the positive effect of delaying marriage and childbirth (see Chapter 4 and Amin et al. 1998). Some studies find that as women's access to outside income rises, they are better able to renegotiate the distribution of resources within the household to the benefit of themselves and their children (Kabeer 2000). The source and stability of this income appears to play a role in influencing women's bargaining power and their overall status and well-being (Haddad et al. 1997).

On the negative side, export-oriented factory employment may have put young female workers at greater risk of early sexual activity and sexual harassment and may have changed the traditional needs for contraceptive services, which in Bangladesh are sought typically after marriage. Moreover, Amin et al.'s (1998) study also points out that the girls recruited by the garment factories are often below the minimum age for child labour, which affects their educational attainment; being in school provides important knowledge about reproductive health. If they live with their families, young female workers are also not likely to have much power to negotiate control over their earnings.

Occupational and environmental health problems have also been associated with export employment, although the extent to which their degree and frequency is greater or less than those in domestic employment is not known. Employment in export processing zones (EPZs) in many countries, for instance, has been associated with high levels of machine-related accidents, dust, noise, poor ventilation and exposure to toxic chemicals. These factors create additional pressure on already highly stressful work, resulting in cardiovascular and psychological disorders. In the young women who work in EPZs, the stress can affect reproductive health, leading to miscarriage, problems with pregnancies and poor foetal health.[17] This has been the case of the horticultural workers in the export sector in Chile, where rates of malformation among newborns were higher among temporary workers in the industry than among workers in the general population (Rodríguez and Venegas 1991; Venegas 1993).[18] Three studies in Mexico suggest that women working in *maquiladoras* may be more likely than other women to give birth to low birth weight babies (Eskenazi et al. 1993; Denman et al. 2003). Thus, the health hazards associated with working with chemical pesticides further dampen the positive employment effects for women (Thrupp et al. 1995; Dolan et al. 1999), although some recent studies report that progress has been made on improving labour conditions as a result of advocacy on the issues (Newman 2001; Friedemann-Sanchez 2004).

Home-based paid work

Another category of female employment that is on the increase with trade liberalization is home-based paid work in which women predominate (Chen et al. 1999; Carr et al. 2000). Not only do informally employed women lack formal contracts and security in their work, but they also do not have access to leave or health benefits (Balakrishnan 2002). The fact that they are invisible in employment statistics prevents their reproductive and occupational health needs from being considered in employment, health or industrial policies.[19] Moreover, although home-based workers bring in income, and this type of work may be a more viable employment option for women with small children, their access to health care may be as limited as those who do not earn income.

Sex work

Several recent studies have pointed to the increase in sex work with globalization (UN 1999; Upadhyay 2000; Subramaniam 2001). The growth of the services sector and the concomitant expansion of the tourism and hospitality industry create a demand for sex work. Under- and unemployment, including that associated with liberalization, can drive women into sex work or to undertake transactional sex to buy a better quality of life (Malhotra and Mathur 2000; Luke 2001). Women who use sex as a tradable commodity have multiple partners and are at greater risk of contracting HIV/AIDS and other sexually transmitted diseases.

Part-time and seasonal work

Job security arising from trade-related employment may be questionable; the increased employment opportunities may be short-lived (Smith et al. 2004). The seasonality of non-traditional agricultural jobs, for example, implies that work is available only at certain times of the year. In the case of the Chilean and South African grape export industries, women are the preferred source of temporary workers and hold a very small share of permanent jobs (Barrientos 2001). The subcontracting system in other sectors entails that employment is only available when the factories need a particular part or product. Women in these types of jobs are often paid by the piece, receive no income for out of season unemployment and are not covered by employer-based health insurance plans.

Work, migration and reproductive health

Trade liberalization has been associated with large-scale migrations in the last few decades (Sassen 1998; Dixon-Mueller and Germain 2000). In fact, the same countries that have opened up to trade in recent years have also had large-scale migration of labour from rural to urban areas. Countries in Southeast and East Asia, notably, have had patterns of female-dominated migration and increased participation of women in the labour force since the 1970s (Dixon-Mueller and Germain 2000; Hugo 2000).

How does migration affect women's reproductive health? Female migrants are exposed to new experiences, ideas, knowledge, skills and communities (see Chapter 5). They may also be able to move out of the family dominated social realm into a more public realm. Often, they have control over their earnings, even though they remit some of their earnings to their families (Kabeer 2000). In addition, moving into urban areas and to more developed countries bring access to reproductive technologies and services that may not have been available near their homes. However, Hugo (2000) points out that migration is only empowering if it is not clandestine, if it is rural to urban, if women work outside the home in formal jobs and if they migrate permanently rather than temporarily.

The process of migration can put women at risk from sexual activity (UN 1999; Hugo 2000). When women migrate in search of employment, they are subject to the same risks from sexual activity as women who enter paid employment for the first time, except that migrant women are more vulnerable. Migrant men seeking sex also put themselves and their sexual partners at risk of contracting HIV/AIDS. Moreover, the provision of public services lags behind migration; for instance, in Sri Lanka, the ratio of pregnant women to public health midwives per service area has increased tenfold in one EPZ, because the government has not redistributed health resources to keep up with regional migration patterns associated with the creation of EPZs (Hettiarachchy and Schensul 2001).

Summary

In summary, the pathway between trade liberalization, female employment and women's reproductive health problems and access to services is complex. The effects of liberalization on women's employment and their reproductive health problems are both positive and negative. Sector and type of employment – whether regular, contractual or seasonal, self-employment or waged, factory or home-based, full-time or part-time – all determine the positive and negative nature of the effects. In addition, the conditions under which women enter the labour force – from a position of strength or weakness – also determine their bargaining power, both in the workplace and at home, which affects their ability to access reproductive health care and translate their reproductive rights into positive outcomes.

Conclusion

This chapter has presented a framework for understanding two of the possible pathways through which the liberalization of trade can affect women's reproductive health and rights. It has specified a direct pathway, through which trade policies affect the supply of reproductive health services, and an indirect pathway, through which trade policies and movements in goods and services affect women's demand for services indirectly through changes in their labour force participation.

Although these are not the only two routes through which the linkages between trade liberalization and reproductive health are established, they nonetheless provide a starting point that can guide future research and advocacy.

As the discussion of direct pathways implied, monitoring current multilateral negotiations and implementation of trade agreements once they are signed can be important for advancing reproductive health and rights. Monitoring efforts should focus on the interrelationship between WTO commitments and the International Conference on Population and Development (ICPD) goals, as well as other international treaties or agreements, such as those human rights conventions that cover reproductive health and rights. Efforts to ensure coherence between international agreements can prevent WTO agreements from undermining the achievement of ICPD goals. It will also be important to track what sorts of reproductive health services for-profit firms are pursuing, to see whether they are concentrating in high-tech care, for example. In some countries, it may not be WTO agreements, but rather domestic regulations that determine whether foreign reproductive health providers can set up operations or invest in a given country.

The discussion of indirect pathways underscores the importance of country and comparative studies for understanding trade-induced employment changes and their impacts on women's reproductive health problems and access to services. Such studies may be particularly useful for policymakers, employers and trade unions or workers' associations because they would identify particular problems in specific places that may be amenable to intervention to improve health and rights.

Notes

This chapter is a consolidated version of two working papers, one co-authored with Maitreyi Das and the other co-authored with Guadalupe Duron, both prepared in 1992–93 as part of an exploratory project undertaken by the International Center for Research on Women (ICRW). Some of the material in this chapter has also been incorporated into a chapter in *Globalization, Women, and Health in the Twenty-First Century* by Kickbusch et al. (2005), as well as an article in *Development*, vol. 48, no. 4, December 2005. Thanks to Palgrave-Macmillan for permission to reproduce parts of those articles, and to Elissa Braunstein and Diane Elson for comments on this chapter.

1. As Lipson (see Chapter 2) states, 'In most countries, trade in health-related goods and services is a relatively minor factor affecting the availability, cost and quality of health services. The ways in which each country organizes, finances and regulates health services are usually much more important determinants of whether countries are able to ensure the delivery of basic health care to their people, without financially burdening the poor. But trade can influence some particularly critical health goods, such as life-saving pharmaceuticals, or the availability of certain services if only foreign-owned companies offer them. It is in these situations where trade and the rules governing such trade come into play.'

2. Most indicators cover the medical and demographic aspects of reproductive health. Indicators are being developed to capture the socio-political dimensions of reproductive health, but they are not available for a large number of countries. There are few indicators for reproductive rights that are agreed upon and available across countries.

3. Although there are distinct country trends and modes of transmission, many analysts highlight gender inequality – especially the rules governing sexual relationships and sexual violence – as a major factor driving the increase of the epidemic (Rao Gupta 2000; UNAIDS 2004).

4. Distinguishing empirically the effects of trade liberalization on reproductive health outcomes (or vice versa) from other policies and forces (such as health sector reform) may be difficult.

5. Thanks are due to Ruth Dixon Mueller who outlined these schemas at a meeting at ICRW on 8-9 April 2002.

6. Other agreements, such as the Agreement on Agriculture, may also affect reproductive health outcomes through changes in food consumption and nutritional status.

7. As of 2003, fifty-four countries, nearly half of the WTO members, have made commitments to at least one of the trading modes under GATS.

8. Several developing countries, including India and Cuba, promote their health services to foreigners.

9. When a GATS commitment is made in a sector, it is legally binding. Governments must wait three years after the commitment is made to modify or withdraw commitments and may be liable for financial losses as a result of the change.

10. Prior to the TRIPS Agreement, a substantial number of developing countries did not adequately cover intellectual property rights for medicines and pharmaceutical products. In addition, patent coverage was highly inconsistent between some developing countries, ranging from as little as three years (Thailand) to as long as sixteen years (South Africa). These conditions generally favoured the local production of less expensive generic medicines where possible (see Williams 2001).

11. Parallel importation (Article 6) is 'importation, without the consent of the patent holder, of a patented product marketed in another country either by the patent holder or with the patent holder's consent.' Parallel importation

is often used to promote price competition between equivalent patented products, one of which is usually marketed at a lower price in other countries. The Bolar provision (Article 30) allows a generic producer to conduct all tests required for marketing approval in advance, so that a generic drug can be put on the market as soon as the patent expires. The TRIPS Agreement does not permit 'stockpiling' or large-scale commercial production of the generic drug before the patent expires.

12. Another indirect pathway is through the household. For instance, changes in the husband's status or in the status of other earners in the household may affect a woman's reproductive health and her access to services (if it is through another earner's health insurance).

13. In Taiwan, Hong Kong, South Korea and Singapore, as well as in Mexico's *maquiladoras*, women's share of manufacturing employment first increased and then fell in later stages of industrialization.

14. The sex trade is also one of the fastest growing and most profitable service industries (see UN 1999).

15. In some countries, such as in Latin America, economic restructuring and globalization have led to the feminization of agriculture as women seek remunerative employment to supplement declining family income (Deere 2004). Countries that export unprocessed primary products (such as ores) do not fit the stylized fact for agriculturally based economies.

16. It is important to recognize that apart from women's own employment, changes in the husband's employment status or that of other earners in the household may affect women's reproductive health and access to services, for example, if husbands lose health insurance that covers all family members. However, these will not be considered further here.

17. Causality is not clear. Women employed in export production frequently enter the workforce in poor health, being undernourished and anaemic (Loewenson 1999).

18. It is important to note that these studies do not control for selection bias; it may be that other characteristics of workers in the horticultural industry are responsible for this outcome.

19. Chikan embroidery workers in the north Indian town of Lucknow have long had serious back- and eye-related problems, but only after the Self-Employed Women's Association organized them did these problems appear on the advocacy agenda (Das and Grown 2002).

References

Amin, S., I. Diamond, R.T. Naved and M. Newby (1998) 'Transition to Adulthood of Female Garment-Factory Workers in Bangladesh', *Studies in Family Planning*, vol. 29, no. 2: 185–200.

Balakrishnan, R. (ed.) (2002) *The Hidden Assembly Line: Gender Dynamics of Subcontracted Work in a Global Economy*, Bloomfield, CT: Kumarian Press.

Barrientos, S. (2001) 'Gender, Flexibility, and Global Value Chains', *IDS Bulletin*, vol. 32, no. 3: 83–93.

Carr, M., M. Alter Chen and J. Tate (2000) 'Globalization and Home-Based Workers', *Feminist Economics*, vol. 6, no. 3: 123–42.

Chanda, R. (2001) 'Trade in Health Services', Commission on Macroeconomics and Health Working Paper Series, Paper No. WG4:5, Geneva: World Health Organization.

Chen, M., J. Sebstad and L. O'Connell (1999) 'Counting the Invisible Workforce: The case of Homebased Workers', *World Development*, vol. 27, no. 3: 603–10.

Das, M., and C. Grown (2002) 'Trade Liberalization, Women's Employment, and Reproductive Health: What are the Linkages and Entry Points for Policy and Action?', International Center for Research on Women Working Paper, Washington, DC: International Center for Research on Women.

Davidson-O'Connell, J., and J. Sanchez-Taylor (1999) 'Fantasy Islands: Exploring the Demand for Sex Tourism', in K. Kempadoo (ed.), *Sun, Sex and Gold: Sex tourism in the Caribbean*, Lanham, MD: Rowman and Littlefield.

Deere, C.D. (2004) 'The Feminization of Agriculture? Economic Restructuring in Rural Latin America', Background paper for UNRISD Policy Report on Gender and Development: An UNRISD Contribution to Beijing Plus Ten, Geneva: United Nations Research Institute for Social Development.

Denman, C., L. Cedillo and S. Harlow (2003) 'Work and Health in Export Industries at National Borders', in J. Heymann (ed.), *Global Inequalities at Work: Work's Impact on the Health of Individuals, Families, and Societies*, New York: Oxford University Press.

Dixon-Mueller, R., and A. Germain (2000) 'Reproductive Health and the Demographic Imagination', in H. Presser and G. Sen (eds), *Women's Empowerment and Demographic Processes*, Oxford: Oxford University Press.

Dolan, C., J. Humphrey and C. Harris-Pascal (1999) 'Horticulture Commodity Chains: The Impact of the UK Market on the African Fresh Vegetable Industry', IDS Working Paper No. 96, Brighton, UK: Institute of Development Studies.

Eskenazi, B., S. Guendelman and E. Elkin (1993) 'A Preliminary Study of Reproductive Outcomes of Female Maquiladora Workers in Tijuana, Mexico', *American Journal of Industrial Medicine*, vol. 24, no. 6: 667–76.

Freeman, Carla (2000) *High Tech and High Heels in the Global Economy: Women, Work, and Pink Collar Identities in the Caribbean*, Durham, NC: Duke University Press.

Friedemann-Sanchez, G. (2004) 'Assets, Wage Income, and Social Capital in Intrahousehold Bargaining Among Women Workers in Colombia's Cut-Flower Industry', Paper presented at the Workshop on Women and the Distribution of Wealth at the Yale Center for International and Area Studies, New Haven, CT, 12–13 November.

Haddad, L., J. Hoddinott and H. Alderman (1997) 'Intrahousehold Resource Allocation, an Overview', in L. Haddad, J. Hoddinott and H. Alderman (eds), *Intrahousehold Resource Allocation in Developing Countries: Models, Methods and Policy*, Baltimore, MD: Johns Hopkins Press.

Hettiarachchy, T., and S.L. Schensul (2001) 'The Risks of Pregnancy and the Consequences Among Young Unmarried Women Working in a Free Trade Zone in Sri Lanka', *Asia Pacific Population Journal*, vol. 16, no. 2: 125–40.

Hilary, J. (2001) *The Wrong Model. GATS, Trade Liberalisation and Children's Right to Health*, London, UK: Save the Children.

Hugo, G.J. (2000) 'Migration and Women's Empowerment', in H.B. Presser and G. Sen (eds), *Women's Empowerment and Demographic Processes: Moving Beyond Cairo*, Oxford: Oxford University Press.

Joekes, S. (1995) 'Trade-Related Employment for Women in Industry and Services in Developing Countries', Occasional Paper No. 5, Geneva: UNRISD.

Kabeer, N. (2000) *The Power to Choose: Bangladeshi Women and Labour Market Decisions in London and Dhaka*, London: Verso.

Kickbusch, I., K. Hartwig and J. List (eds) (2005) *Globalization, Women, and Health in the Twenty-First Century*, New York: Palgrave-Macmillan.

Kucera, D., and W. Milberg (2000) 'Gender Segregation and Gender Bias in Manufacturing Trade Expansion: Revisiting the "Wood Asymmetry"', *World Development*, vol. 28, no. 7: 1191–1210.

Loewenson, R. (1999) 'Women's Occupational Health in Globalization and Development', *American Journal of Industrial Medicine*, vol. 36, no. 1: 34–42.

Luke, N. (2001) 'Cross-Generational and Transactional Sexual Relations in Sub-Saharan Africa: A Review of the Evidence on Prevalence and Implications for Negotiation of Safe Sexual Practices for Adolescent Girls', Paper prepared for the International Center for Research on Women as part of the AIDSMark Project, Washington, DC: International Center for Research on Women.

Malhotra, A., and S. Mathur (2000) 'The Economics of Young Women's Sexuality in Nepal', Paper presented at the IAFFE Conference Istanbul, Turkey.

Newman, C. (2001) *Gender, Time Use and Change: Impacts of Agricultural Employment in Ecuador*, Washington, DC: World Bank.

Pan American Health Organization (2002) *36th Session of the Subcommittee on Planning and Programming of the Executive Meeting*, Washington, DC: Pan American Health Organization.

Rao, J.M. (1999) 'Globalization and the Fiscal Autonomy of the State', *Background Papers: Human Development Report 1999*, New York: United Nations Development Program.

Rao Gupta, G. (2000) "Gender, sexuality, and HIV/AIDS: the what, the why, and the how." Plenary address at the 13th International AIDS Conference, Durban, South Africa.

Rodríguez, D., and S. Venegas (1991) *Los Trabajadores de la Fruta en Cifras*, Santiago: GEA.

Sassen, S. (1998) 'Informalization in Advanced Market Economies', Issues in Development Discussion Paper 20, Geneva: International Labour Organization.

Scherer, F.M., and J. Watal (2001) 'Post-TRIPS Options for Access to Patented Medicines in Developing Countries', Commission on Macroeconomics and Health Working Paper Series, Paper No. WG4: 1, Geneva: The World Health Organization.

Smith, S., D. Auret, S. Barrientos, C. Dolan, K. Kleinbooi, C. Njobvu, M. Opondo and A. Tallontire (2004) 'Ethical Trade in African Horticulture: Gender, Rights and Participation', IDS Working Paper 223, Brighton, Sussex: Institute for Development Studies.

Subramaniam, V. (2001) 'The Impact of Globalization on Women's Reproductive Health and Rights: A Regional Perspective', *Development*, vol. 42, no. 4: 145–9.

Thrupp, L.A., G. Bergeron and W.F. Waters (1995) *Bittersweet Harvests for Global Supermarkets: Challenges in Latin America's Agricultural Export Boom*, Washington, DC: World Resources Institute.

UN (1995) 'Population and Development', Programme of Action Adopted at the International Conference on Population and Development, Cairo, 5–13 September 1994, New York: United Nations (Document No. ST/ESA/SER.A/149).

UN (1999) *1999 World Survey on the Role of Women in Development: Globalization, Gender, and Work*, New York: United Nations.

UN (2002) *Demographic Yearbook*, New York: United Nations.

UNAIDS (1998) 'A Global Overview of the AIDS Epidemic', in *1998 Report on the Global AIDS Epidemic*, Available from: http://www.unaids.org.

UNAIDS (2004) 'A Global Overview of the AIDS Epidemic', in *2004 Report on the Global AIDS Epidemic*, Available from: http://www.unaids.org.

UNAIDS/WHO (2004) *The AIDS Epidemic Update*, Geneva: UNAIDS.

UNCTAD (2004) *Trade and Development Report 2004*, Geneva: United Nations.

UNCTAD/WHO (1998) *International Trade in Health Services, a Development Perspective*, Geneva: United Nations.

UNDP (2004) *Making Global Trade Work for People*, London: Earthscan Publications.

Upadhyay, U.D. (2000) 'India's New Economic Policy of 1991 and Its Impact on Women's Poverty and AIDS', *Feminist Economics*, vol. 6, no. 3: 105–22.

Venegas, S. (1993) 'Programas de apoyo a temporeros y temporeras en Chile', in S. Gomes and E. Klein (eds), *Los Pobres del Campo, El Trabajador Eventual*, Santiago: FLACSO/PREALC/OIT.

Williams, M. (2001) 'The TRIPS and Public Health Debate: An Overview', International Gender and Trade Network Research Paper, Geneva: International Gender and Trade Network.

World Bank (2002) 'Trade in Services: Using Openness to Grow', in *Global Economic Prospects*, Washington, DC: World Bank.

World Bank (2004) *World Development Indicators*, Available from: http://devdata.worldbank.org/wdi2005.

World Health Organization and World Trade Organization (2002) *WTO Agreements and Public Health*, Geneva: World Health Organization and World Trade Organization.

World Trade Organization (2003) *Understanding WTO*, Available from: http://wstream.hq.unu.edu/presentations/wtoenglish/e-doc/understanding_e.pdf.

World Trade Organization (2004) *International Trade Statistics 2004*, Available from: http://www.wto.org/english/res_e/statis_e/its2004_e/its04_toc_e.htm.

2

Implications of the General Agreement on Trade in Services for Reproductive Health Services

Debra J. Lipson

Introduction

As awareness grows about ways in which international trade and health interact, concern has increased about how multilateral trade rules of the World Trade Organization (WTO) will affect health services and systems around the world. In the last three years, world attention has focused on the effect of multilateral trade rules protecting intellectual property (patent) rights on the access to and affordability of essential drugs for the treatment of HIV/AIDS by poor people in developing countries. This is but one of the many tensions created between global trade rules and the ability of countries to promote equitable access to health care services.

This chapter provides a foundation for understanding how liberalization in services trade, through the rules and commitments of the WTO General Agreement on Trade in Services (GATS), affects health services generally, and then examines some particular issues that arise in reproductive health services. Trade liberalization can occur unilaterally, that is, as an autonomous decision of a government to relax rules regarding imports or exports. But it more typically occurs as a result of multilateral trade negotiations of the WTO, through regional or bilateral trade agreements, or via conditions attached to IMF or World Bank loans. This chapter focuses on services trade liberalization through the WTO GATS since these rules apply most widely.

First, this chapter presents a conceptual framework for tracing the routes and mechanisms by which trade liberalization affects health care generally. It then explains the provisions of the GATS Agreement and their relevance to health services. Then it examines how GATS rules and specific commitments in the health sector may influence reproductive health services and rights in certain situations. It then reviews some implications of the current WTO negotiations on GATS for reproductive health service policy development. The chapter concludes with recommendations for reproductive health advocates if they wish to ensure that GATS, as it is now structured or as modified by WTO negotiations, does not interfere with national efforts to assure rights to reproductive health care.

International Trade and Health: a Framework for Analysis

There are widely differing views on how cross-border trade and global trade rules affect national policy-making, how they influence economic growth and income distribution between and within countries, and the nature of their consequences in a wide range of sectors. To make sense of the relationships and linkages between international trade, global trade rules and health, it is helpful to draw on a framework that takes into account the complex nature of determinants and pathways in both directions – from trade to health and health to trade.

A framework developed by WHO (Woodward et al. 2001) identifies three aspects of globalization, each of which has a correlate in the trade context: (1) cross-border flows – for example, trade in goods and services among countries; (2) global rules and institutions – for example, those of the WTO and regional integration agreements; and, (3) greater opening of economies to foreign goods, services, capital and investment through national policies, IMF/World Bank loan conditions or deregulation. There are both direct and indirect ways by which these three elements affect the health system, as shown in Figure 2.1. Direct effects (in dotted line arrows) occur via impacts of WTO or regional trade agreement rules on national health policies or on international markets for health goods and services. Indirect effects (solid black arrows) of international trade on health operate through the national economy, for example, trade balances affecting national public health expenditures, or through the household economy, which influences

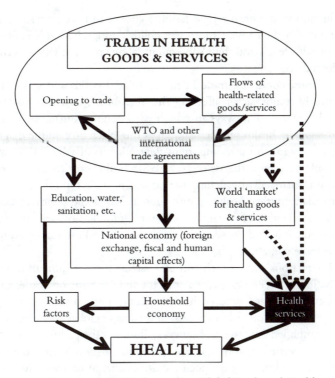

Figure 2.1   Framework for Understanding Global Trade and Health
Linkages.

the ability to pay for health goods and services. The figure also shows
that trade in other services (e.g. education, water supply) can affect
health risk factors, such as access to safe water, and has effects on health
apart from services supplied in the health system.

   This framework is a very simplified portrayal of a complex set of
driving forces, facilitating or constraining factors, and mediating
dynamics that influence the relationships between international trade
and health. The effects of trade and trade rules on health services are
likely to be multiple, separated in time and country-specific depending on the policies and market conditions that prevail at any given
time in a country. Furthermore, the linkages shown in the figure may
go in the other direction, that is, from health outcomes and health
services, or from household and national economies, to trade flows.
For example, improved access to prenatal and delivery services can
help to lower infant mortality rates and contribute to a subsequent

reduction in the birth rate as families choose to have fewer children. Parents can then invest more per child, raising children's education and health levels and their subsequent labour productivity in a trade-oriented economy.

In most countries, trade in health-related goods and services is a relatively minor factor affecting the availability, cost and quality of health services. The ways in which each country organizes, finances and regulates health services, shown as the 'black box' in the diagram, are usually much more important determinants of whether countries are able to ensure the delivery of basic health care to their people, without financially burdening the poor. But trade can influence some particularly critical health goods, such as life-saving pharmaceuticals, or the availability of certain services if only foreign-owned companies sell them. It is in these situations where trade and the rules governing such trade come into play.

Interactions among such complex factors make it difficult to prove causation between one particular factor and a specific outcome, and to measure the magnitude of health system effects attributable to the exogenous (and often amorphous) influences of globalization and trade. This simplified framework, however, illustrates the pathways by which WTO agreements, and GATS in particular, may influence the availability or affordability of specific components of reproductive health services, while underscoring the multitude of factors and forces other than trade or trade agreements that may also affect these outcomes.

GATS Rules and Their Application to Health Services

The GATS Agreement was one of the first multilateral trade agreements to address trade in services, and thus provides the framework and principles adopted by other regional or bilateral trade agreements for services trade. GATS provides WTO members with a range of policy options to allow them to liberalize services trade on a gradual basis, in line with their development objectives.

GATS defines four types, or modes, of trade in services, and health services trade occurs via each mode. Mode 1 is cross-border supply; that is, when a service is delivered via telecommunication or by mail – for example, telemedicine. Mode 2 is consumption abroad, which occurs when consumers travel across borders to obtain health services in another country. Mode 3 is commercial presence, which occurs when companies establish operations or make investments in health service entities in another country. Mode 4, the presence of natural persons, refers to health professionals travelling across borders to deliver services on a temporary basis. Commercial presence (mode 3) is the most important mode of supply for trade in many service sectors. This does not appear to hold true for health services, where mode 2 (consumption abroad) appears to be the dominant mode of supply for trade.[1]

Certain GATS obligations apply to all WTO members and affect trade in all service sectors, regardless of whether members have made sector-specific commitments. One of the most significant is the most-favoured nation (MFN) treatment rule, which stipulates that if a country permits trade in services in a particular sector, then suppliers from other member countries must be granted market access on terms at least as favourable as the MFN. If no trade is permitted in a particular sector, MFN rules require that the prohibition apply to suppliers from all member countries. For example, a country can prohibit foreign investment in private health insurance companies but the ban must apply to companies from all WTO members.

Exempt from GATS obligations are purely public services – those supplied in the exercise of governmental authority. Article I(3) defines these services as those supplied by any level of government (national, regional, local) or by non-governmental bodies exercising delegated authority, such as regional health authorities, and requires that such services be 'supplied neither on a commercial basis, nor in competition with one or more service suppliers'. There are some services to which these criteria clearly apply, such as the provision of health care under statutory social security plans and free medical treatment in public facilities.

But common features of national health care systems raise questions about whether certain public services would be subject to GATS rules. For example, where government-sponsored health services are similar to those supplied by privately sponsored health services, could they be regarded as competing? Where governments charge user fees, could services be regarded as commercial? As these questions and issues have not yet resulted in a dispute between WTO members, there is no definitive interpretation of the governmental services exception. For WTO members that have already made GATS health services commitments, if the government 'carve-out' provision did not apply to public services with competitive features, they might be required to apply market access and national treatment rules to foreign health providers from all WTO member countries. The uncertainty surrounding this provision has made many WTO member governments, such as Canada, decline from making GATS commitments in the health sector where government-provided and -financed services have a strong role.

Article XIII also exempts from GATS rules concerning market access and national treatment the purchase (procurement) by governmental agencies of services to be used for governmental purposes. Subsidies or grants to health services providers are not considered to be government procurement, and therefore would be subject to requirements that prohibit discrimination against foreign suppliers.

Under Article XIV of GATS, member governments are entitled to take any measure necessary to protect public order or morals, and human, animal or plant life or health, regardless of their obligations under the agreement. Any such exception to GATS, however, cannot arbitrarily or unjustifiably discriminate between the WTO members, nor constitute a disguised restriction on trade in services. If a government adopts a trade-restricting measure to protect health, other WTO members may challenge them, in which case it would be subject to scrutiny by a dispute panel regarding what is 'necessary' to protect health.[2]

GATS allows WTO members to choose which service sectors to open to foreign trade and foreign competitors and which modes of service to liberalize. Since adoption of GATS, about half of the WTO members made some type of commitment in health services in some form, compared with 70 per cent on financial and/or telecommunications services (Adlung and Carzaniga 2001). Developing countries tend to make more extensive GATS commitments in the health sector than developed countries, possibly because vested interests in the latter want to protect their health systems from foreign competition. For the sectors in which WTO members choose to make commitments, they develop schedules for each sector, and specify any terms, limitations and conditions in three areas: market access, national treatment and other. Market access and national treatment commitments specified for each mode of trade within each sector may be: (1) full, that is, without limitations; (2) limited (or partial), involving some restrictions or qualifications; or (3) unbound, which allows restrictions at any time in the future. A GATS commitment in a sector, once made, is legally binding. Governments may modify or withdraw commitments, but only three years after its entry into force, and the country proposing the change must negotiate with affected trading partners on the amount of compensation for any losses that occur from such a change.

A market access commitment means the WTO member agrees not to maintain or adopt measures that restrict the number of service suppliers, the value of service transactions, the number of persons employed in a scheduled sector, the types of permissible legal entities and foreign capital participation. However, GATS allows members to make exceptions by specifying 'limitations'. Members making such commitments still retain some scope for national policy and regulations. For example, a requirement for hospitals to devote 10 per cent of beds to care for the uninsured, if applied to all foreign suppliers, does not interfere with market access. The national treatment rule requires members to treat all services and service suppliers of any other member no less favourably than its domestic services and service suppliers. However, GATS regards national treatment as a conditional (and therefore negotiable) obligation and as such it may be subject to conditions or qualifications that members have inscribed in their commitment schedules. In the previous example, GATS permits countries to require just foreign-owned hospitals to reserve 10 per cent of beds for the uninsured, but only if it is scheduled as a limitation on national treatment.

GATS and Reproductive Health Services in Developing Countries

With this general description of GATS, this section examines how its rules might affect access to, or the quality of, reproductive health services. This discussion includes within the scope of reproductive health those services identified by the 1995 International Conference on Population and Development (ICPD).[3]

Three important caveats apply to the following discussion. First, because WTO principles and legal texts are often interpreted differently by the parties to the agreements, one cannot predict exactly how the rules will apply to any particular health policy adopted by a WTO member government. Second, this discussion only addresses GATS; other WTO agreements with implications for the delivery of reproductive health care, such as those concerning intellectual property rights (TRIPS) or tariffs and other rules governing traded health products (e.g. GATT), are discussed in the other chapters of this book. Third, as the trade and health framework indicates, international trade policies interact with many other factors to influence the availability, access, cost and quality of health services. These factors include national health policies and regulations, local health care market conditions, international assistance programmes and loans, and local norms and cultural practices. Thus, this discussion illustrates the potential influence of GATS on reproductive health services; its role or impact in practice depends on the specific mix and interaction of these factors in each country.

This discussion uses several examples to illustrate how GATS commitments in health-related service sectors and the modes within them might affect reproductive health services. Among the four modes of supply, it focuses on mode 2 (consumption abroad) and mode 3 (commercial presence), which appear to have the greatest relevance to the cross-border delivery of reproductive health services. The discussion also explains the potential effect on reproductive health services of commitments in the financial services sector, which covers health insurance. It also touches on GATS rules under consideration in the current round of negotiations, which if adopted would affect health services since they would apply to all sectors, regardless of country commitments in specific sectors.

With regard to health services trade via mode 1, the highly personal nature of reproductive health services means they are unlikely to be delivered via telemedicine on a cross-border basis, except perhaps for highly specialized diagnostic services. To the extent that such trade increases, those seeking such services might benefit if it means easier or cheaper access to otherwise unavailable or costly services.

With regard to the temporary movement of labour (mode 4), countries experiencing a shortage of trained reproductive health providers might benefit by making GATS commitments that ease the way for the entry of foreign professionals. For example, some Arabic countries recruit female obstetricians/gynaecologists or female nurse midwives to serve women seeking reproductive health care. Countries such as India, Bangladesh and the Philippines operate health profession schools that explicitly train graduates for positions abroad. However, these countries do not use GATS as a tool for facilitating cross-border migration of health personnel. Instead, they rely on national immigration or health workforce training and recruitment policies. For this reason, this issue is not discussed in this chapter.[4]

Country commitments for consumption abroad (mode 2)

In some countries, the lack of specialized services, such as obstetric or infertility services in the reproductive health realm, may lead some people to seek such care abroad. Abortion is a relatively rare example of a health service that is unavailable in some countries because it is illegal. In such countries, many women travel to neighbouring countries, where the procedure is legal, to obtain one. In countries where AIDS treatment is readily available, people with HIV/AIDS in the neighbouring countries may migrate or travel across the border to receive care. In all of these cases, the ability to obtain reproductive care in another country depends on the ease and cost of travel, the cost of the services relative to the person's income and whether public funds or insurance coverage is available to cover care obtained abroad, among other factors.

Theoretically, people travelling abroad to obtain health services, whether reproductive or otherwise, should not face any restrictions on this activity in the 50 or so WTO member countries that have made full or partial GATS commitments in medical and hospital services in mode 2. These commitments mean that WTO members agree not to impede residents travelling to other countries to obtain health care. Thus, there are more commitments in this mode relative to the other modes of health services trade; 28 countries made full commitments in market access for mode 2 for medical and dental services and 38 for hospital services – although only 10 did so for nursing and midwifery services. This compares to 15 full commitments in medical and dental services in market access for mode 3 and 16 for hospital services.[5] The differences reflect governments' belief that they cannot or should not interfere with consumer demand, and that allowing people to obtain care abroad lessens the need to import foreign providers or foreign investment for health services that are in short supply.

Interestingly, a common limitation in WTO members' GATS schedules on mode 2 trade in health services is an exclusion of health services obtained in other countries from reimbursement under public health or medical insurance programmes. One could argue that such a limitation is unwarranted since GATS commitments in mode 2 do not explicitly oblige coverage under public health programmes for services obtained abroad. However, in two recent cases the European Court of Justice (ECJ) ruled that the EU's treaty governing the right to free movement of services guaranteed EU citizens the right to reimbursement for health services received in other EU countries under certain circumstances. In an earlier case, the ECJ agreed with reproductive health advocates that EU treaties similarly guaranteed Irish women the right to obtain abortions abroad, based on a finding that abortion was an economic service under the meaning of the treaty.[6] These cases indicate that trade agreements (in these cases, EU treaties on the free movement of services) can have unintended health policy consequences (Mossialos and McKee 2002).

Nonetheless, the EU cases may not be good predictors of GATS' impact on abortion access outside common market areas. In a country where abortion is illegal, the fact that it may have made a GATS mode 2 commitment in health services would not protect women from potential prosecution for travelling abroad to obtain an abortion. It is likely that GATS would provide no legal recourse in such cases, since WTO members retain the right to make exceptions to GATS to protect public morals or health, under which abortion bans would probably fall.

In practice, the lack of public funds and insurance portability for care obtained in other countries means that GATS commitments in mode 2 have little or no benefit for the majority of low- and middle-income people who cannot afford to travel abroad, and cannot afford to pay for health services out of pocket. Even in border cities and towns, where people regularly cross the border for all sorts of reasons, GATS commitments in mode 2 does not make it easier for them to obtain health care. This is because local or national rules restricting eligibility for care to citizens, based on the ability to pay, would constitute stronger determinants of access to reproductive or other types of health services in another country. For example, despite provisions allowing for free movement of services across the US–Mexico border in the North American Free Trade Agreement (NAFTA), it is the state and local rules governing access to free health care that make it very hard for poor, pregnant Mexican women to obtain health services in the US, other than emergency deliveries.

Country commitments on foreign health investment (mode 3)

Foreign investment in hospitals, clinics, laboratories and other health services has grown in some countries. In the years leading up to the Asian economic crisis, Thailand experienced a rapid increase in foreign investment in the hospital sector, increasing the number of private sector beds by 65 per cent between 1992 and 1998. The last decade has also seen a strong increase in investment in Latin American health facilities by American and European-based companies. Yet recent analyses by UNCTAD[7] indicate that relative to other industries, there is very low growth in foreign investment in health services, and that health services continue to represent a minuscule proportion of total foreign direct investment (FDI), or sales of foreign affiliates, by service firms operating in other countries. While FDI statistics in the health field are extremely limited and incomplete, there also appears to be very little foreign investment in the reproductive health field.

Nonetheless, private sector organizations are expanding their operations in reproductive health services in many developing countries, often with support from developed countries. For example, from 1985 to 2001, USAID provided approximately $6.2 billion in population and reproductive health assistance to developing countries. Some of these funds supported efforts to identify investment opportunities in health and family planning services and provide technical assistance to the private sector.[8] In addition, more for-profit firms are entering or expanding operations in the reproductive health field in developing countries, while the number of private providers – doctors, nurse-midwives and pharmacists – providing reproductive health services and supplies is large and growing in many countries. Finally, in many countries, the public sector has initiated or raised user fees for reproductive health services. Such charges are one of the threshold criteria under GATS Article I(3) that can determine whether an activity is 'commercial', as discussed earlier. If such fees become widespread, the service sector may fall under GATS rules regarding market access to foreign suppliers. The growth of the private sector, whether for profit or non-profit, has implications for national policy choices under GATS. As noted before, GATS covers services that are provided on a commercial or competitive basis. As a service sector becomes more private, foreign suppliers can more easily argue that general GATS rules should apply to the sector overall. For example, under the MFN rule, if a WTO member allows private reproductive health suppliers from abroad to set up clinics in their country, it must allow suppliers from all other WTO members to do so, regardless of whether the country made a specific commitment in the health service sector.

If a country has made mode 3 commitments in the health sector, reproductive health services would be covered under the market access rules, unless they were specifically excluded in a country's GATS schedule. Or if a country wanted to require only foreign-owned or invested reproductive health services to provide a minimum amount of services to the indigent, it would have to negotiate with

other WTO members for the right to do so as part of its GATS commitments in mode 3 of the health service sector. Countries that want
to retain the most flexibility to regulate all such foreign investment
would refrain from making GATS commitments in mode 3 of the
health service sector – if they have not done so already.

Country commitments in financial services/insurance

Reproductive health services, though nominally an entitlement in many
developing countries, are poorly funded and thus often unavailable to
poor people. Even when reproductive health services are included in
the health benefits of statutory health insurance programmes, coverage
under such programmes often excludes families working in the informal sector, and controversial or very expensive reproductive health
services may not be covered under such programmes. Middle- and
upper-income individuals and households may therefore turn to the
private health insurance sector to seek coverage for such expenses.

GATS classifies health insurance as a financial service, so country
commitments regarding market access rules for foreign private health
insurance companies would fall under this sector. More than 100
WTO members have made a commitment in the financial services
insurance subsector, which covers health insurance unless a country
explicitly excludes it (but few have done so). Nearly all the countries
that have not made a commitment in insurance are developing countries, either because there is low demand for insurance or because of
concerns about allowing unlimited foreign entry into the sector.
However, both developed and developing countries that have made
GATS commitments in the sector scheduled numerous restrictions or
limitations, for example, on the form of commercial presence (subsidiary, joint venture and level of equity participation) or the number
of foreign service suppliers.

Some WTO members have limited market access or national treatment commitments in the insurance market by excluding certain types
of health insurance plans from their GATS obligations. Chile, for
example, excluded private health insurance plans from qualifying as
government-approved health plans (known as ISAPREs) in its GATS
insurance commitments. The Czech Republic and Slovakia prohi-
bited foreign suppliers from offering compulsory statutory health
insurance, while Estonia specified that their GATS insurance commitments do not apply to compulsory social security services. Despite such

exclusions, there is still room for foreign suppliers to offer private health insurance to cover health care benefits supplementary to those included in mandatory insurance plans, or to people not covered under them. For example, companies based in the US or Western Europe have invested in health insurance plans in Latin America and Eastern Europe.

There may be some benefit in having foreign participation in health insurance by offering a greater choice of options, if government-sponsored plans exclude sensitive reproductive health services such as abortion or costly ones like infertility treatment. However, for-profit firms could be expected to market such policies to the best 'risks' – higher-income people in good health. This underscores the importance of having an adequate regulatory system to guard against insurance companies engaging in consumer fraud, and to set rules so that they contribute to social policy objectives. Some countries, for example, prohibit insurers from rejecting people who have had high health costs and, in the US, some states mandate coverage of mammograms under private insurance policies.

GATS rules could also constrain government policy options under certain conditions. For example, if a country wanted to cover all reproductive health services in the national social health insurance plan, or provide services free to all through the public sector, private providers already operating in the country might suffer business losses as a result. If the government had made commitments in GATS mode 3 of health services, foreign-owned or foreign-invested private providers already operating in the country could argue that market access conditions as promised under the government's GATS commitments had been altered, and that they were entitled to compensation. Canadian health advocates have warned about such scenarios with respect to home health and pharmaceutical coverage under the national health plan, and have therefore urged the government to refrain from further trade negotiations that would increase this risk (Sanger 2001).

Reproductive Health Services Issues in the WTO GATS Negotiations

The GATS negotiations that concluded in 1994 contained relatively modest commitments to trade liberalization in the services sector, in part because it was the first time that such trade was subject to global trade rules. Country negotiators, however, committed themselves to conduct further negotiations designed for 'achieving a progressively higher level of liberalization' (GATS, Article XIX). Negotiations on GATS within the WTO began in February 2000.

Civil society groups around the world have watched these negotiations closely, concerned about their potential to expand GATS commitments in health, education, and water and sanitation. Current GATS rules allow WTO members to set limits on the sectors they will open to foreign suppliers in order to minimize the risks to health or to achieve national health objectives, such as assuring universal access to basic human services. But civil society advocates fear that GATS negotiations will put pressure on countries to liberalize policies in ways that would harm public health systems.

By December 2004, virtually all WTO members had received requests to liberalize market access or national treatment of one or more service sectors from ninety developed and developing countries.[9] Yet few of these requests pertained to the health sector. While this has allayed some concerns of health advocates, ongoing negotiations in a number of so-called 'horizontal' issues – those affecting all service sectors covered by GATS – and other GATS rules may still pose risks to basic human service sectors to the extent they limit countries' regulatory options. These issues include: establishment of an emergency safeguard mechanism to counteract the damage caused by a large volume of imports flooding a domestic market, government subsidies in services, government procurement of services, and disciplines on domestic services-related regulations. Some proposed changes in the domestic regulation area have potential implications for reproductive health services and therefore warrant more detailed discussion. Moreover, some observers believe that the rules in domestic regulation may be among the only ones to produce concrete results at the end of the current round of GATS negotiations, which are currently scheduled to end in 2006.[10]

GATS rules concerning domestic regulation

In most countries, reproductive health services are subject to many national and subnational regulations. The right of countries to promulgate such 'domestic regulations' is recognized in the preamble to GATS, 'in order to meet national policy objectives'. However, Article VI.4 of GATS requires the development of necessary disciplines to ensure that certain types of domestic regulations, including those related to service provider qualification requirements and procedures, technical standards, and licensing requirements: (1) do not constitute 'unnecessary barriers' to trade in services, and (2) that such disciplines are not 'more burdensome than necessary' to ensure the quality of the service. Public health advocates worry that this could require health regulations to be not more trade restrictive than 'necessary'. They also worry that if a WTO member's domestic health regulations were challenged in a dispute resolution, trade officials rather than health officials would determine whether such rules were necessary. In previous WTO disputes, panel and appellate decisions have interpreted the term 'necessary' quite narrowly; that is, few trade restrictions have survived scrutiny under the necessity test.

One of the debates in the most recent round of GATS negotiations has focused on whether any new GATS disciplines on domestic regulation should apply to service sectors in which WTO members have not made commitments. If this were to be adopted, it would require all WTO members to adhere to the domestic regulation disciplines in the health service sector, even if they did not make any commitments on market access in health care or health insurance. This would in turn require that all domestic health regulations affecting trade in services in any sector could be subject to the GATS necessity test.

Concerns have also been raised that new disciplines in domestic regulation might make it more difficult for countries to develop rules designed to achieve equity in access to services, which is a major goal of the ICPD and central to the UN human rights declarations.[11] Any domestic regulation – even one that does not discriminate against foreign suppliers – could be challenged by trading partners if it is perceived to be more burdensome than necessary to ensure the quality of service. The sole or primary focus on quality of services could make it difficult to argue against trade restrictions designed to ensure universal access to key services. For this reason, a group of developing countries proposed to expand the necessity test by revising GATS Article VI to specify that domestic regulations should 'not be more burdensome than necessary to pursue national policy objectives'. This would give countries greater leeway to impose trade restrictions for a broader range of public goals.

In one respect, new GATS rules governing domestic regulations could expand market access to foreign suppliers of reproductive health services if they make the rule-making process more transparent and less arbitrary. For example, such guarantees might make it easier for international NGOs to enter and set up operations in a country. Countries might still claim an exception to this rule for public morals or health reasons – for example, if they want to exclude providers of abortion or domestic violence services.

Reproductive Health Advocacy in the Context of GATS Negotiations

There is little evidence that GATS rules and individual country commitments have had a direct or significant impact on national policies concerning reproductive health so far. This is due to two factors. First, reproductive health services are delivered largely by the public sector, or by non-profit organizations, because they tend to be not very profitable. Thus, the reproductive health sector largely excludes the type of for-profit commercial activity that trade, by definition, involves. Second, the flexibility accorded by GATS to WTO member governments to liberalize market access in specific sectors of their choice, and to make exceptions for public morals or health reasons, have allowed governments to adopt reproductive health policies without any constraints.

But for-profit companies are making inroads in the delivery and financing of reproductive health services. According to Population Action International (1999), 'The commercial sector share of the family planning market is just under 50 per cent in Latin America and the Caribbean and the Middle East and North Africa, and near 25 per cent in sub-Saharan Africa and Asia excluding China and India. Consumers rely more often on commercial sources for temporary than for longer-acting contraceptive methods.'

To the extent that for-profit commercial activity in the sector expands, GATS and its rules governing the regulation of providers could have a greater impact. Private, commercial activity in a service sector brings into play basic GATS rules concerning foreign supplier participation. In those situations where reproductive health services are profitable, such as infertility services for the elite, abortion and other surgical procedures, or sales of certain contraceptive supplies, foreign providers may seek to influence the rules governing their entry and operations in other countries' markets. Some of these rules may be under GATS jurisdiction, while others would be subject to national regulations that govern licensing requirements, quality standards and service obligations of health delivery organizations. The entry of foreign providers into any particular market sector therefore calls attention to both international trade agreements and domestic regulations. Reproductive health service advocates in countries with an expanding for-profit provider market must therefore examine regulations in both arenas with a view to protecting consumer rights and promoting reproductive health policy objectives.

For example, if universal access to a full range of reproductive health services is a national policy goal, the role of foreign for-profit providers in achieving it and the rules governing their entry into the market under GATS should be structured to support this goal. Lessons from the sequencing of trade liberalization and the introduction of market forces in other sectors suggest that achieving universal service or other development goals requires a strong regulatory framework prior to privatization and before the opening of a sector to foreign investors (Wallsten 2002). Within the health sector, the WHO–WTO guide to trade agreements concurs that, 'Trade liberalization heightens the need for effective regulatory frameworks to ensure that private sector activity in the health system generates the expected benefits' (WHO and WTO 2002: 123).

Chile's failure to create such frameworks for its private health insurance market when it was first created in 1980, for example, led to inequities in the health care financing system that were more difficult to correct later on (WHO 2000: 109). If it was difficult for Chile, one of the more advanced developing countries, to put in place adequate regulations, imagine how much more difficult the task would be for much less developed countries, which have even fewer budgetary resources and lack the technical knowledge required to create, implement and enforce effective regulatory systems.

The push for further trade liberalization in the services sector at the global, regional and bilateral level makes it important for reproductive health advocates to understand how trade rules can limit the ability of governments to adopt national health and social policies. The GATS negotiations to date suggest that developed countries are not actively pursuing greater access to developing countries' health care service markets through trade agreements. But as the discussion before shows, health services can be affected by commitments in non-health sectors, such as financial services, or through rules and obligations that apply to all sectors.

In addition, since health care delivery depends on the ability to provide affordable medicines, medical equipment or supplies, trade negotiations focusing on the latter could affect national health services policy. In the US–Australia free trade agreement that came into force on 1 January 2005, for example, negotiations focused on Australia's pharmaceutical benefits policy. The final text of the agreement contains a number of ambiguities that some Australian health advocates say 'could undermine the integrity and basic framework of the Pharmaceutical Benefits Scheme (PBS)'.[12] The PBS is part of Australia's national policy apparatus that helps to hold down drug costs. If the US were successful in challenging how some provisions are interpreted, it could delay the marketing of low-cost generic drugs, for example (Metherell 2004).

Keeping track of trade negotiations is not easy since countries' individual requests and offers on specific service sector commitments are usually confidential. However, some countries publish their requests to trading partners. A few countries have established government bodies to coordinate policy on issues at the intersection of trade and health, which can serve as a source of information and a focus for advocacy.[13] Countries without such groups should create them to help the Ministry of Health and the health research community to understand better the impact of trade agreements, and to serve as a locus for consultation with the public, the health profession and civil society groups. More knowledgeable ministers of health can, in turn, push the WHO to provide greater assistance to its member countries in dealing with the health consequences of trade agreements.

Reproductive health advocates can also obtain information and updates from civil society groups that monitor and publicize trade negotiations. In the US, for example, the Center for Policy Analysis on Trade and Health (www.cpath.org) fills this role, and Consumers International (www.consumersinternational.org) provides information through its global campaign to promote provisions in trade agreements that will benefit consumers.

To be proactive, advocates can also establish lines of communication with the Trade Ministry in their own countries, and ask to be consulted before any trade commitments that affect health services, medicines or health products are made. This will give reproductive health advocates the ability to evaluate requests from other countries for market access liberalization in the health service sector, assess their potential impact on reproductive health and decide if any exceptions are needed to maintain flexibility to regulate reproductive health services and rights. For example, to ensure that trade in services improves the quality of, or access to, reproductive health care, foreign suppliers may be subject to minimum requirements to serve the poor.

Continued vigilance and monitoring by reproductive health advocates are important, particularly during a period of GATS negotiations. While services trade issues usually take a back seat to agriculture trade issues in the overall WTO negotiations, there is always the possibility that countries will be pushed to liberalize services trade more than they might otherwise, to compensate for the lack of progress in liberalizing agriculture trade rules. In addition, services trade issues are increasingly included in bilateral and regional trade negotiations, so they also need to be followed closely. Such efforts will ensure that reproductive health services and rights do not suffer intentional harm or unintentional consequences from trade liberalization.

Notes

1. Based on data presented by Guy Karsenty, Trade in Services Section, Statistics Division, World Trade Organization, at the World Health Organization International Consultation on Assessment of Trade in Health Services and GATS: Research and Monitoring Priorities, January 2002. Available from: http://www.who.int/health-services-trade/.

2. Two famous trade disputes involving health matters focused on the interpretation of what is 'necessary' to protect health. These were the US vs. Thailand cigarette case (DS10/R- 37S/200) litigated under the GATT system before the creation of the WTO, and the more recent Canada vs. European Communities (WT/DS135), which focused on a ban on asbestos. Because both of these cases concerned products with well-established hazards to human health, it is unclear if the standards and criteria for determining whether trade barriers were 'necessary' in these cases would apply to health service practices or policies.

3. The ICPD Programme of Action defined reproductive health services as including: family planning counselling, information, education and services; education and services for prenatal care, safe delivery and post-natal care; prevention and treatment of infertility; abortion, including its prevention and management of complications; information, education, prevention, screening, testing and counselling, as well as treatment of reproductive tract infections and sexually transmitted diseases (including HIV/AIDS); and information, education and counselling on human sexuality, reproductive health and responsible parenthood.

4. Calls in the current round of GATS negotiations for greater liberalization by developed countries in mode 4 would allow health professionals from developing countries to gain easier entry into their labour markets. This would probably not improve access to reproductive health services in developing countries; instead, it could exacerbate access problems by contributing to shortages of trained health professionals in developing countries, unless provisions were made to ensure the return of migrating health professionals after a reasonable period of time. One proposal in the current GATS negotiations for a 'GATS visa' would simplify immigration rules for people travelling internationally to work on a temporary basis; if it were adopted, it could facilitate the movement of health personnel for short-term assignments and assure that such personnel return to their country, mitigating concerns about long-term loss of such people, that is, 'brain drain'. As of November 2005, this proposal has not been the subject of serious negotiations in the WTO.

5. See Adlung and Carzaniga (2001), table 2. The number of commitments reflects those as of July 2000, excluding nine countries or customs area that have since joined the WTO and may have made GATS commitments as part of their WTO accession negotiations.

6. R. Fletcher, 'National Crisis, Supranational Opportunity: The Irish Construction of Abortion as a European Service', presented at the meeting 'Guaranteeing Reproductive Health and Rights: What is the Role of Trade Agreements?' 10–11 September 2002, Washington, DC, sponsored by the International Center for Research on Women.

7. Based on a data presented by M. Fujita, United Nations Conference on Trade and Development (UNCTAD) Division on Investment, Technology and Enterprise Development, at the WHO's International Consultation on Assessment of Trade in Health Services and GATS: Research and Monitoring Priorities, Geneva, Switzerland, January 2002. Available from: http://www.who.int/health-services-trade/.

8. See USAID website: http://www.usaid.gov/pop_health/pop/techareas/privatesector/index.html for more information. USAID supports private sector development in the reproductive health field by funding Commercial Market Strategies (www.psishare.org/partners/CMSproject), a project of Deloitte Touche Tohmatsu's Emerging Market Group, which works to strengthen, expand and develop the private sector to promote access to high-quality reproductive health care. The Summa Foundation, under the auspices of CMS, provides financing (mostly loans) and technical assistance to private and commercial reproductive health providers in developing countries.

9. See, for example, 'Trade in Services', Doha Round Briefing Series, International Centre for Trade and Sustainable Development, December 2004, vol. 3, no. 3; and 'Services Week Shows Dynamism despite Stalled

Doha Talks', *Bridges Weekly Trade News Digest*, vol. 7, no. 42, 11 December 2003, International Centre for Trade and Sustainable Development (www.ictsd.org/weekly/03-12-11/story3.htm).

10. For further details, see 'Domestic Regulation of Services Trade: Key Issues and Perspectives for Hong Kong', Bridges – ICTSD Analysis, no. 8, August 2005: 10–11. Available from: http://www.ictsd.org/monthly/bridges/BRIDGES9-8.pdf.

11. For views of the UN Commission on Human Rights on this issue, see the 2002 report 'Liberalization of Trade in Services and Human Rights', Report of the High Commissioner. Available from: http://daccessdds.un.org/doc/UNDOC/GEN/G02/141/14/PDF/G0214114.pdf?OpenElement Or, you can find it by scrolling down to document no. E/CN.4/Sub.2/2002/9 located at http://ap.ohchr.org/documents/dpage_e.aspx?s=115.

12. 'Leading Health Experts say Ambiguities in Trade Deal Puts PBS at Risk', 27 September 2004, Media Release by Public Health Association of Australia and other groups. Available from: http://www.phaa.net.au/Media_Releases/OpenLetteronPBSandFTA.pdf.

13. See the discussion on Canada and Thailand's collaboration among health and trade officials in *WTO Agreements and Public Health* (WHO and WTO 2002: 138–42).

References

Adlung, R. and A. Carzaniga (2001) 'Health Services under the General Agreement on Trade in Services', *Bulletin of the World Health Organization*, vol. 79: 352–64.

Metherell, M. (2004) 'Backdown on Drug-Subsidy Scheme Sickens Experts', *Sydney Morning Herald*. Available from: http://www.smh.com.au/articles/2004/02/09/1076175104568.html, accessed 10 February 2005.

Mossialos, E., and M. McKee (2002) 'Health Care and the European Union', *British Medical Journal*, vol. 324: 991–2.

Population Action International (1999) 'How Expanding the Private Commercial Sector's Role Can Help Meet Reproductive Health Needs', Fact Sheet Number 11. Available from: http://www.populationaction.org/resources/publications/gdtb/gdtb_factsheet11.htm.

Sanger, M. (2001) *Reckless Abandon: Canada the GATS and the Future of Health Care*, Ottawa, Canada: Canadian Centre on Policy Alternatives. Available from: http://www.policyalternatives.ca/documents/National_Office_Pubs/reckless_abandon_summary.pdf.

Wallsten, S. (2002) 'Does Sequencing Matter? Regulation and Privatization in Telecommunications Reforms', Working Paper 2817. Washington, DC: World Bank, March.

Woodward, D., N. Drager, R. Beaglehole and D. Lipson (2001) 'Globalization and Health: A Framework for Analysis and Action,' *Bulletin of the World Health Organization*, vol. 79: 874–81.

World Health Organization (2000) *The World Health Report 2000, Health Systems: Improving Performance 'The Chilean Health Insurance Market'*, Geneva: Switzerland.

World Health Organization and World Trade Organization (2002) *WTO Agreements and Public Health*, Geneva: Switzerland.

3

Women's Work, Autonomy and Reproductive Health: The Role of Trade and Investment Liberalization

Elissa Braunstein

Introduction

Women's empowerment and autonomy is a central theme of the global agenda for reproductive health and rights. At the 1994 International Conference on Population and Development, the Plan of Action stated, 'The empowerment and autonomy of women and the improvement of their political, social, economic, and health status is a highly important end in itself [and] is essential for sustainable development' (United Nations Population Fund 1994). The increasing significance of women's empowerment in population policy has come about partly as a result of empirical correlations between women's status, often measured in the aggregate by education or income, and lower fertility in many countries (Sen 1993; Barroso and Jacobson 2000). But women's empowerment is also a part of policy discussion and implementation because of the work of the global women's movement, which sees gender inequality and poverty as the key factors in high fertility, and at the core of the 'enabling conditions' for securing women's reproductive health and rights (Barroso and Jacobson 2000).

At the same time, trade and investment liberalization have introduced the prospect of lessening gender inequality because they have been associated with an increase in the demand for women's labour. This trend underlies the nearly universal increase in women's share of the non-agricultural labour force among high-growth developing countries in the past few decades (UN 1999), a result of the tremendous growth in the manufacturing trade and export processing from developing countries (Standing 1989, 1999). This increased demand is not just a matter of expanding the available labour force when male labour is in short supply. With labour costs being such a crucial part of international competitiveness, labour-intensive exporters prefer to hire women both because women's wages are typically lower than men's, and because employers perceive women as more productive in these types of jobs (Elson and Pearson 1981). By extension, women may lose their comparative advantage in these job markets as industries upgrade, leading to a de-feminization of manufacturing employment, as has happened in Mexico, India, Ireland and Singapore (Elson 1996; Joekes 1999; Fussell 2000; Ghosh 2001). Subcontracting also may have a role to play, as women doing own account work for subcontractors linked with international trade may underlie de-feminization in formal manufacturing sectors. Women working in the informal sector are seldom counted in official employment statistics (Carr et al. 2000). For the purposes of this chapter, however, we take the positive association between trade and investment liberalization and women's employment as a given, and work from the presumption that it is associated with increases in the demand for women's labour.

This chapter will consider the set of enabling conditions that are introduced by trade and investment liberalization by asking under what circumstances liberalization results in an improvement in women's autonomy, or bargaining power, in the household.[1] Our approach involves two interrelated questions, taken at different levels of social activity. First, we will explore the microissue of how liberalization-induced changes in the demand for women's labour affect women's autonomy using an intra-household bargaining model. To the extent that waged work and associated changes in women's autonomy in the household are coincidental with improvements in reproductive health, using an intra-household bargaining model provides a structure for understanding the indirect pathways between trade and investment liberalization and women's reproductive health. Second, we address the macro-question of how trade and investment liberalization change the capacity of communities and states to meet gendered needs for the types of social supports that are central to women's empowerment and reproductive health – both in terms of direct health services, and in terms of creating the social conditions necessary for greater female autonomy.

Putting these micro- and macro-perspectives together gives a clearer picture of the complexities of the trade-reproductive health link from the perspective of women's autonomy.

The next section presents an intra-household bargaining model of the determinants of female labour supply. Focusing on how women exercise power over their labour market participation contextualizes how market work enhances women's autonomy and, ultimately, their well-being. The third section draws on this model to show how trade and investment liberalization also have non-wage effects on women's autonomy, via their impact on the enabling conditions of autonomy proffered in the community and by the state. We conclude that while investment liberalization may increase women's autonomy through raising the demand for female labour, it may limit the scope for employment to result in fundamental improvements in gender inequality.

Bargaining and Autonomy in the Household

Female labour supply and the structures of constraint

It is important to begin by situating the choices of women and men within a social and material context. This context is what Nancy Folbre (1994) terms 'the structures of constraint'. Structures of constraint fall into four categories: preferences, norms, assets and rules.

Beginning with preferences, women make decisions about whether or not to look for waged work, a process sometimes referred to as exercising agency or, in the language of utilitarian economics, 'desire fulfilment'. But self-perception, what individuals value, and what choices they perceive as possible are constituted by the social world (Sen 1990; Folbre 1994; Kabeer 1994, 2000; Agarwal 1997), and so the putative preferences that underlie an individual's objectives must be understood in this light. The objectives that drive women into the labour market can be different from those governing men, with implications for the price of labour and household consumption. Women who expect to leave the labour force for full-time motherhood may prefer the structure of easy-access, high-turnover jobs that give them a chance to live away from home and exercise freedoms they would not otherwise be able to enjoy.

Norms are the traditional structures of gender and kinship that constitute the meaning and social expectations of women and men in the household. They typically change throughout the course of a woman's or household's life cycle. Perhaps the most salient factor here – one that underlies many of the other household-level constraints we discuss – is the sexual division of labour. Women are primarily associated with the care and reproduction of the family, and much of their work time is spent outside of the market, whereas men's work is typically viewed as more directly productive and more fully incorporated into the market sphere. These divisions not only have implications for whether women look for market work at all but also what types of jobs are considered suitable, and to what extent market work affects women's positions in the household and larger society.

Norms about divorce and remarriage also underpin household-level structures that shape women's labour. They partly determine the possibility and terms of exit from a conjugal union and affect daughters' attitudes about market work. In East Asia, where divorce rates are extremely low, waged work for married women is less important as insurance against the economic stress of divorce. Conversely, in parts of Southeast Asia, divorce and remarriage rates are high (Lim 1990: 106). Women's high labour force participation rates and active household management in this region provide a way of insuring against the costs of divorce (Papanek and Schwede 1988: 79).

Household assets, or wealth, structure women's labour supply in two distinctive ways: (1) the combined assets of all household members determine how much waged employment the household requires to meet its consumption needs; and (2) a woman's own assets help determine the extent to which she controls her own labour supply. In a bargaining framework, a woman's own wealth (in the form of land, housing, financial savings, etc.) can have different effects on her labour supply than wealth controlled by others in the household. Owning assets provides economic security, and at times, streams of non-wage income, enhancing a woman's bargaining power vis-à-vis other household members. In, perhaps, a less instrumental way, own assets and income can also give women an increased sense of their own individuality and well-being, the chance to form and benefit from peer relationships, and a general 'widening of horizons' (Salaff 1981; Sen 1990; Lim 1990; Baden and Joekes 1993; Agarwal 1997).

In terms of rules, property rights and family law are crucial determinants of the relationship between women's labour-market decisions and their empowerment, because male authority in the household can be buttressed by law. Patriarchal property rights, where eldest men have the right to claim and apportion the fruits of all household members' labour time, can create incentives for high fertility (Braunstein and Folbre 2001). Agarwal (1994) links the evolution of inheritance rules with gender asymmetries in contemporary property law, and argues that achieving independent land rights is a basic requirement for women's empowerment. Not having a legal claim on a spouse's income in the event of separation means that a paying job can be an insurance policy against loss of that support (Folbre 1997).

Modelling gender regime and female labour supply

This section develops a stylized household model to illustrate how different family systems determine female labour supply, as represented by their reservation wage, and the extent to which working for income may, in turn, affect women's power in the household. The theoretical model is described in the Appendix to this chapter, and the more intuitive version of the framework is discussed in the following section. A central factor in both approaches is family structure, or the extent to which women and men share the costs of social reproduction (i.e. the time and money that go into maintaining a family). This delineation of responsibility is paralleled by autonomy in decision-making. The organizing principle behind the model is that individuals live in households where one's input into resource allocation and distribution decisions depends both on one's alternatives to remaining in the household (exit) and one's right or ability to try and influence household decisions (voice or autonomy), including decisions about one's own strategic life choices.[2] The conceptualization of autonomy is based on a typology of three gender regimes that mark a continuum of women's input into household decision-making processes.

At one extreme is 'complete dominance', where women are members of male-headed families and have little or no influence over decision-making but typically enjoy some male support; at the other is 'defection' or families maintained by women alone, where women are decision-makers but seldom receive financial assistance from men. In between lie a diversity of intra-household bargaining structures termed 'contested dominance', where a woman's input into decisions over resource allocation and distribution is largely determined by her fall-back position, should her husband or parents dislike her actions enough to withdraw their cooperation.

The notion of complete dominance parallels what the anthropological literature identifies as systems of household organization centred around paternal power and the conjugal bond, embedded in cultural rules that prescribe male authority as well as responsibility for the protection and provisioning of women and children, and including traditions of patrilineal descent and inheritance (Kabeer 1994: 115). Its clearest instances are found in geographical areas that include North Africa, the Muslim Middle East and South and East Asia (Kandiyoti 1991: 107–8).

Defection, where families are maintained by women alone, can be thought of as the mirror image of complete dominance, with the added and important caveat that these households typically face more dire economic circumstances. Reliable data on households maintained by women alone is hard to find because much is based on census data, which varies in definition and quality by country (Folbre 1991; Chant 1997). In the developing world, the majority of households maintained by women alone are the result of widowhood, desertion and migration. In Latin America and the Caribbean, unmarried parenthood is a significant factor. In the Caribbean, for example, two-thirds of all births take place outside of official marriage (Chant 1997: 85).

Contested dominance, or bargaining, describes situations where household members interact in a spirit of cooperation and conflict. There are gains to cooperation in household production, but choosing among a multitude of bargains, all of which are better for some than others, entails conflict (Sen 1990).[3] These household systems are characterized by weaker conjugal ties than in the case of complete dominance, and women and men may assume specific responsibilities for household provisioning and exercise access to separate resources to enable them to discharge their obligations (Kabeer 1994: 116). The weaker conjugal ties found in the Caribbean, parts of Latin America and sub-Saharan Africa provide examples of such terms, as do some parts of Southeast Asia. Most households probably fall into this category. Even the process of development itself, and the accompanying increased visibility of women's productive roles and access to their own income, may serve to transform regions that were at one time closer to complete dominance.

An intuitive approach

This section presents an intuitive version of the theoretical model in the Appendix. The advantage of the theoretical model is that it uses mathematical rules to illustrate more precisely how bargaining factors come into play. However, the main pathways between waged employment and autonomy can be amply demonstrated graphically as well.

Figure 3.1 illustrates the flows of the model. Starting at the top with the bargaining dyad, denoted by the symbols for male and female (or alternatively, by a parent and child), it is apparent that both individuals begin with a set of constraints; these include time, market wages, prices, non-wage income, the probability of getting market employment, and the relationship between non-market labour inputs and outputs. Time captures the notion of labour inputs, and as such sexual and reproductive health and other capabilities are an essential part of

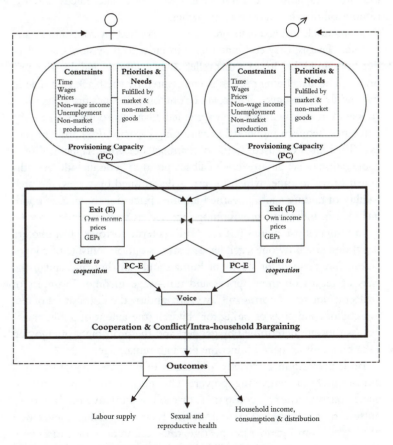

Figure 3.1 A portrait of intra-household bargaining.

the bargaining problem. Together, these constraints correspond to equations (2)–(5) in Table 3.1. Priorities and needs correspond to what economists typically refer to as a person's objective or utility function, and include all their desires and responsibilities relative to household production; they capture equation (1). They are fulfilled by market and non-market goods, with the latter including commodities and goods produced exclusively by time, such as childcare. And they can be gender-specific, in that there is likely to be a gender-based division of financial or household responsibilities. Hence, they are strongly determined by factors such as social norms or stage in the life cycle. The set of individual constraints and priorities/needs combine to form an individual's 'provisioning capacity', which captures each person's individual capability to fulfil their own wants and needs and the responsibilities they have towards others.

Households are taken to produce in a context of cooperation and conflict. That is, they combine their capacities to provision as a collective household, but in ways that reflect their common and differing priorities. This bargaining process is represented by the black rectangle in the middle of the figure. The result or outcome depends first on gains to cooperation and then ultimately on voice. Gains to cooperation are the difference between individual provisioning capacity (PC) and terms of exit (E). Exit is captured by the determinants of what happens, should cooperation break down – one's fallback position. This includes an individual's own income, which in turn is determined by wages, the probability of finding a job, unearned income, prices for the market goods included in individual provisioning capacity, as well as gender-specific environmental parameters (GEPs). GEPs (a term borrowed from Folbre 1997) describe how one's gender determines options outside of cooperation, independent of stocks of human and non-human capital, the rates of return on them, prices and non-wage income. Examples of GEPs include social norms and laws surrounding the distribution of responsibilities and costs of caring for children, the extent of public transfers (as they are determined by gender) and the probability of enjoying a share of another person's income through remarriage.

Both provisioning capacity and terms of exit are central to one's intra-household bargaining power. The greater one's priorities or needs, relative to one's constraints, or the less attractive one's options outside of household cooperation, the lesser bargaining power one will have. From a gender perspective, these differences are clearly very significant, as women tend to have greater needs and constraints, and lower terms of exit, than men. Waged employment will be discussed in the following section, but it is already clear how it is just one of the many factors that determine power in the household.

One of the main factors in this model is family structure, or autonomy in decision-making, as denoted by voice in Figure 3.1. Voice is the socially determined capability women have to transmit a given bargaining position into power in the family, and it ranges between zero (for complete dominance by the male head), and one, indicating complete female autonomy (defection by the male head). The bargaining between these two individuals, as represented by equation (6) in Table 3.1, is the application of voice to the interplay of the two individuals' gains to cooperation.

The result is dependent on all the factors discussed previously. These types of models typically focus on issues of household income, consumption and distribution. But they can also give significant insights into how women's market and non-market labour supply are determined, the capacity of wages to increase female autonomy and the conditions under which work may contribute to greater sexual and reproductive health. Because outcomes feed back into the individual, the entire model helps explain the dynamics of power and social reproduction in the household.

Household bargaining, work and gender equality

The bargaining model developed in this chapter specifies the parameters to consider in order to answer the question of when working for a wage contributes to gender equality and women's autonomy at the household level. In the short-term, the malleable elements of women's power in the household are given by their gains to cooperation. These gains are captured by women's individual abilities to fulfil their provisioning needs, relative to the parameters of exit. So parameters given by time, income, prices, unemployment, the productivity of non-market work and gender-specific environmental parameters, such as child support laws, are all determinants of women's bargaining power. Changes in any of these parameters will yield immediate and tangible household bargaining effects. An increase in the female unemployment rate, an exchange rate devaluation that makes the price of consumer imports higher, the expansion or contraction of state supports for reproductive labour – all of these factors, by changing the gains to cooperation or terms of exit from household membership, will shift the balance of power. Likewise, an increase in male gains to cooperation will also tip the balance towards women.

The mapping of one's gains to cooperation into bargaining power is mediated, though, by voice, which is fixed in the short term. Achieving gender equity in property rights by legal fiat, for instance, may do little in the short run to alter the terms of exchange between women and men when social norms prevent women from even negotiating. In the longer term, norms do change (sometimes as the result of legal fiats), and voice becomes a variable determined by the same sort of parameters as fallback positions.

To see how the model creates a better understanding of the relationship between work and women's autonomy, consider what the model indicates about the importance of working for a wage. In extremely patriarchal societies where women have no voice, working for a wage contributes only to family income and purchases as controlled by the male household head. As one moves through varying degrees of contested dominance, women's ability to translate working for a wage into having a say in household decisions is enhanced until one arrives at the defection model, where women provision themselves and their families on their own.

In the longer term, working for a wage may enhance voice; it depends on the extent to which work challenges traditional sources of patriarchal power. In economies where social norms inhibit women from exercising their exit options, gender inequalities will persist in the household and society at large, despite high levels of female labour force participation. For instance, forms of employment that do little to challenge traditional gender relations in the household, such as industrial homework, may draw women into market labour while conferring few of the benefits in terms of autonomy (Kabeer 2000).

There are ways by which public policy can enhance the linkages between work and autonomy. Strong public provisions for the enforcement of parental child support take a significant proportion of intra-household transfers out of the household bargain. By doing so, it not only shores up women's intra-household bargaining power, it protects children from the economic risk of single-parent families. Taxation policies and extensive systems of social insurance can also have these effects, as would enhancing women's rights to own assets, such as land rights. And, enforcing anti-discriminatory policies in education and employment would lower gender wage differentials and increase women's fallback positions.

The challenge posed by this analysis is the following: wages and employment can be transformative in and of themselves. But these resources are utilized in social and material contexts – the non-wage components of exit and voice – that ultimately determine women's abilities to translate wages and employment into real shifts in bargaining power. Taken in this context, trade and investment liberalization do not just have a wage or employment effect on female autonomy. They also impact the non-wage components of exit and voice by affecting the supply of the types of social interventions enumerated previously that help guard against a gender inequality trap.

Empowerment and reproductive health in the household model

This section addresses the differences between the notions of autonomy as it was used in the bargaining model, and the idea of 'empowerment'. The difference between the two is important because empowerment is a central feature in the discourse on development and reproductive health, and the connection between autonomy and empowerment is not immediately clear.

Our definition of empowerment is drawn from Kabeer (1999) and entails 'the processes by which those who have been denied the ability to make choices acquire such ability' (Kabeer 1999: 437). She proposes three dimensions to empowerment: resources, which are preconditions; agency, which is a process whereby individuals define their goals and act upon them; and achievements, which are the outcomes of empowerment. In the intra-household bargaining model above, the notion of constraints and exit parallel 'preconditions', in that they encompass the resources that individuals draw on to effect decision-making power. And voice, or one's ability to exercise choice, in conjunction with the objective function that details preferences, or how one defines one's goals, is akin to the notion of 'agency'. 'Achievements' are measured in the same way for autonomy and empowerment as they have been defined here.

The key difference between autonomy and empowerment is that empowerment implies a process, and autonomy is more like a snapshot that takes agency as an exogenous parameter, a static version of empowerment. Making agency endogenous and introducing dynamics into the model can illustrate the process of empowerment, but it also results in a much more challenging modelling task.

Still, autonomy has been defined on an individual basis in relation to
bargaining in the household, with particular reference to the conjugal
relationship. Empowerment is a term that is used much more expan-
sively, with direct linkages to meso- and macro-level indicators. Even
though autonomy is operationalized at the microeconomic level, meso-
and macro-level factors determine autonomy as well. For instance,
gender wage inequality, women's unemployment, anti-discrimination
laws, female literacy, community norms around age at marriage, divorce,
migration and women's legal rights are all determinants of women's
gains to cooperation – the difference between women's provisioning
capacities and terms of exit. They underlie women's bargaining power
in the short-term, and ultimately shape their ability to bargain in a
dynamic context by influencing voice, preferences and norms.

There are, however, meso-level processes that are interdependent
with the household, and constitute a sort of feedback loop that is
difficult for the household bargaining approach to reflect. Basu and
Bechtold (1998) link a household bargaining model of endogenous
parenting preferences with a lobbying process whereby women lobby
government to impose a tax on employers of men; the after-tax marginal
contributions to production of new mothers (who must take time off
from paid labour after giving birth) and fathers are consequently equa-
lized. The result of the external lobbying process is that men and
women split up the childcare more equally. Women's household
choices are partly determined by political processes at the state level.

There are instances where empowerment effects happen entirely
outside the household, with discernibly few repercussions at the household level. Community-based health centres could well enhance
women's sense of empowerment to control their own reproductive
health and rights, without an appreciable household autonomy effect.
Yet, if one were interested in measuring a woman's control over her
health using a microeconomic approach to autonomy, it would certainly make sense to include the availability of community services in
such an evaluation. The availability of women's health services is a
gender-specific environmental parameter that may ultimately play a
part in shaping household autonomy, as it improves women's physical
capacities and expands their choices.

Furthermore, focusing on equality in the conjugal relationship is
significant for achievements that fall outside the approved boundaries
of women's activities, a key part of improvements in women's reproductive health. Kabeer (1999) illustrates this point in a close reading of

some empirical studies of women's empowerment and health. In discussing a study by Kishor (1997) of Egyptian data that explored the effects of women's empowerment on infant survival rates and infant immunization, Kabeer noted that women's education and employment, as well as 'equality in marriage', all had a direct influence on the likelihood of child immunization. Conversely, only women's employment affected their children's survival chances. She suggests that this is the result of childhood immunization requiring more active agency on the part of mothers than the more routine forms of health-seeking behaviour that are linked with improved child survival.

While power in the conjugal relationship can be a critical component in determining the scope of women's choice, it is also the case that meso- and macro-level factors can shape women's choices. Different sorts of decisions about sexual and reproductive health can have varying relationships with bargaining power and autonomy. In general, work can contribute to greater reproductive health by reducing the dependence of women and girls on men and boys, and by providing them with leverage to challenge patriarchal controls over their sexual and reproductive lives (Gage 2000). But because different aspects of reproductive health challenge traditional sources of male power in different ways, employment is also more likely to have strong reproductive health effects where there is less gender inequality to begin with, where women are most able to translate income gains into enhanced provisioning for themselves and their families. Meso- and macro-level factors can be very significant in challenging these larger systems of gender inequality. The next section explores one such pathway, the effect of trade and investment liberalization on the supply of, and demand for, social protections.

Investment Liberalization and Women's Autonomy

This section illustrates the community or state-level effects of trade and investment liberalization on women's autonomy. By developing an intra-household bargaining model of women's autonomy, the preceding section introduced two liberalization effects at the microeconomic level: the wage/employment effect, and the social protection effect. Social protection refers to social provisions that boost women's bargaining power or autonomy in the household, including legal measures, such as anti-discrimination or equal inheritance laws, or provisions that support women in their reproductive responsibilities, such as childcare services, healthcare, sanitation, clean drinking water or fuel supplies. All of these supports boost women's provisioning capacities, their fallback positions, and ultimately, via changes in social norms, their voice or autonomy in the household.

Direct supports, such as the provision of reproductive health services, education about reproductive health and associated services and passing and enforcing laws against violations of sexual and reproductive rights all may affect women's power in the household, as well as their reproductive health. In addition, governments can provide more indirect supports for women to enhance their negotiating capacities and boost their self-confidence via reproductive health interventions, such as strengthening women's direct participation and role in reproductive health programmes, and enabling women to plan, monitor and evaluate reproductive health plans and facilities (Sen and Batliwala 2000). Whether one refers to social protections that support the translation of waged work into greater autonomy, or those that more directly address women's reproductive health, both types are essentially about the 'enabling conditions' of empowerment provided by the community and the state. But while the social protection effect plays out in the household by constraining or enhancing bargaining power and ultimately voice, the provision of social protection happens at the level of the community and the state. This is the starting point for the model developed next.[4]

The model uses as its framework the basic idea that as trade and investment liberalization increase, two opposing tendencies will operate on the policy structures of domestic economies. On the one hand, there will be pressures toward a race to the bottom – pressures for cutting the role of the government and firms in supplying the social protections of the welfare state. Trade liberalization means cutting trade tariffs, with direct and potentially significant consequences for developing country government budgets, for which trade taxes are a significant source of revenue (Khattry and Rao 2002).[5] Investment liberalization (both in terms of long- and short-term flows) means that government budgets are beholden to global financial markets. Global financial markets can constrain government spending via the spectre of financial outflows and crisis should that spending result in budget deficits that the market deems unsustainable. Some of these budget constraints result from prior financial crisis and current debt servicing; others are due to conditionalities imposed by international financial institutions like the IMF. In exchange for aid and loans, developing country governments restructure their economies via marketization and privatization, and cut government spending, despite the persistently high demands of debt servicing to pay for prior crises. In an empirical study of these issues, Rao (1999) shows that trade and financial liberalization are indeed positively correlated with what is termed the degree of liberalization-related 'fiscal squeeze' – changes in the growth of trade taxes and interest expenses as a proportion of GDP.

Firms have a role to play in the supply of social protections, as well. Although firms may contribute relatively little to tax revenue in developing countries (Barnett and Grown 2004), a number of social protections are delivered through employment, such as minimum wages, maternity leave and occupational health and safety. Trade and investment liberalization enhance exit options available to firms because it is easier for them to move abroad in search of lower production costs, and increase the international competition facing domestic firms from transnational corporations. As such, liberalization may also contribute to a race to the bottom by suppressing the ability or willingness of firms to be a conduit for social protections, even if they do not finance the protections themselves. Furthermore, part of the logic behind decreasing trade taxes is that they will increase incomes and change the structure of the economy, resulting in greater tax revenues from the domestic private sector. Liberalization makes it more difficult for governments to shift their tax structures in these ways, as firms can threaten to leave.

On the demand side, trade and investment liberalization may bring increases in the demand for social protections. Globalization creates losers and winners, and may generate more insecurity by accelerating the pace of change (Rodrik 1997). From a gender and development perspective, trade liberalization and increasing integration within the global economy widen the scope of the cash economy, requiring women to earn money to meet their traditional household responsibilities. Expanding marketization and the commodification of different aspects of local economies may add to women's double burden, in that they must take on two jobs – paid and unpaid – to provision their families (Pearson 2004). Traditional sources of subsistence, such as a household garden, are less tenable when families move to urban centres in search of trade-related work. Also, to pursue new opportunities offered by liberalization, children must be educated and in good health. All of these factors combine to increase the support that women need from the community and state to carry out their provisioning responsibilities.

These conflicting pressures can operate simultaneously: the demand for more social protection, and the declining capability of governments or willingness of capital to supply protection as liberalization increases. Figure 3.2 illustrates these in a simple diagram, the supply and demand for social protection. The demand for social protection is upward sloping, reflecting the fact that as liberalization and openness to the global economy increase, women and men need more social support from the state. The supply of social protection represents two related dynamics that depend on the level of development and economic structure: the decreasing ability of the state to provide social supports, and firms' willingness to support social protection, either through paying taxes to government, providing it directly to their own employees or tolerating legislation that strengthens citizens' ability to demand greater social protection. The line **G** represents the exogenously given level of liberalization, reflecting the vulnerability of governments to budgetary pressures from liberalization, and firms' exit options as well as competition from transnational corporations.

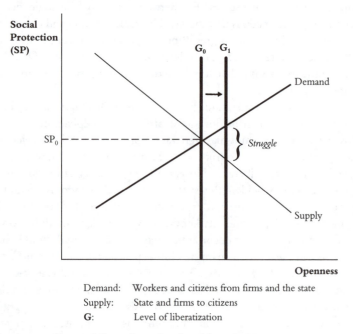

Figure 3.2   Demand for and supply of social protection.

A shift out in **G** represents an exogenous increase in the level of liberalization. Such a shift may be the result of a new trade or investment liberalization agreement, which lowers government revenue (and strains government budgets), or opens the domestic market to greater import competition (and increases the competitive pressures facing domestic firms). As **G** shifts out, a wedge develops between the social protection that citizens and workers need and that which the state or firms can or want to provide. This sets up a power struggle for institutional change. The outcome depends on the relative power of citizens, workers, firms and the state, the institutional structures in place, and, significantly, the level of liberalization itself. Figure 3.3 illustrates this relationship in the case of investment liberalization, where increasing levels of liberalization result in increased bargaining power for transnational corporations. The outcome is illustrated by the 'contract curve', which represents the locus of bargains settled on as liberalization increases. By enhancing the exit options of firms, investment liberalization enhances their power relative to citizens, workers and the state. This allows firms to win a better deal in the struggle for social protection.

The supply of social protection may be upward sloping. Through agglomeration effects and economies of scale, more openness may be associated with greater demands for infrastructure, education and high performance work structures on the part of firms (Milberg 1998).

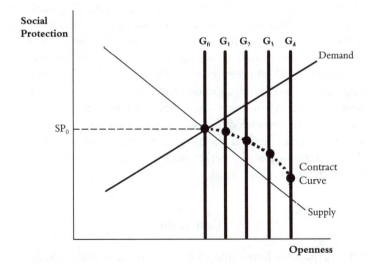

Figure 3.3 Effects of investment liberalization.

By generating this sort of climb to the top, these effects may moderate or even eliminate the negative impacts of liberalization. But as long as the need for social protection increases at a faster rate than the supply (the slope of the demand curve is higher than that of the supply curve), the same dilemma, though quantitatively smaller, will still exist.

To the extent that trade and investment liberalization exert downward pressure on the supply of social protections, it lessens the capacity of the community and state, and the willingness of firms, to provide the social welfare supports necessary for women to translate employment opportunities into greater autonomy. For instance, lower social spending on healthcare, either as a result of lower government tax revenue or cuts in job benefits offered by firms, will lower women's fallback positions. This is because where women work for a wage, and bear continued responsibility for the health and welfare of their families; their ability to assert themselves in the household is dampened by their continued need for access to male income. Furthermore, because women's employment gains are happening in sectors that are the most exposed to international competition, the bargaining power of employers vis-à-vis workers will be higher in female-dominated industries relative to other economic sectors. As a result, women are less likely to access job benefits than their male counterparts, and their intra-household bargaining power is concomitantly lower.

Sexual and reproductive health services supplied by the state or community are an essential part of social protections. They constitute both an input into and an outcome of women's autonomy. Tighter government budgets, lower healthcare spending or the institution of user fees will have direct effects on women's access to reproductive health services. These pressures also make governments less capable of using reproductive health education and services as a tool of women's empowerment. At the same time, liberalization may contribute to increases in women's needs for reproductive health services as factors like desire for fewer children, and greater sexual activity pursuant to urban or extra-household workplaces for young women may accompany the take-up of paid work.

Conclusion

In this chapter, we have explored the circumstances under which trade and investment liberalization result in an improvement in women's well-being, as reflected in their autonomy or bargaining power in the household. The intra-household bargaining model shows that working for a wage has direct autonomy-enhancing effects via increasing women's bargaining power. But these wage effects are mediated by the social and material contexts in which they are earned, including the extent of social supports for countering the sources of gender inequality. This is where trade and investment liberalization may also introduce counter pressures to improvements in women's autonomy: by increasing pressure on government budgets, and by raising the bargaining power of firms relative to workers and the state, it can also lower the supply of social protection, and undermine the provision of social supports for countering gender inequality. Despite higher incomes, liberalization may also put stress on the 'enabling conditions' that are conducive to women's empowerment.

From a reproductive health perspective, then, we may not see appreciable changes in women's reproductive health outcomes via the autonomy pathway because of the indirect effects that liberalization has on the supply of social protections. While wages may enhance women's field of reproductive health choices by expanding their ability to assert themselves, higher incomes may not be enough in circumstances where non-wage sources of gender inequality persist or even deepen.

Appendix: A Theoretical Model of Women's Bargaining Power

The model below integrates a consideration of the three gender regimes discussed in this chapter, taking as a framework the standard Nash cooperative bargaining solution and deriving a specification for the female reservation wage. Table 3.1 summarizes the equations and variables of the model. It is based on a two-person household, which can represent either a husband and wife or a parent and child, but the bargaining dyad will be referred to as 'male' and 'female'. Labour markets are segmented by gender: men work only in the market sector producing goods that are not traded internationally (y); women work either in the internationally traded goods sector (x) or in the home sector producing non-market goods (h), including children.[6]

Each household member has their own utility function, as described in equation (1), which depends positively both on market and non-market goods.[7] Equations (2)–(5) specify constraints on the household's decision-making problem. The first constraint indicates that women's total labour time available is divided between market and

Table 3.1 Bargaining and autonomy

Individual objective function	$U^i(y, h) \quad i = f, m$	(1)

Constraints

Female labour time	$\ell^h + \ell^x \leq L^f$	(2)
Male labour time	$\ell^y \leq (1 - \mathrm{UER}^m)L^m$	(3)
Household money income constraint	$w_f \ell^x + w_m \ell^y + I^f + I^m \leq py$	(4)
Non-market production function	$h = \beta \ell^h$	(5)

Household objective function

$$N = [U^m(y, h) - V^m(w_m \rho_m, p, I^m, \alpha_m)]^{(1-\theta)}$$
$$\times [U^f(y,h) - V^f(w_f \rho_f, p, I^f, \alpha_f)]^\theta \qquad (6)$$

Female reservation wage

Contested dominance

$$\frac{w_f^\star}{p} = \beta \left[\frac{U_h^m(1-\theta)(U^f - V^f) + U_h^f(\theta)(U^m - V^m)}{U_y^m(1-\theta)(U^f - V^f) + U_y^f(\theta)(U^m - V^m)} \right] \qquad (7)$$

Complete dominance

$$\frac{w_f^\star}{p} = \beta \frac{U_h^m}{U_y^m} \qquad (8)$$

Defection

$$\frac{w_f^\star}{p} = \beta \frac{U_h^f}{U_y^f} \qquad (9)$$

where

y	=	domestic market good
x	=	MNC sector good
h	=	non-market good
ℓ^h	=	non-market labour time
ℓ^x	=	female market time
ℓ^y	=	male market time
$L^i \ (i = f, m)$	=	available labour time
$V^i \ (i = f, m)$	=	fallback position
$\rho_i \ (i = f, m)$	=	probability of employment
$\alpha_i \ (i = f, m)$	=	GEP
θ	=	female voice, $0 \leq \theta \leq 1$
UER^m	=	male unemployment
$w^i \ (i = f, m)$	=	market wage
$I^i \ (i = f, m)$	=	non-wage income
p	=	market price
β	=	household technology

non-market labour.[8] On the other hand, men, who work only in the market sector, are assumed to take as much market labour as they can get, so their actual market labour time depends on the total available labour time and the male unemployment rate, as indicated in equation (3).[9] Equation (4) is the household's money income constraint, and indicates that the family pools its income;[10] I represents unearned income, and could be things like inherited wealth or social welfare payments from the government. Equation (5) is the non-market production function, and is the simple multiplicative result of a technological parameter β and women's non-market labour time.

$$U^i(y, h) \qquad i = \text{f, m} \tag{1}$$

$$\ell^h + \ell^x \leq L^f \tag{2}$$

$$\ell^y \leq (1 - \text{UER}^m)L^m \tag{3}$$

$$w_f \ell^x + w_m \ell^y + I^f + I^m \leq py \tag{4}$$

$$h = \beta \ell^h \tag{5}$$

In order to derive a set of demands for the household, we must specify exit and autonomy. Exit options, as represented by the threat point or fallback (V^i, $i = $ f, m), depend on an individual's market wage times the probability of employment (ρ_i, $i = $ f, m), prices, unearned income and a vector of determinants represented by α, GEPs. The precise manner in which fallbacks enter the household's objective function is by specifying male and female gains to cooperation ($U - V$).

Female autonomy, or the socially determined capability women have to transmit a given fallback position into bargaining power in the family, is represented by the parameter θ in equation (6) and weights these gains to cooperation. Autonomy ranges between zero and one, with a value of zero indicating that women cannot influence household decisions at all (complete dominance by the male head) and a value of one indicating complete female autonomy (defection by the male head).

$$\left[U^m(y, h) - V^m(w_m \rho_m, p, I^m, \alpha_m)\right]^{(1-\theta)}$$
$$\times \left[U^f(y, h) - V^f(w_f \rho_f, p, I^f, \alpha_f)\right]^{\theta} \tag{6}$$

The resulting household objective function as written in equation (6) represents the bargaining pair as maximizing the product of their utility gains to cooperation, $(U^m - V^m)$ or $(U^f - V^f)$, a standard form in Nash cooperative bargaining models, weighted by autonomy (θ for female, $1 - \theta$ for male).

The solution to the constrained maximization problem represented by equations (2)–(6), where the household chooses its consumption of market and non-market goods as well as the allocation of women's market and non-market labour time, indicates that the female reservation wage can be represented by equation (7) below. The nominal female reservation wage, $w_f^\star$, indicates the minimum market wage at which a woman will engage in market labour; any level below $w_f^\star$ indicates that the household is better off (in the sense of fulfilling its objective function) allocating all of the woman's labour time to the household. (The same equations for complete dominance ($\theta = 0$) and defection ($\theta = 1$) are represented by equations (8) and (9) respectively in Table 3.1.)

$$\frac{w_f^\star}{p} = \beta \left[\frac{U_h^m(1-\theta)(U^f - V^f) + U_h^f(\theta)(U^m - V^m)}{U_y^m(1-\theta)(U^f - V^f) + U_y^f(\theta)(U^m - V^m)} \right] \tag{7}$$

Equation (7) indicates that the household's marginal rate of substitution between non-market and market goods (the fraction inside the brackets) is a ratio of the weighted sums: the numerator is the sum of the marginal benefit of non-market goods to the male and the marginal benefit of non-market goods to the female, each multiplied by the other's utility gains from cooperation and their autonomy. A lower fallback position indicates a higher potential utility gain from cooperation, and a heavier 'weight' put on the other's preferences. Autonomy has a similar effect except that a higher level of independence weights one's preferences more heavily ceteris paribus; $\theta = 1/2$ indicates symmetry or equal power in the household. The denominator is the weighted sum of the marginal utility of market goods. Hence, the allocation between productive and reproductive labour for women depends on the marginal rate of substitution between market and non-market goods, with the preferences of the male and the female (or parent and child) weighted by their effective bargaining power in the household.

Notes

1. For a review of the empirical literature on the connections between women's empowerment and health outcomes, see Malhotra et al. (2002).

2. This system of voice and exit reflects points made in Katz (1997), based in turn, on the work of A. Hirschman.

3. This separation between complete dominance and bargaining does not imply that intra-household bargaining never occurs in patriarchal systems. 'Complete dominance' represents the extreme of a class of systems where norms surrounding gender and age prohibit the meaningful participation of particular groups in household decision-making, regardless of what their fallbacks are. In a more technical parlance, complete dominance represents an extreme case of asymmetric bargaining.

4. This model is taken from Braunstein and Epstein (1999), and informed by Rodrik (1997).

5. In 1995–98, trade taxes were 35 per cent of the total revenue in low-income countries, 20 per cent in lower–middle-income countries and less than 1 per cent in high-income countries (Khattry and Rao 2002; Barnett and Grown 2004).

6. The female market sector is limited to traded goods only for ease of exposition. The only difference between women and men's market work that need be assumed in this model is a gender gap in pay.

7. We assume positive but diminishing marginal utility for both market and non-market goods.

8. Considering leisure as well adds the substantial complexity of another choice variable without much additional analytical insight in terms of how the model works. The total labour time available can be thought of as twenty-four hours less the time required for sleep and other necessary personal maintenance; pressures on women's leisure time can be incorporated as changes in this exogenous variable.

9. The implication here is that only men face unemployment – when women cannot find paid labour (if they want to work in the market), they replace this job with labouring more in the home.

10. Whether or not one assumes the pooling of income is important, working confers property rights over income earned (Katz 1992). In this set of models, degrees of pooling are represented by family structure, but only incompletely. An extension of these models could usefully focus on the implications of different degrees of income pooling.

References

Agarwal, B. (1994) *A Field of One's Own: Gender and Land Rights in South Asia*, Cambridge: Cambridge University Press.

Agarwal, B. (1997) 'Bargaining and Gender Relations: Within and Beyond the Household', *Feminist Economics*, vol. 3, no. 1: 1–51.

Baden, S., and S. Joekes (1993) '*Gender Issues in the Development of the Special Economic Zones and Open Areas in the People's Republic of China*', Paper presented at Fudan University Seminar Women's Participation in Economic Development, Shanghai, People's Republic of China, 15 April.

Barnett, K., and C. Grown (2004) *Gender Impacts of Government Revenue Collection: The Case of Taxation*, London: Commonwealth Secretariat.

Barroso, C., and J. Jacobson (2000) 'Population Policy and Women's Empowerment: Challenges and Opportunities', in H. Presser and G. Sen (eds), *Women's Empowerment and Demographic Processes*, Oxford: Oxford University Press.

Basu, B., and B. Bechtold (1998) 'Endogenous Determination of Parenting Preferences by Interaction of an Internal and an External Game', *Review of Radical Political Economics*, vol. 30, no. 2: 31–45.

Braunstein, E., and G. Epstein (1999) 'Creating International Credit Rules and the Multilateral Agreement on Investment: What are the Alternatives?', in J. Michie and J. Grieve Smiths (eds), *Global Instability: The Political Economy of World Economic Governance*, London and New York: Routledge Press.

Braunstein, E., and N. Folbre (2001) 'To Honor and Obey: Efficiency, Inequality and Patriarchal Property Rights', *Feminist Economics*, vol. 7, no. 1: 25–44.

Carr, M., M. Alter Chen and J. Tate (2000) 'Globalization and Home-Based Workers', *World Development*, vol. 6, no. 3: 123–42.

Chant, S. (1997) *Women-Headed Households, Diversity and Dynamics in the Developing World*, New York: St. Martin's Press.

Elson, D. (1996) 'Appraising Recent Developments in the World Market for Nimble Fingers', in A. Chhachhi and R. Pittin (eds), *Confronting State, Capital and Patriarchy: Women Organizing in the Process of Industrialization*, New York: St. Martin's Press, Inc.

Elson, D., and R. Pearson (1981) 'Nimble Fingers make Cheap Workers: An Analysis of Women's Employment in Third World Export Manufacturing', *Feminist Review*, vol. 7: 87–107.

Folbre, N. (1991) 'Women on their Own: Global Patterns of Female Headship', in R. Gallin and A. Ferguson (eds), *The Women and International Development*, Annual Volume 2, Boulder, CO: Westview Press.

Folbre, N. (1994) *Who Pays for the Kids? Gender and the Structures of Constraint*, London and New York: Routledge.

Folbre, N. (1997) 'Gender Coalitions: Extrafamily Influences on Intrafamily Inequality', in L. Haddad, J. Hoddinott, and H. Alderman (eds), *Intrahousehold Resource Allocation in Developing Countries. Models, Methods, and Policy*, Baltimore, MD: The Johns Hopkins University Press.

Fussell, E. (2000) 'Making Labor Flexible: The Recomposition of Tijuana's Maquiladora Female Labor Force', *Feminist Economics*, vol. 6, no. 3: 59–79.

Gage, A. (2000) 'Female Empowerment and Adolescent Demographic Behaviour', in Harriet Presser and Gita Sen (eds), *Women's Empowerment and Demographic Processes*, Oxford: Oxford University Press.

Ghosh, J. (2001) 'Globalisation, Export-Oriented Employment for Women and Social Policy: A Case Study of India', Paper prepared for UNRISD project on Globalization, Export-Oriented Employment for Women and Social Policy, July.

Hirschman, A.O. (1970) 'Exit, Voice, and Loyalty: Responses to Decline in Firms, Organizations and States', Cambridge, MA: Harvard University Press.

Joekes, S. (1999) 'A Gender-Analytical Perspective on Trade and Sustainable Development', in *Trade, Sustainable Development and Gender*, New York and Geneva: UNCTAD.

Kabeer, N. (1994) *Reversed Realities: Gender Hierarchies in Development Thought*, London and New York: Verso.

Kabeer, N. (1999) 'Resources, Agency, Achievements: Reflections on the Measurement of Women's Empowerment', *Development and Change*, vol. 30: 435–64.

Kabeer, N. (2000) *The Power to Choose: Bangladeshi Women and Labour Market Decisions in London and Dhaka*, London and New York: Verso.

Kandiyoti, D. (1991) 'Bargaining with Patriarchy', in J. Lorber and S. Farell (eds), *The Social Construction of Gender*, New Park, CA, London and New Delhi: Sage Publications.

Katz, E. (1992) 'Intra-Household Resource Allocation in the Guatemalan Central Highlands: The Impact of Non-Traditional Agricultural Exports', PhD Dissertation, University of Wisconsin-Madison.

Katz, E. (1997) 'The Intra-Household Economics of Voice and Exit', *Feminist Economics*, vol. 3, no. 3: 25–46.

Khattry, B., and J. Rao (2002) 'Fiscal Faux Pas? An Analysis of the Revenue Implications of Trade Liberalization', *World Development*, vol. 30, no. 8: 1431–44.

Kishor, S. (1997) 'Empowerment of Women in Egypt and Links to the Survival and Health of the Infants', Paper presented at the seminar on 'Female Empowerment and Demographic Processes', Lund, 20–24 April.

Lim, L. (1990) 'Women's Work in Export Factories: The Politics of a Cause', in I. Tinker (ed.), *Persistent Inequalities: Women and World Development*, Oxford: Oxford University Press.

Malhotra, A., S. Schuler and C. Boender (2002) 'Measuring Women's Empowerment as a Variable in International Development', Paper commissioned by the Gender and Development Group of the World Bank.

Milberg, W. (1998) 'Technological Change, Social Policy and International Competitiveness', Working paper on Globalization, Labor Markets and Social Policy, New York: New School for Social Research.

Papanek, H., and L. Schwede (1988) 'Women are Good with Money: Earning and Managing in an Indonesian City', in D. Daisy and J. Bruce (eds), *A Home Divided: Women and Income in the Third World*, Stanford, CA: Stanford University Press.

Pearson, R. (2004) 'Women, Work and Empowerment in a Global Era', *IDS Bulletin*, vol. 35, no. 4: 117–20.

Rao, M. (1999) 'Globalization and the Fiscal Autonomy of the State', Background paper for the Human Development Report 1999, New York: UNDP.

Rodrik, D. (1997) *Has International Economic Integration Gone too Far?*, Washington, DC: Institute for International Economics.

Salaff, J. (1981) *Working Daughters of Hong Kong: Filial Piety or Power in the Family?*, Cambridge: Cambridge University Press.

Sen, A. (1990) 'Gender and Cooperative Conflicts', in I. Tinker (ed.), *Persistent Inequalities: Women and World Development*, New York and Oxford: Oxford University Press.

Sen, G. (1993) 'Paths to Fertility Decline: A Cross-Country Analysis', in P. Bardhan, M. Chauduri and T.N. Krishnan (eds), *Development and Change: Essays in Honour of K.N. Raj*, Bombay: Oxford University Press.

Sen, G., and S. Batliwala (2000) 'Empowering Women for Reproductive Rights', in H. Presser and G. Sen (eds), *Women's Empowerment and Demographic Processes*, Oxford: Oxford University Press.

Standing, G. (1989) 'Global Feminization through Flexible Labor', *World Development*, vol. 17, no. 7: 1077–95.

Standing, G. (1999) 'Global Feminization through Flexible Labor: A Theme Revisited', *World Development*, vol. 27, no. 3: 583–602.

United Nations (1999) *World Survey on the Role of Women in Development. Globalization, Gender and Work*, New York: United Nations.

United Nations Population Fund (1994) *Plan of Action of the International Conference on Population and Development*, New York: United Nations.

PART II

Country Case Studies on Trade Liberalization, Women's Employment and Reproductive Health

4

Implications of Trade Liberalization for Working Women's Marriage: Case Studies of Bangladesh, Egypt and Vietnam

Sajeda Amin

Introduction

This chapter explores how trade liberalization affects the position of women through marriage and work in the export sector. As with many other aspects of social change, the impact of trade liberalization on marriage as an institution, and therefore on women's position, is likely to vary considerably depending upon the context. I present case studies of Bangladesh, Egypt and Vietnam to describe women's experiences with trade expansion policies, and how these impacts were shaped by the economic and social contexts.

The chapter is informed by a perspective that emphasizes the importance of marriage as an institution in shaping the status and livelihoods of women. Economist Gary Becker's (1991) work suggests a retreat from marriage resulting from women's workforce participation. Economic growth and increasing opportunities for women threaten the social institution of marriage. Marriage becomes less essential in economic terms when women become financially independent. However, a number of other studies have suggested that this relationship is not straightforward because even when the structural underpinnings of marriage are eroded by broader economic change, values and perceptions can intervene to bolster the institution of marriage. Studies exploring marriage change in relation to women's work in Asia have found that, contrary to the modernization theory, traditional family forms show remarkable resilience in the face of considerable change (Greenhalgh 1985; Malhotra 1991; Malhotra and De Graff 1997; Malhotra and Tsui 1996).[1]

A range of studies in contemporary Asia show that change in marriage is highly context-dependent and that the resultant mix of modern and traditional practices is as varied as the contexts themselves. In Taiwan, Greenhalgh (1985) found that single women work, but their income is used primarily to fulfil traditional filial obligations and work exacerbates women's disempowerment. In Indonesia, the impact of expanding opportunities for work is greater for rural than urban women (Malhotra 1997). Even though more women marry spouses of their own choice now than in the past, they continue to marry at relatively early ages (Malhotra 1991). In Sri Lanka, on the other hand, where the age pattern of marriage was traditionally late, women continue to have arranged marriages and live in extended households. Thus, a body of evidence has evolved seeking to explain how social and cultural factors, particularly attitudes and norms, mediate tradeoffs between women's independence and the benefits of marriage. This evidence can help us understand the transformations occurring under regimes of trade liberalization in developing countries in a number of ways. Perhaps the most relevant lesson to derive is the cultural specificity of the influence of economic change on marriage, a warning against overly simple generalizations.

In this chapter, I focus on the role of aspirations and expectations in shaping the nexus between marriage and trade liberalization, and the social context in which these changes occur. Marriage timing, aspirations related to marriage and transactions taking place during and after marriage can be important factors affecting and mediating the broadranging changes brought about by globalization. The timing of marriage determines the onset and pace of childbearing, and works as a proximate determinant of fertility, but the consequences of marriage also extend far into later stages of reproduction. The type of marriage arrangement and age differences between spouses affect reproductive decision-making within the household through gender and age dynamics. Women who are married early tend to marry men much older than themselves and hence face a high likelihood of spending a part of their lives as widows (Cain 1984). Circumstances around marriage are correlated with marital stability, and marriage transactions have implications for women's bargaining position within the household (Suran et al. 2004).

The specific policy impetus of interest in this chapter is changing trade regimes. The overall architecture of trade liberalization was similar in all three countries, but took place under very different economic conditions with varying success levels and hence had considerably different impacts. In every country that has approached the World Bank or the International Monetary Fund for debt relief or development assistance, structural adjustment and export promotion have been the key features of this assistance. In addition, the Multifibre Arrangement (MFA) (1974–95) was an important factor in conditioning the experience of trade since the garment sector played an important role in export expansion.

Country Case Studies of Trade Liberalization

Bangladesh

Bangladesh began removing barriers to trade relatively early in the 1980s, and was among the first countries formally to adopt a structural adjustment package. The first factories for garment production were set up in 1978 during a period of economic recession, high unemployment and poverty. During the mid- to late 1970s, in the decade preceding trade liberalization, poverty levels were the highest ever experienced, with 64 per cent of all households estimated to be below the poverty line at income levels that allow households to subsist at minimal levels.[2] As shown in Table 4.1, in 1980 the GNP per capita was $210, 71 per cent of the adult population was illiterate, and life expectancy was forty-eight and forty-nine years for women and

Table 4.1 Economic and social indicators for Bangladesh (1980, 1990 and 1998)

	1980	1990	1998
Per capita GNP (Atlas method) (US$)	210	280	360
Illiteracy (15+ population illiterate) (%)	71.0	65.0	59.9
Female life expectancy (years)	48.0	55.0	58.6
Male life expectancy (years)	49.0	54.6	58.4
Fertility (births per woman)	6.1	4.1	3.1
Urban population as percentage of total	15.0	19.3	23.4

Sources: World Development Indicators and Asian Development Bank.

Table 4.2 Total export earnings and earnings from manufactured exports (Bangladesh) (US$ millions)

	1982	1992	2001	2002
Total exports	769.4	1,986	6,476	5,929
Total manufactured exports	382	1,593	5,766	5,367
Export of garments (subcategory of manufactured exports)	11.39	1,041.2	4,261	4,584

Sources: Comtrade, World Bank, Economic Intelligence Unit Country Profiles (EIU 2004), Bangladesh Bank, International Financial Statistics, Asian Development Bank and International Trade Statistics.

men, respectively. The total fertility rate was more than six births per woman. Only 15 per cent of the population lived in urban areas. Throughout the period of trade expansion, these economic and social indicators improved considerably. By 1998, per capita income rose to $360, adult illiteracy declined to 59.9 per cent, life expectancy increased by ten years for men and women, and fertility fell to 3.1 births per woman, half the level observed in 1980. The population still remained predominantly rural with 23.4 per cent of the population living in urban areas.

Table 4.2 shows that total export earnings grew from US$769.4 million in 1982 to US$5,929 million in 2002, most of which was due to garment exports, which grew from US$11.39 million in 1982 to US$4,584 million in 2002. Exports peaked in 2001 and fell by about US$0.5 million as a result of the US economic slowdown following the attacks on 11 September. Somewhat surprisingly, the decline in exports did not emanate from the garment sector but from other export commodities.

As shown in Figure 4.1, the first significant change in export figures occurred in 1985 when an embargo on new factories was lifted. Manufactured goods led the growth of exports, which grew steadily to almost 12 per cent of GDP by the year 2000. The embargo was originally put in place by regulators attempting to control the quota distribution process. The lifting of specific sanctions against new factories was most likely associated with the new economic policy implemented in 1982 as part of a structural adjustment programme undertaken by Bangladesh in 1981. The reform package also included measures to remove barriers to foreign direct investment, give tax relief and rebates, bonded warehouse facilities and other facilities to all

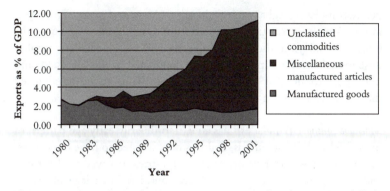

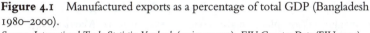

Figure 4.1   Manufactured exports as a percentage of total GDP (Bangladesh 1980–2000).

Sources: International Trade Statistics Yearbook (various years), EIU Country Data (EIU 2004).

garment-producing firms located within and outside export processing zones (EPZs) (Sobhan 1995).

Export production in Bangladesh takes place in over 3,000 factories employing an average of 300 workers per site in the major urban centres of Dhaka and Chittagong. More than 90 per cent of these workers are women. Overall, the industry requires relatively little capital investment and also has low value added, a matter of some concern to policy-makers (Sobhan 1995). Strong and highly effective employers' associations exist, which have most likely been instrumental in collective bargaining, lobbying in the US Congress for quotas and exemptions.

Social context at the time of trade liberalization

Education   In Bangladesh, the overall level of literacy in the early 1980s (during structural adjustment and the first garment production boom) was very low by international standards. The majority of adults had no formal education (Cleland et al. 1994). During the period of trade liberalization, educational indicators improved considerably among children and young adults, but the majority of adults were still illiterate in 2002 (Table 4.1). The 1990s were declared the 'education decade' and important measures to subsidize and promote primary and secondary education helped to boost primary and secondary school enrolment in rural areas. However, school dropout rates remained high among adolescents, with most boys and girls leaving school before completing eight years of education (Amin et al. 2002). Employers in the garment sector thus recruited from a largely uneducated workforce and adapted their recruiting strategies in order to employ unschooled workers. Indeed, surveys conducted in the late 1980s and mid-1990s found that workers were more likely to be uneducated than their non-working counterparts (Amin et al. 1998).

Marriage timing   Bangladesh has an extraordinarily early age pattern of marriage by global standards, and was documented to have the earliest age of all the World Fertility Survey countries surveyed in the 1970s and early 1980s (Smith 1980). Girls are considered marriageable at the time of puberty or soon after. The overall median age at marriage for marriages taking place in the 1980s was 15.4 years. Marriage age was slightly higher in urban areas at 16.8 years. Seventy-nine per cent of all girls are married by age 18 (Table 4.3).

Table 4.3   Age at marriage among women in the 1980s

Marriage and related indicators	Bangladesh	Egypt	Vietnam
Percentage of women aged 15–19 years never married	49.0	86.1	95.2
Percentage of women aged 20–24 years never married	12.0	43.4	46.2
Percentage of women aged 25–29 years never married	2.3	13.4	14.2
Percentage of women aged 30–34 years never married	0.3	4.9	8.8
Median age at first marriage in the late 1980s			
All women	15.4*	19.9*	21.0
Urban women	16.8	22.0	23.7
Rural women	15.1	18.4	20.5
Percentage of women married before the age of 18**	79.0	30.0	14.7

*Data for women aged 25–29 years from Demographic and Health Surveys (various years). The year of survey was chosen so that retrospective marriage data would reflect the experience of marriages taking place in the late 1980s or the closest available date. The years of survey were: 2000 for Bangladesh, 1992 for Egypt and 1997 (earliest available) for Vietnam.

**Data compiled by Mensch et al. from DHS surveys, Bangladesh 1992, Egypt 1994 for women aged 25–29 years, and by the author from the DHS report on Vietnam (1997).

While there exists widespread consciousness about the drawbacks of early marriage, with efforts to institute legal and social reform dating back to the nineteenth century (Basu and Amin 2000), the incidence of early marriage has been slow to change. With such early patterns it is difficult to argue that marriage was significantly earlier in the past, but several studies claim that mean age at marriage has increased by about one to two years each decade for the past three decades. These trends imply that a substantial number of pre-pubescent or child marriages were prevalent in the past (Cleland and Huq 1990).

Marriage transactions   In Bangladesh, there is an unabated trend in increasing dowry demands. By one estimate, 80 per cent of marriages in recent years were contracted with a dowry (Amin and Cain 1997), with an average demand for dowry (varying substantially from district to district within the country) of about US$200, roughly half of the average per capita income in 2001 (Amin et al. 2002). Dowry demands have not led to delayed marriages in the aggregate, as one would have expected given the time it takes to accumulate dowry, because younger brides require less dowry and so families are motivated to marry their daughters even earlier. Work in the garment industry was welcomed as a way to accumulate savings to pay for dowry. The garment sector remains one of the few sectors where young girls and women can earn wages.

Response to emerging opportunities   Despite long hours, low wages and harsh working conditions, work in garment factories in Bangladesh is generally viewed as bringing in a new era of positive opportunities for women (Kabeer 1991; Paul-Majumdar and Zohir 1994; Amin et al. 1998). Data collected by the author showed that women who are able to enter work before marriage and delay marriage and childbearing seem to be the most positive about their experiences in factory work.[3] Domestic work is the main alternative to factory work. Domestic workers earn considerably less but work equally long hours as factory workers. While in some urban homes domestic work may imply access to television, good food and clothing, there are also widespread reports of physical and sexual abuses of female and child domestic workers. Domestic work is, therefore, not seen as an attractive alternative to factory work under most circumstances. Nor do factory workers see many professional or even clerical role models among women. Although affirmative action policies are in place to recruit women, these are of relatively recent origin and the educational requirement of these jobs place them well outside the reach of most factory workers.

Impact on marriage timing Expanded opportunities for work may affect women's relative positions in a variety of ways. In societies where gender specialization is high and women are traditionally excluded from access to wage work, trade liberalization can reduce gender inequality in income by providing access to income-earning opportunities for women. Who avails these opportunities also matters. In the case of Bangladesh, my colleagues and I have argued (see Amin et al. 1998) that work opportunities are particularly consequential in the garment sector because it employs young, unmarried women who then delay marriage in order to spend some time working. Most workers eventually quit work to get married and have children because the long hours demanded are not compatible with marriage and childcare.

Bangladesh had a pattern of very early marriage that undermined the position of women in society. Early marriage and large differences in age at marriage lessen women's bargaining position in the conjugal relationship. The marriage regime and the perception that marriage is the 'peril to escape' enhance the perception of Bangladeshi girls towards their factory work. The reason marriage is viewed in a negative light by girls and their families is almost solely a product of the increasingly high dowry demands.

Even after more than twenty years of substantial growth, the garment sector still remains one of the few sectors where young girls and women can earn wages. While women can engage in some forms of self-employment largely through micro-credit and home-based activities, these opportunities are typically limited to older women who are in stable stages of the life cycle – a necessary precondition to minimize risk of default. Otherwise, opportunities are practically non-existent.

Egypt

Unlike Bangladesh, where export growth began during a time of economic crisis, the Egyptian experience with economic reform followed a long period of economic growth and rising economic aspirations. A programme of structural adjustment and reform was formally instituted in 1991 in response to an economic crisis characterized by growing budget deficits and rising inflation. Structural reforms coincided with the return of a large number of overseas migrants from Iraq and Kuwait following the Gulf War, and with the labour force entry of a baby-boom generation. Courbage (1995) and Cassandra (1995) argue that the timing of structural adjustment reflected bad policy judgement and led to long-term negative consequences for the Egyptian economy and society.

Egypt was considered a middle-income country in 1980, with per capita income at US$530. It has long been an urban society with 50 per cent of the population living in urban areas. However, increases in education are recent and the majority of adults were illiterate in 1980. Life expectancy at birth was reasonably high and reflected income levels. The total fertility rate was five births per woman. By 1990, all economic and social indicators suggested modest improvements in the quality of life indicators and these improvements continued through the 1990s. Per capita income rose to more than double the levels of 1980. Illiteracy declined due to universal education and life expectancy increased. Total fertility declined moderately to four births per woman (Table 4.4).

Migration of men to the oil-producing Gulf States had important implications for family and household structure. When men migrated and were absent from their households for long periods, women assumed important roles in the household and as female heads assumed considerable economic responsibility. The return of the men after the Gulf War may have led to the restitution of more traditional roles for women within the family and to the curbing of decision-making power among them (Hoodfar 1997).

Table 4.4 Economic and social indicators for Egypt (1980, 1990 and 1998)

	1980	1990	1998
Per capita GNP (Atlas method) (US$)	530	810	1270
Illiteracy (15+ population illiterate) (%)	61.0	53.0	46.3
Female life expectancy (years)	57.0	64.0	68.1
Male life expectancy (years)	54.0	61.4	65.0
Fertility (births per woman)	5.0	4.0	4.0
Urban population as percentage of total	44.0	44.0	43.0

Sources: Male and female life expectancy – World Development Indicators and Asian Development Bank.

Economic reform had two other important implications for Egypt. Prior to reform, the public sector in Egypt was large and accounted for a considerable proportion of employment. Thus, an important agenda for the reform was to reduce the size of the public sector through privatization. Export promotion was also an important part of the reform package, including such specific measures as the reduction of import tariffs and the implementation of special tax holidays to attract foreign investment. Because Egyptian labour laws are considered a disincentive for investors, reform of labour laws also formed part of the agenda.

Efforts at export-led growth have not had much impact on female employment for a number of reasons. To attract investors, the Egyptian government created several industrial zones and invested in infrastructural development. But attracting investment in the more productive, labour-intensive sectors remained difficult because the location of the industrial zones in areas far from the urban centres made it difficult to attract a large number of workers. In firms that employ female labour, workers are bussed from significant distances. Assaad and Arntz (2004) suggest that the inability to travel long distances for work may be one reason why women's employment has suffered more than men's during a period of economic expansion. Even compared with other countries in the Middle East and the North African region, the expansion of exports in Egypt was limited (Moghadam 1995) and did not show anywhere near the kind of growth witnessed by Bangladesh and Vietnam. While Egypt experienced good overall economic growth it was not fuelled by exports. In general, exports have never accounted for more than 4 per cent of GDP.

Social context at the time of trade liberalization

Education Schooling levels in Egypt were much higher compared with Bangladesh, but also increased rapidly at the onset of structural adjustment and resulted in a narrowing of the gender gap. Between 1988 and 1998, the proportion of young adults continuing in school increased rapidly. However, there is some evidence that overcrowding in schools resulting from large adolescent cohorts, combined with a reduction in investments in schooling, led to a decline in the overall quality of education (Lloyd et al. 2003).

Marriage timing In Egypt, early marriage for girls was the norm in the past but by the late 1980s things had changed and marriage occurred at a relatively late median age of 19.9 years (Table 4.3). Demographic trends in the proportion remaining single suggest that there was a significant change in the mean age at marriage that occurred in the late 1960s or early 1970s. Coale (1989) attributes this change to mobilization for the war effort with Israel when large numbers of young men went to fight. Some part of the explanation may also lie in rising education among girls that began with increased investments in girls' schooling in the late 1950s. Since then, there has been a gradual increase in the age at marriage without a parallel increase in workforce participation among young unmarried women. Rather, the proportion of girls engaged in wage work actually decreased between 1988 and 1998 according to national labour force surveys (El-Kogali and Al-Bassusi 2001).

Marriage transactions   Like Bangladesh, Egypt has witnessed a well-documented escalation in marriage costs (Singerman and Ibrahim 2001). The reasons for these changes are not fully understood, but they appear to be linked to globalization to the extent that they are related to rising consumerism and a rising preference for nuclear living arrangements among the newly married. Unlike marriage transactions that involve dowry, a specific transfer from the bride's family to the groom's, Egyptian marriage expenses are specifically designated for the household of the newly weds. Young men and women, and their families, save up for years before marriage to buy durable goods for the household, such as stoves, refrigerators and furnishings. Normally, expectations and norms are rigid regarding the contributions of the bride's and the groom's side, and there is even an explicit understanding between them about the quality of these items. Discussions about these contributions begin much before marriage and items brought to the marriage are listed (Al-Qaema) as part of the marriage contract. The contract is resorted to in the event of a divorce to divide up property. The Al-Qaema is considered to be an important means of ensuring economic security for the bride and empowers her in the marriage. Thus, documentation of a woman's contribution is thought to be an important determinant of her future well-being (Hoodfar 1997). Families expend considerable energy to ensure their children marry well and in negotiating appropriate terms of exchange at the time of marriage.

Rising consumerism and urbanization have strong influences on the material aspirations of couples and, therefore, globalization has a direct implication for the cost of marriage. In a study of young women working for wages conducted by the Population Council, young women often spoke of items they bought for marriage in ways that indicated a preference for imported goods (Amin and Al-Bassusi 2002). References to imported brand names were not idle ruminations. Even single women with no definite prospect of marriage saved actively for marriage. Women report that income from their employment helps to expedite marriage (Amin and Al-Bassusi 2004).

Another important feature of rising marriage costs in Egypt is that both bride and groom contribute to marriage accumulation with the groom bearing the majority of the cost including the price of a home, whereas in the case of dowry demands in Bangladesh, women and their families bear the entire burden of expenses. Qualitative evidence from the Population Council study suggests falling expectations about supporting families on one income, which makes it all the more important that a household is well equipped at the start (Singerman and Ibrahim 2001; Amin and Al-Bassusi 2004). As the price of real estate rises, aspirations of setting up a separate household becomes increasingly difficult to attain, resulting in marriage delays.

Response to emerging opportunities   During the 1980s and 1990s, unprecedented numbers of young women entered the workforce but unemployment was high. Assaad and Arntz (2004) suggest that the location of export jobs in places that required women to commute long distances may have been a factor. The demanding nature of factory employment has been a major deterrent in the recruitment and retention of large numbers of women in garment and textile factories.

In Egypt, work in export-oriented factories is considered harsh (El-Kogali and Al-Bassusi 2001). Respondents who work in garment production factories complain about long working hours and high production demands. Although workers report appreciating the opportunity to earn wages, garment factory workers have been found to complain more than workers in other sectors about the pace of work and pressure to be productive.

High expectations regarding working conditions set up by the terms of employment in the public sector for previous generations of women may also play a part. Prior to the reform, the majority of employed women worked in professional or white-collar and clerical jobs. The public sector was the dominant source of employment in the Egyptian economy and was particularly important for the employment of women through the graduate employment guarantee scheme. Under this scheme, every university graduate was guaranteed a job. The dominance of professional and white-collar public sector jobs for women thus set the tone for worker expectations. During the reform, opportunities in state-owned enterprises contracted, as did opportunities for waged labour in agriculture.[4] These contractions in employment were not compensated by growth in the manufacturing, trade and service sectors in the economy.

According to respondents in the Population Council study, public sector-like jobs are the only kind of job that a factory worker is willing to do after she gets married. Most young workers in the private sector work considerably longer hours, as do workers in other sectors of the economy. These hours are given as the main reason why young women are reluctant to continue working after they marry. The hours are not considered compatible with role expectations in marriage and childbearing in the nuclear family setting that is also held as the ideal by these young workers.

Vietnam

Vietnam's economic reform programme was officially announced in 1986. The reform policy under *Doi Moi* (renovation) was premised on the notion that central economic planning had failed (National Human Development Report 2001). Like Bangladesh, conditions of extreme poverty and deprivation in the period preceding *Doi Moi* induced the Vietnamese government to adopt these measures (National Human Development Report 2001). The earliest macro-indicators available are for 1990 which show that the per capita income was very low at US$130, considerably lower than that for Bangladesh. By 1998, income levels had reached levels comparable with Bangladesh. However, income figures are somewhat suspect and may reflect poor national income accounting as literacy, life expectancy and fertility levels for 1980 suggest that a reasonably high quality of life prevailed in 1980. The vast majority of the population was rural but literate. Life expectancy was comparable with Egypt's although average income levels are considerably higher there. Bangladesh and Vietnam had similar rural populations but the Vietnamese life expectancy was much higher. Income and other indicators continued to improve through the 1990s. Female life expectancy increased to 70.8 years and total fertility fell from 5 births in 1980 to 2.3 births in 1998 (Table 4.5).

Table 4.5 Economic and social indicators for Vietnam (1980, 1990 and 1998)

	1980	1990	1998
Per capita GNP (Atlas method) (US$)		130	350
Illiteracy (15+ population illiterate) (%)	13.0	10.0	8.0
Female life expectancy (years)	62.0	67.0	70.8
Male life expectancy (years)	58.0	63.0	66.0
Fertility (births per woman)	5.0	3.6	2.3
Urban population as percentage of total	19.0	20.0	23.0

Sources: World Development Indicators and Asian Development Bank.

Table 4.6 Total export earnings and earnings from manufactured exports (Vietnam) (US$)

	1982	1992	2001	2002
Total export in million	527	2,475	15,027	16,706
Export of manufactured goods	219	756	3,175	3,270
Export of garments		221	1,867	2,710

Sources: Comtrade, World Bank, Economic Intelligence Unit Country Profiles (EIU 2004), Bangladesh Bank, International Financial Statistics, Asian Development Bank and International Trade Statistics.

The intention of the reform was to shift to a market-based incentive scheme that emphasized growth in manufacturing and manufactured exports (Nadvi et al. 2004). Table 4.6 shows that Vietnam's overall exports grew more than tenfold between 1982 and 2002 from US$527 million to US$16,706 million. Less than 25 per cent of total exports in 2002 were from manufactured goods and only a sixth of it was from export of garments, however. Agriculture and aquaculture products dominated export earnings.

The growth of manufacturing in Vietnam began with direct foreign investment, with many brand-name manufacturers of garments and other consumer goods setting up factories, although there was some manufacturing for export in the state-owned sector as well (Nadvi et al. 2004). An educated and low-cost workforce attracted foreign investment. The location of industrial development was in industrial parks and EPZs mostly situated near the major cities. There is strong government support for export-led growth, and Nadvi et al. (2004) conclude that workers have benefited from the robust growth of exports.

Although Vietnam's garment exports grew tenfold during the 1990s, from US$221 million to US$2,710 million between 1992 and 2002, Vietnam was a relative latecomer as an exporter in the garment sector and was barred from participating in the MFA because of a long-standing trade embargo imposed by the US. Japan was the main importer of garments from Vietnam in the initial years. But exports to the US grew quickly after a bilateral trade agreement was signed in 2001 (Nadvi et al. 2004). Presently, the overall size of the garment-manufacturing sector is comparable with that of Bangladesh and is much larger than that of Egypt.

Not much is known about the Vietnamese economy prior to the reform period. After reunification of the North and South following the American War, the entire country witnessed a decade of socialist policies prior to reform. Kerkvliet (1995) argued that the process probably began long before the official pronouncements of *Doi Moi*. Citing observations on village dynamics, she argues that there was resistance to collective farming evident in village politics from the beginning, and collectivization never really took hold. Changes in agrarian practices predated the official pronouncements of *Doi Moi*, and happened much more gradually but in a manner hidden from official statistics. In a similar vein, argued that a significant underground economy existed in urban Vietnam, in Saigon in particular, that remained undocumented and unreported in official statistics. These gradual processes of change were hidden because of the absence of official recognition and may have been brought to light once *Doi Moi* legitimized these activities. Indeed, the pressures from below may have brought on *Doi Moi*. In other words, changes in the Vietnamese economy attributed to *Doi Moi* and trade liberalization may be exaggerated in part because previously illegal economic activities became officially sanctioned post-*Doi Moi* and could therefore be recorded in official data.

Social context at the time of trade liberalization

Education   Despite high levels of poverty, Vietnam had a very strong legacy of education. According to the Human Development Report this legacy is reflected in high literacy among the adult population who grew up during times of extreme poverty. Less than 7 per cent of the adult population of Vietnam was illiterate in 2001. Following reunification in 1975, the education system mandated compulsory primary education (Grades 1–5 at ages 6–10 years). *Creche*s and kindergartens are widely available for preschoolers but the official age for starting school is six years. Enrolments fell during the early reform years between 1989 and 1995 due to both early dropout rates and high-grade repetition. Poor school continuation/performance among the poor was partially attributed to *Doi Moi*-related policies that introduced tuition and other fees in public institutions and also encouraged private education. School dropout rates were higher among girls than boys. Analysing school attainment differences by gender, Liu (2001) concluded that cultural and economic factors led to stronger incentives to invest in boys rather than girls. Gender differences in wage returns suggest that returns to girls' education are lower than for boys.

Data from a later phase of reform suggests that school performance did not, in fact, suffer as much as was feared. Vietnam Living Standard Measurement Surveys conducted in 1993 and 1998 showed considerable improvement in education during that period for all socio-economic classes. Enrolments rose at the primary level from 78 to 93 per cent, at the lower secondary level from 36 to 62 per cent, and at the upper secondary level from 11 to 29 per cent. Returns to education are particularly strong for waged workers but are reasonably strong for non-wage earners as well. Pay-offs to education are reflected both in higher wages, and in a higher probability of gaining waged employment (Belanger and Liu 2004).

Marriage   Vietnam has a relatively late age at marriage for women and age differences between spouses are typically small. In the years preceding *Doi Moi*, mean age at marriage may have been artificially high because of temporary distortions in the marriage market due to unbalanced sex ratios. In 1988, the median age at marriage was estimated to be twenty-one for the country as a whole. High death rates among adult men during the 'American War' created a marriage squeeze in the 1960s and 1970s and may explain the high rates of non-marriage among older women in the late 1980s. The proportion of single women aged 45–49 rose to an all time high of 9.9 per cent in 1997 and declined by almost half to 5.1 per cent by 2002, suggesting that the marriage squeeze is on its way to being resolved. Belanger and Hong's (2002) qualitative data suggest that there may have been more indirect long-term effects. By observing 'war spinsters' among them, Vietnamese women have been able to envision lifelong single-hood in a manner they perhaps could not in the past. Belanger and Hong (2002) argue that socialist laws encouraging individual choice in marriage, combined with women's ability to earn income, contributed to changes in the position of daughters in the family. They are more likely to resist marriages that they consider unacceptable and thereby exercise more agency in their own lives. These trends suggest that the relatively high levels of non-marriage of a couple of cohorts may have implications for delayed marriage for younger generations of women even if spinsterhood per se is not sustained.

Other than the effects of the marriage squeeze on rates of non-marriage associated with the war, there is no evidence of any impact on age at marriage among those who were married. Cohort comparisons among younger and older women interviewed in Demographic and Health Surveys who were married in the 1970s and 1980s suggest that Vietnam has had a relatively stable age pattern of marriage for some time.

Marriage is shaped by a socialist legacy that attempts to regulate by law marriage practices considered detrimental to women, such as early marriages, traditionally arranged marriages, concubinage and polygamy. Owing to these laws, first enacted in 1960 in the North and in 1975 in the South, the state acting through commune officials substituted for community elders and traditional leaders and played an important part in the arrangement and celebration of marriages. During the height of socialist rule, commune officials often matched couples according to political criteria (Goodkind 1996). Belanger and Hong (1996) found, however, that through these times of socialist experimentation, as well as during the period of relative individual freedom that followed the *Doi Moi* reforms, parents continued to exert considerable influence in final marriage decisions – young people always had to gain parental approval before they could marry, and thus the parental role had remained considerably stable.

The primary concern about marriage change in Vietnam post-*Doi Moi* has been with a return to traditional practices as well as with influences of increasing consumerism (Wisensale 1999). Several studies have explored marriage practices during these changing regimes. Goodkind (1996) did not find much evidence of the re-emergence of traditional practices in the two communities he studied. However, given that *Doi Moi* had been in place for only three or four years this finding is not conclusive. He also suggests that parents of those getting married in the early 1990s would have been sufficiently influenced by the socialist system, preventing a full-scale return to traditional practices.

Response to emerging opportunities for women's work   In Vietnam, women are more likely than men to be employed in export-oriented factories. Factory work is considered harsh. In general, there does not appear to be consensus in the literature either on whether expanding opportunities are on balance positive, as in Bangladesh, or negative, as in Egypt.

According to a 2003 study of four communes in Vietnam (Committee for Population, Family and Children, 2003), recent economic developments created new employment opportunities for men and women. However, women wageworkers were not new. Vietnam has a long history of women having relatively high rates of labour force participation, with women likely to work in trade and commerce as well as in cultivation alongside men. There is some suggestion of socialist legacies playing a role in how new opportunities are crafted and perceived. Many of the garment factories, for example, are previously public sector factories that were handed over to private investors. The harsh working conditions in terms of longer hours, relative absence of job security and benefits such as medical and health insurance have a negative impact on perceptions, but the fact that there is still significant social control in the system means that it is not a complete free-for-all for employers. According to economist Naila Kabeer (personal communication), evidence from her on-going study of garment workers suggests that there are sufficient controls in place to guarantee assurance of labour rights at a considerably high level.

Relatively late marriages mean that women can work for some years before they marry. However, because labour force activity by women has always been acceptable, opportunities for women's work does not have the kind of novelty effect in Vietnam as we have argued to be the case in Bangladesh. Work also cannot be viewed as singularly responsible for marriage delays since a significant proportion of women are staying on in school and delaying marriage for this reason. A particularly striking trend is the high proportion of unmarried men and women attending vocational training. These opportunities for training are provided in the private sector and families invest considerable amounts of money because of perceived higher wage returns. There is some evidence to suggest that households engage in economic activities in multiple sectors and that women spend more time in agricultural activities than men. Agriculture is considered women's work, as are many market activities. Young women and men are equally likely to engage in formal labour before marriage although there is some evidence to suggest that men are more likely to migrate and travel further for work than women (data from Population Council Study).

Discussion

The case studies of Bangladesh, Vietnam and Egypt show how the nature of export-led growth can vary in terms of success, physical location and social patterns. Workers experience these transformations differently as well. The major argument that I have tried to build in this chapter is that important socio-economic factors, such as the marriage regime, alternative work opportunities and education levels play important roles in how trade liberalization affects women workers. Where marriage is already late, as in Egypt and Vietnam, the impact of new opportunities in work will be of lesser social consequence, because an important consequence of work is in how it legitimizes later marriage. More educated workforces are desirable and attractive for new entrepreneurs, but education also raises aspirations and dampens the enthusiasm for the work that export factories have to offer. Studies of Bangladeshi factory workers report that the novelty of waged work has had a palpable effect. It does not appear to have the same psychological impact in Egypt or Vietnam, where factory work has been around for women for some time.

Egypt's experiment with economic liberalization took place when it had already achieved a relatively late age at marriage, but increasing marriage delays still took place for men and for women after the reforms. Yet economic reforms did not increase young women's workforce participation. Rising costs of marriage, housing shortages and rising expectations for a high standard of living after marriage gave rise to later marriage even as opportunities for work declined for young women (Amin and Al-Bassusi 2004). While concerted efforts have been made to encourage export-oriented production, these policies were not particularly successful in increasing female employment. Locational aspects of industrial development policies may bear some of the responsibility.

Vietnam, like Egypt, also experienced economic opening during a relatively late marriage age regime. Like Egypt, marriage continued to take place at later ages. At the time of economic opening, male and female workforce participation rates were similar since Vietnamese women have always played a significant role in the paid economy.

Gender equity was also aggressively promoted during communist rule. Thus, while there was high economic growth and increasing opportunities for work after the *Doi Moi*, factory work did not hold the novelty it did for the women of Bangladesh, and thus did not have comparable effects on marriage.

Patterns of very early marriage in Bangladesh made marriage an all-important transition for adolescent girls so that when new opportunities became available they posed a direct challenge to early marriage. Although overall levels of change were low, marriage change was strongly associated with going to work. The substantial workforce in the garment sector is young, enters work at young ages and delays marriage considerably because of work (Amin et al. 1998). Women's work in factories brought large numbers of women out of their homes for the first time, with a substantial social impact in terms of women's presence and mobility in public places. Even though one million women working in the garment sector may not have a macro demographic impact in a country of 130 million, the social influence of such large numbers of women migrating for work for the first time is considerable.

The three country studies together offer important insights into the diverse implications of trade liberalization. I have tried to establish that preconditions and institutions – specifically what marriage regime existed and how effectively social policies were implemented – matter in all three cases. Even as countries implement economic policies that are very similar, their interactions with pre-existing contexts have led to divergent, intended and unintended, social and economic outcomes.

Notes

1. Modernization theories suggest that new norms, such as exercise of greater choice in marriage as opposed to arranged marriages, and a preference for nuclear as opposed to extended living arrangements, arise after structural change, to bring about change in marriage.
2. Analysis of trends through the 1980s established that Bangladesh finally emerged out of this nature of impoverishment in the mid-1980s.
3. The data are drawn from several secondary sources and in-depth studies on adolescents and livelihoods carried out by the author. In addition, the author accessed several nationally representative surveys from each country that provide trend data on work and marriage patterns among young

people: the Demographic and Health Surveys for Bangladesh, Egypt and Vietnam, the Egypt Labour Force Survey of 1988, the Egypt Labour Market Survey of 1998, and the Vietnam Living Standards Measurement Surveys of 1993 and 1998. In addition, qualitative studies on young people's livelihood opportunities were conducted in all three countries. For more information on these studies, contact the author.

4. The downturn in agriculture as a sector of employment appears to have been a global phenomenon during the 1970s.

References

Amin, S., and N. Al-Bassusi (2002) 'Wage Work to Prepare for Marriage: Labor Force Entry for Young Women in Egypt', Paper prepared for the Annual Meetings of the Population Association of America, Atlanta, USA, 9–11 May 2002.

Amin, S. and N.H. Al-Bassusi (2004) 'Education, Wage work and Marriage: Perspectives of Egyptian Working Women', *Journal of Marriage and Family* 66 (December: 1287–1299).

Amin, S., and M. Cain (1997) 'The Rise of Dowry in Bangladesh', in G. Jones, J. Caldwell, R. Douglas and R. D'Souza, (eds), *The Continuing Demographic Transition*, Oxford: Oxford University Press, pp. 290–306. Paper was also presented at 'The Continuing Demographic Transition', the J. Caldwell Seminar, Australian National University, 14–17 August 1995, Canberra, Australia.

Amin, S., I. Diamond, R. Naved and M. Newby (1998) 'Transitions to Adulthood of Female Garment-Factory Workers in Bangladesh', *Studies in Family Planning*, vol. 29, no. 2: 198–200.

Amin, S., L. Huq and S. Mahmud (2002) *Rural Adolescents in Bangladesh, 2001*, A report drawn from the baseline survey for the Bangladesh adolescent girls' livelihood Kishori Abhijan project', Dhaka, Bangladesh: UNICEF.

Assaad, R., and M. Arntz (2004) 'Constrained geographical mobility and gendered labor market outcomes under structural adjustment: Evidence from Egypt'. Paper presented at the Economic Research Forum Workshop on Gender, Work and Family in the Middle-east and North Africa, Mahdia, Tunisia.

Basu, A. Malwade and S. Amin (2000) 'Some Preconditions for Fertility Decline in Bengal: History, Language Identity and an Openness to Innovations', *Population Development Review*, vol. 26, no. 4: 761–94. Also published as Policy Research Division Working Paper No. 142, New York: Population Council.

Becker, G. (1991) *A Treatise on the Family*, Cambridge, MA: Harvard University Press.

Belanger, D., and K. Hong (1996) 'Marriage and the Family in Urban North Vietnam, 1965–1993', *Journal of Population*, vol. 2, no. 1: 83–105.

Belanger, D., and K. Hong (2002) 'Too Late to Marry: Failure, Fate or Fortune? – Female single-hood in rural North Vietnam', in J. Werner and D. Belanger (eds), *Gender, Household, State: Doi Moi in Vietnam*, Ithaca: South East Asia Program Publications, Cornell University, pp. 98–110.

Belanger, D., and J. Liu (2004) 'Social Policy Reforms and Daughters' Schooling in Vietnam', *International Journal of Educational Development*, vol. 24: 23–38.

Cain, M. (1984) 'Women's Status and Fertility in Developing Countries: Son Preference and Economic Security', Working Paper No. 682, Washington, DC: World Bank.

Cassandra (pseudonym) (1995) 'The Impending Crisis in Egypt', *Middle East Journal*, vol. 49, no. 1: 9–27.

Cleland, J., and N. Huq (1990) *Bangladesh Fertility Survey, 1989: Main Report*, Dhaka: NIPORT.

Cleland, J., J. Phillips, S. Amin and G. Kamal (1994) The Determinants of Reproductive Change in Bangladesh: Success in a Challenging Environment, Washington, DC: World Bank.

Coale, A.J. (1989) A reassessment of fertility trends, taking account of the Egyptian Fertility Survey. In A.M. Hallouda, S. Farid, and S.H. Cochrane (Eds.), Egypt: Demographic responses to modernization, 21–42. Cairo: Central Agency for Public Mobilization and Statistics.

Committee for Population, Family and Children (2003) *Vietnam: Demographic and Health Survey*, Calverton, MD: ORC Macro.

Courbage, Y. (1995) Fertility transition in the Mashriq and the Maghrib: Education, emigration and the diffusion of ideas. In C.M. Obermeyer (Ed.), Family, gender and population in the Middle East: Policies in context, 80–104. Cairo: American University in Cairo Press.

The Economist Intelligence Unit (2004) *EIU Country Data*, London: EIU. Available from: http://www.countrydata.bvdep.com/cgi/template.dll?product=101&user=ipaddress, accessed on 19 May 2004.

El-Kogali, S., and N. Al-Bassusi (2001) *Youth Livelihood Opportunities in Egypt*, Cairo: Population Council.

Goodkind (1996) 'State Agendas, Local Sentiments: Vietnamese Wedding Practices Amidst Socialist Transformations', *Social Forces*, vol. 75, no. 2: 717–42.

Greenhalgh, S. (1985) 'Sexual Stratification: The Other Side of Growth and Equity', Population and Development Review, vol. 11, no. 2: 265–314.

Hoodfar, H. (1997) 'The Impact of Male Migration on Domestic Budgeting: Egyptian Women Striving for an Islamic Budgeting Pattern', *Journal of Comparative Family Studies*, vol. 28, no. 2: 74.

Kabeer, N. (1991). 'Cultural Dopes or Rational Fools?: Women and Labor Supply in the Bangladesh Garment Industry', *The European Journal of Development Research*, vol. 3, no. 4: 133–60.

Kerkvliet, B., and J. Tria (1995) 'Village-State Relations in Vietnam: The Effect of Everyday Politics on Decollectivization', *Journal of Asian Studies* vol. 54 (May: 396–418).

Liu, A. (2001) 'Flying Ducks?: Girls' Schooling in Rural Vietnam', *Asian Economic Journal*, vol. 15, no. 4: 385–403.

Lloyd, C.B., S. El Tawila, W.H. Clark and B. Mensch (2003) 'The impact of educational quality on school exit in Egypt', Comparative Education Review, vol. 47, 444–467.

Malhotra, A. (1991) 'Gender and Changing Generational Relations: Spouse Choice in Indonesia', *Demography*, vol. 28, no. 4: 549–570.

Malhotra, A. (1997) 'Gender and the Timing of Marriage: Rural Urban Differences in Java', *Journal of Marriage and the Family*, vol. 59, no. 2: 434–450.

Malhotra, A., and A.O. Tsui (1996) 'Marriage timing in Sri Lanka: The role of modern norms and ideas', *Journal of Marriage and the Family*, vol. 58, no. 2: 476–490.

Malhotra, A., and D. DeGraff (1997) 'Entry versus success in the labor force: Young women's employment in Sri Lanka', World Development, vol. 25, no. 3: 379–394.

Mensch, B., J. Bruce, and M. Greene (1998) The Unchartered Passage: Girls adolescence in the Developing world, New York: Population Council.

Moghadam, V. (ed.) (1995) *World Development Studies 4: Economic Reforms, Women's Employment, and Social Policies*, Paino Oy: UNU World Institute for Development Economics Research.

Nadvi, K., J. Thoburn, B. Thang, N. Ha, N. Hoa, D. Le and E. Blanco de Armas (2004) 'Vietnam in the Global Garment and Textile Value Chain: Impact on Firms and Workers', *Journal of International Development*, vol. 16: 111–23.

National Centre for Social Sciences and Humanities (2001) *National Human Development Report, 2001: Doi Moi and Human Development in Viet Nam*, Hanoi: The Political Publishing House.

Paul-Majumdar, P., and S. Zohir (1994) 'Dynamics of Wage Employment: A Case of Employment in the Garment Industry', in S. Amin (ed.), *Bangladesh Development Studies, Special Issue on Women, Development and Change*, vol. 22, no. 2/3: 179–216.

Singerman, D., and B. Ibrahim (2001) 'The Cost of Marriage in Egypt: A Hidden Variable in the New Arab Demography', *Al-Raida*, vol. 17–24, no. 93–94 (Spring/Summer): 20–6.

Smith, D. (1980) 'Age at First Marriage', *World Fertility Survey Comparative Studies, No. 7*, London: Spottiswoode Ballantyne Ltd.

Sobhan, R. (ed.) (1995) *Experience with Economic Reform: A Review of Bangladesh's Development in the 1950s*, Dhaka: Centre for Policy Dialogue and University Press Ltd.

Suran, L., S. Amin, L. Huq, and K. Chowdury (2004) 'Does Dowry Improve Life for Brides: A Test of the Bequest Theory of Dowry', Population

Council Policy Research Division Working paper No. 195, www. popcouncil.org/pdfs/wp/195.pdf.

United Nations (various years) *International Trade Statistics Yearbook*, Vol. 1, New York: United Nations Department of International Economic and Social Affairs, Statistical Office.

Wisensale, S. (1999) 'Marriage and Family Law in a Changing Vietnam', *Journal of Family Issues*, vol. 20, no. 5: 602–16.

5

Trade Liberalization, Women's Migration and Reproductive Health in China

Lin Tan, Zhenzhen Zheng and Yueping Song

Introduction

As a key characteristic of globalization, trade liberalization aims to eliminate international trade barriers, thereby promoting development. With the increasingly free flows of global investment and trade, domestic labour markets adjust and restructure in conjunction with changes in capital, technology, industry and the availability of human resources. In China, one of the most visible and significant manifestations of this restructuring process has been the tremendous increase in migration from rural areas to the relatively industrialized urban areas, particularly the special economic zones where wholly owned foreign enterprises, joint-venture enterprises, domestic private enterprises (DPEs) and the informal economy are encouraged. While these new opportunities are a significant draw for rural labour, it is impossible for rural–urban migrant workers to live in cities as permanent residents because of tight restrictions on residential mobility. This special group of migratory workers is referred to as 'unofficial temporary migrants' or the 'floating population', meaning they have migrated into urban areas for work without any official registration for permanent residence. In the late 1990s, it was estimated that there were about 100 million temporary migrants in China. Most of them were rural to urban migrants (Cai 2002), and about one-third of them were women, many of whom were young and single. In areas where labour-intensive industries predominate, such as in Guangdong, the percentage of young female migratory workers of the whole migrant work force is as high as 75 per cent (Sun 1996).

This trade-related rural–urban migration has had both positive and negative impacts on the health conditions of female migrants, especially on their reproductive health (RH). By analysing these effects, this chapter intends to link the terms and conditions of female migrants' employment to their RH, assessing the impact that trade-related employment and migration have on health status.

Data review and methodology

There are no survey data that directly link trade liberalization with migration and health. As a result, we use macro-level statistics on trade liberalization, and survey data on the living conditions, attitudes, knowledge and behaviour of female migrants as related to sexual and RH, to analyse and discuss the possible links between trade liberalization, migration and RH.

Published research on China's floating population mainly focuses on its macroeconomic effects and the challenges of administration, particularly in terms of population control. After the 1994 International Conference on Population and Development and the United Nations' 1995 Fourth World Conference on Women, the notion of 'reproductive health' was soon used by some Chinese women's studies researchers and demographers, resulting in a number of new surveys on the RH status of female migrants in different cities (see Table 5.1). Most of these analyses focused on deficiencies in the family-planning administration, the lack of RH services, the main factors contributing to RH problems among female migrants and their consequent demand for specific kinds of services. However, few studies integrated these issues with the social and economic contexts, much less linked them with trade liberalization. Although these studies focus on the administrative and population control problems caused by rural–urban migration, they neglect the catalytic, even determinant, role of trade liberalization and globalization. Thus the association between the RH issues of migrants and trade liberalization, to the extent that trade liberalization affects migration and consequently poses challenges to RH, is still ambiguous.

Using data derived from some of the surveys listed in Table 5.1, the 2000 Chinese Census and data published in the *Chinese National Statistics Yearbook*, compiled by the National Statistics Bureau, this

Table 5.1 A brief review of selected published surveys on the RH condition of female migrants

Topic	Date/City/Sample	Sponsors	Issue and main conclusion
RH status of migrating women in Pudong Area in Shanghai	2000–01 Shanghai 1,070	Population Research Institute, Fudan University	Personal hygiene habits and knowledge were improved after migration, while living and working conditions still impaired their RH status.
RH conditions of female migrants in Jiading District, Shanghai	1998 Shanghai 1,072	Jiading Family Planning Committee and Fudan University	Unmet demand for government RH services for female migrants, little knowledge of RH in migrant women.
Effect of population migration on rural women	2000 Sichuan and Anhui Province 3,186	Ford Fund	Migrating experience changed female migrants' knowledge and attitudes towards RH very much.
Study on high risks of RH of unmarried young female migrant workers	1999 Shenzhen and Gaoming City 19 (FDGs)	WHO Special Programme for Research and Training	Sexual activity was active among migrating young women, which resulted in unsafe sex, unwanted pregnancy, induced abortion and RTI.
Knowledge, attitude and pattern of AIDS and STDs among migrant females in Pudong New District, Shanghai	March–April 2002 Shanghai City 53 (FDGs)	Public Health Institute, Fudan University, Shanghai	Migrant population in Pudong District lacks the necessary knowledge to protect themselves against AIDS and STD.

Continued

Table 5.1 *Continued*

Topic	Date/City/Sample	Sponsors	Issue and main conclusion
Investigation on RTI among migrant married women of childbearing age in Fengtai District in Beijing	June–July 2001 Beijing City 2,069	Beijing Family Planning Committee	Higher rate of RTI in migrant women than rural women in the outskirts of Beijing, with weak initiative to seek medical assistance.
Reproductive and sexual health status and related service needs of young female migrant workers in five cities	1997–1999 Beijing, Shanghai, Guiyang, Guangzhou, Taiyuan 146 (FDGs)	UNDP/UNFPA/WHO/ Development and Research Training in Human Reproduction	A host of barriers have inhibited migrant young women from seeking sexual and RH services, particularly those from public sector facilities.

chapter first describes China's trade liberalization; then it discusses how the economic development promoted by trade liberalization has fuelled the demand for cheaper labour in urban areas and led to rural–urban migration, particularly among young women. It then discusses both the positive and the negative impacts of migration on women's sexual and reproductive health, exploring the work- and non-work-related conditions of migrant women, as well as local regulations and official services.

Trade Liberalization and Labour Migration

For the last two decades China has attracted more foreign direct investment (FDI) than any other developing country in the world. In 2003, China surpassed the United States as the most popular destination for FDI ($53.5 billion in China and $30 billion in the US).[1] China has secured this commanding position as the top destination for FDI over a short period. In 1980, there were only seven foreign enterprises in China; this figure increased to 25,389 in 1990 and 212,436 in 1999, with an increase in total investment from $470 million in 1980 to $52.7 billion by 2002. The policy of 'reform and openness' (of which trade liberalization was a central part) first promoted in the late 1970s is, of course, widely seen as a great success. So successful, in fact, that by 2001 China reached a historic and far-reaching agreement to accede to the World Trade Organization (WTO). Accession to the WTO marks China's full-fledged acceptance into the global economy, and shows the determination of its leaders to continue to pursue increased liberalization in trade and foreign investment, as well as dramatic reform of the domestic economy.

China's early decision to open its borders to inflows of FDI has meant that foreign-invested enterprises (FIEs) play a prominent role in the economy. FDI flows were more than $50 billion in 2002 (4 per cent of GDP); accumulated net FDI inflows from 1980 to 2002 were $440 billion. In 2002, the output of FIEs accounted for 33.4 per cent of China's industrial output (see Figure 5.1); tax revenue from FIEs accounts for about 20.5 per cent of national tax revenue; exports and imports by FIEs were more than 50 per cent of China's total trade in 2002. With accession to the WTO, FIEs will play an even more prominent role in the development of China's market economy.

Besides liberalizing trade, Chinese economic reforms also liberalized the domestic economy through marketization. In addition to FIEs,

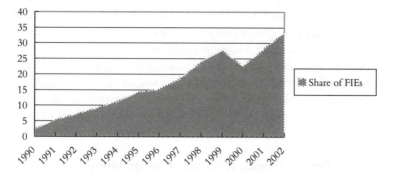

Figure 5.1   Share of FIEs in national industrial outputs (%) (1990–2002).
Source: Based on the data provided by Ministry of Commerce of the People's Republic of China. China State Administration Bureau of Industry and Commerce (2003): 'China Industry and Commerce Administration Yearbook'.

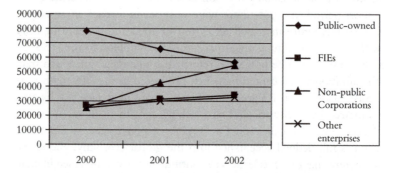

Figure 5.2   Number of industrial enterprises established per year (2000–02).
Source: Compiled by the data provided by Ministry of Commerce of the People's Republic of China. China State Administration Bureau of Industry and Commerce (2003): 'China Industry and Commerce Administration Yearbook'.

other kinds of non-state-owned entities such as private enterprises and informal businesses flourished in the liberalized policy environment. Figure 5.2 illustrates this shift over the past few years: between 2000 and 2002, the number of new publicly owned enterprises, including state-owned enterprises (SOEs), declined while the number of non-public domestic enterprises increased at a surprising speed and scale. The private sector (including FIEs) now accounts for more than 60 per cent of China's GDP and two-thirds of its industrial value-added (from less than one-third in the late 1970s).[2]

China's labour market has changed in response to FDI inflows and the flourishing domestic sector, primarily through the expansion and diversification of labour demand. As with its increasing share of GDP and industrial output, the non-state-owned economy represents an increasing share of labour demand. At the beginning of the reform period, private firms were virtually non-existent in urban China. In 1980, 76 per cent of urban employees were employed in the state sector, 23 per cent in urban collective enterprises (UCEs) and only 0.8 per cent in private businesses. By the end of 2002, the urban employment structure had changed significantly: 47 per cent of urban employees worked in the state sector, 7.4 per cent in UCEs, 28 per cent in private enterprises, including FIEs, DPEs and firms with other forms of ownership.[3] Growth in the non-state-owned economy also created a new path to employment for rural residents. Many FIEs and DPEs are in labour-intensive industries such as manufacturing, garments and processing industries. China's rural surplus labour force was a ready source of supply for the demand of these industries for low-cost labour. Currently, eastern rural areas are undergoing a period of industrial upgrading, absorbing local labour more effectively, but private investors are still able to obtain cheap labour from less-developed central or western China.

Rural labourers, attracted by urban economic development, are considered temporary residents when they migrate into cities. This type of rural–urban migration was restricted in the period before economic reforms, and it is still difficult for jobseekers in the state sector, due to the limitations maintained by the urban household registration system.

As a developing country, China is in a unique position because of its household registration system, which is still used to maintain a strict division between rural and urban areas and to control migration in the course of economic reforms and trade liberalization. According to the criterion of 'whether registered', migration can be classified in two ways. First, there are illegal rural–urban migrants without appropriate registration, many of whom live on the streets, below bridges, in makeshift shelters or with friends and relatives. Some of them find casual work in the informal sector (e.g. in small–medium private enterprises and as street peddlers); others engage in criminal activities. Authorities do not recognize their residential rights, and they are legally required to return to their villages or rural towns. Second, there is the semi-official 'floating population' of workers from rural areas – the migrant labour that we discuss in this chapter. Authorities tolerate them as long as the urban enterprises (including most FIEs and DPEs) that have hired them have received proper permission from labour authorities. Working migrants are registered with local labour authorities and are supposed to stay only temporarily. They usually do not have urban residential status and are still registered as agricultural population in their home village or town. As a result, they do not have any rights to the social welfare benefits commonly enjoyed by urban residents, including basic medical insurance. According to the 2000 census, the floating population is estimated to number more than 100 million, and most of them have lived in urban areas for years. These migrant workers are socially vulnerable due to China's restrictive residential policy. SOEs and public administrative departments and organizations ask for local urban household registration records when recruiting, so it is almost impossible for rural–urban migrants to be recruited by the urban formal sector, including SOEs.

In sum, due to the labour market changes that were ushered in by economic reforms and trade liberalization in recent years, the long-time labour market segmentation that has existed between urban and rural areas has been broken down by labour migration. During the last decade, a large proportion of the rural labour force in China has migrated to provincial capitals and large coastal cities where FIEs, DPEs and the informal sectors are concentrated. But most of these migrants remain marginalized and vulnerable, as the household registration system denies them stability or access to the social welfare benefits of living in an urban area.

Women, Rural–Urban Migration and the Private Sector

FDI has become a significant source of demand for female labour, which directly and indirectly triggered the rural–urban migration of women. Labour-intensive industry is the most popular sector for new domestic and foreign investments, where traditionally female-intensive manufacturing predominates. These industries can generally be characterized as light industries, ranging from food processing, textiles and garments to chemicals, rubber and plastics, and electronics. The proportion of women workers in these light industrial enterprises is much higher than in industry as a whole, especially among enterprises located in the developed and large coastal cities. Data provided by China's Ministry of Labour and Social Security shows that the proportion of women in FIEs and other types of private enterprises is much higher than in SOEs and UCEs. Between 1997 and 2000, the proportion of women workers in FIEs was higher than 50 per cent, while their proportion in SOEs was 36 per cent and in UCEs 40 per cent. In terms of absolute numbers, FIEs employed 3.02 million women in 1997, which increased to 3.29 million women by 2000. In contrast, SOEs employed 4.03 million women in 1997, which declined to 2.95 million in 2000. In the context of trade liberalization, FIEs and DPEs offer more opportunities for women, especially unmarried women, to find jobs easily and migrate out of rural areas.

Though national statistics about the exact number of migrant women engaged in non-state-owned sectors are not available, some inferences about the proportion of female migrants can be made from the data gathered on Shenzhen, the most prominent of four special economic zones in China. A study undertaken by CASS in 1997 (Tan 1998) showed that of the 1.29 million rural labourers migrating into Shenzhen in 1996, 836,000 were women, accounting for 68 per cent. The study found that most local government officials believed that women accounted for more than 60 per cent of rural–urban migrant labourers. The same study found that in the Pearl River Delta migrant women were concentrated in FIEs (among whom 62.1 per cent worked in FIEs), while more migrant men entered local DPEs (36.7 per cent) (Tan 1998).

The Impact of Women's Migration and Employment on Their RH in the Context of Trade Liberalization: Positive versus Negative

Rural–urban migration has a complicated impact on women's RH. Working in a new environment changes living conditions, lifestyle, social networks, personal hygiene, attitudes and behaviour about sexuality – especially with regard to premarital sexual activity, and knowledge of, access to and utilization of family planning services, as well as the specific service options available (i.e. private versus government providers, services at the workplace, etc.).

There are, on the one hand, clearly some benefits of employment-induced migration on women's RH. The development of non-SOEs has enabled many rural women, especially young women, to move into non-farm work. Their urban experiences promote improved health relative to their fellow rural villagers because of higher incomes, lifestyle changes and increased access to services. On the other hand, migration to work in private urban enterprises can have negative effects on the RH of female migrant workers. These negative effects emanate from the limits of official RH services, the pressure exerted by family planning administrations, the sometimes unsafe working and living conditions in private enterprises, and the increased likelihood that these women will engage in unprotected sex. This section reviews these factors, assessing whether and how trade liberalization and the consequent rural–urban migration of many Chinese women have impacted their RH.

Higher incomes and urban RH care

Rural women working in private enterprises typically receive higher pay than they would earn in rural farming work. In 2000, the per capita annual pay in enterprises invested from Hong Kong, Taiwan and Macao was RMB 12,210; for other FIEs the annual pay equalled RMB 15,692. Rural per capita annual net income reached just RMB 2,253 in that year, one-seventh of that in FIEs. Thus, higher incomes should increase women's ability to pay for health care.

However, compared with urban residents, rural migrant female workers earn very little. According to a survey on the RH status of female migrants in Jiading District, Shanghai City, in 1998, on average, a migrant woman earned only RMB 571 per month, less than half of what a female urban resident earned during the same year. The model on which DPEs and FIEs have based their success is one in which they minimize their labour costs, and temporary workers, especially women workers, tend to be the most vulnerable to these pressures to lower wages. Some enterprises try to lower wages indirectly by extending work time, or refusing to pay for overtime by basing wages on a piece rate system. According to a study carried out by The Women's Research Institute of All China Women's Federation in 1996 on 36 private and foreign-invested enterprises in eight cities (Zhuhai and Dongguan, Guangzhou, Hangzhou and Wengzhou, Zhejiang, Wuhan and Xuantao, Hubei, Shenyang and Dalian, Liaoning), over 80 per cent of non-SOEs used fines to discipline workers, 46 per cent docked wages for no plausible reason in the year prior and 21 per cent have at one time delayed payment of wages. Lower wages for women doing the same work as men still persists, despite a labour law that forbids such practices (Jiang and Zhang 1997).

Thus, although the income of female rural–urban migrants is typically much higher than their rural counterparts, their pay is low by urban standards, and they work in environments that thrive on their hard work and low pay. In addition, because female migrants have no access to the urban social security system, their effective wages are even lower by urban standards. Private enterprises, especially small- and medium-sized ones, do little to increase the affordability of health care for temporary rural female workers. Low incomes and having to pay for all of their health care induce migrating women to give up health care, especially RH care.

Working and living conditions in private enterprises

To sustain high labour productivity, enterprises generally provide a basic living environment. For migrant workers, many DPEs, especially FIEs, provide room and board with basic sanitary facilities such as a bathroom and a toilet. Some even provide health care facilities. In a report on the survey carried out by the All China Federation of Trade Unions in 1999 provided by the National Statistics Bureau, 87.5 per cent of the Hong Kong-, Macao- and Taiwan- invested enterprises, and 50 per cent of other FIEs, have established provisions for regular testing for gynaeco-logical diseases.

However, living and working conditions are still problematic. According to the survey by The Women's Research Institute of All China Women's Federation in 1996, many working girls live in dormi-tory rooms provided by employers. The rooms were crowded, with an average of eight to twenty girls in one room and at times as many as fifty. Many dorms were shabby with not enough light, ventilation or heating and cooling facilities. The food lacked nutrition and the dining environ-ment was unhealthy. Living conditions of this kind can damage physical and mental health. Research on Taiwanese enterprises in Tianjin found that the move-in working girls suffered from insomnia and depression because of the crowded and noisy sleeping rooms (Jiang and Zhang 1997).

Sometimes private and foreign-invested enterprises resist improving working conditions to pursue profits. This means that many migrant women work in an environment of noise, dirt, poisonous gases, radiation and other dangers. In the research by the Women's Union mentioned above, only 64 per cent of the enterprises provided protective facilities. The rest had no protection at all. Some enterprises ignore legal requirements for special protection during menses, pregnancy and lactation period for women, and most of the enterprises manage to avoid providing health care for pregnant women or new mothers. Some enterprises even clearly state in labour contracts that pregnancy and childbirth are not allowed. Among Taiwanese-owned enterprises, pregnant working girls were dismissed and dispatched to their home-towns. Such working conditions and the lack of physical and legal protection mean that urban migrant work carries with it more than just higher incomes; it can be discriminatory and harmful to health.

The survey mentioned above also shows that overtime work is common in private enterprises or those invested in by overseas funds. About 76 per cent of the women surveyed had to work overtime continuously in the busy season, at an average of 10.9 hours a day and 8.4 days in a row, which could be extended to 12 days. One-third of the women said they were not always allowed to go to the bathroom when they wanted, and 44 per cent said they had no choice when asked to work overtime. All of these factors have seriously influenced move-in female workers' rights and their health, especially their RH.

Trade liberalization has promoted the private economy significantly, but the recruitment and management behaviour in this sector sometimes violates ILO labour standards and basic human rights. Increasingly, rural female migrants are a key force in the rapid development of this sector, but slow progress in establishing integrated social institutions, such as labour unions, means that women's organizations cannot effectively pressurize enterprises to take care of women's health rights and interests.

With accession to the WTO, the private sector is under increasing pressure to conform to international labour standards, taking on more social responsibility and accounting for workers' human rights. According to the first international standard of moral regulation, Social Accountability 8000 (SA 8000), enterprises should provide safe and healthy working conditions for workers, insure workers' room and board conditions, and observe legal working hour limits. Private enterprises should also implement more hygiene facilities, free gynae-cological exams, special care during menstruation, continued employment during pregnancy and public education on RH issues. In this way, a new corporate pattern that includes government ser-vices and enterprise support together can be established, one that is much more effective and suitable for the sustainable development of trade liberalization.

Exposure to urban lifestyles

During the course of migration, urban atmospheres exert a subtle influence on migrants' habits (Jiang and Zhang 1997: 22). Migrants come to accept the information, culture, behaviours and community health service institutions in their living and working environments. The improvement of sanitary habits is a significant indicator of these changes. In 2001, a study in the Pudong New Area in Shanghai (Chen, Y. 2001) found that women from rural areas significantly changed their personal sanitary habits after migrating to Shanghai for factory work. For example, after migrating, women were more likely to shower during menses and use a dedicated washcloth for their private parts (see Tables 5.2 and 5.3).

Migrant life exposes women to other types of knowledge as they adapt to urban life. Information from books, magazines, TV, the Internet and other media vividly shows a relatively healthy life to the migrants. Migrant women have more opportunities to meet people outside their hometowns to learn about health care. Preliminary findings from a WHO-funded, multi-city qualitative study of young female migrants' RH status and needs while in urban areas (Zheng 2001) show that in the cities young women from rural areas are greatly influenced by their migration experience and urban lifestyle. They tend to get married later; some talked about how classmates at home already had children, while they are still single. They enjoy their work in the city, not only because they can earn more money but also because they can learn more about life outside their villages. Among the interviewees, 14 per cent stated that in addition to family and health care professionals, they get information about health, including RH, from their factory

Table 5.2 Bath manner during menses before and after migration (%, N = 1,070)

	Shower	Towel	In tub	No bath	Total
Present manner during menses period	50.3	20.7	15.5	13.5	100.0
Manner before migration	26.8	26.5	21.5	25.2	100.0

Table 5.3 Whether a dedicated washcloth is used for private parts and feet before/after migration (%, $N = 1,070$)

	No	Yes	Total
Whether a different towel is used at present	4.4	95.6	100.0
Whether a different towel was used before migration	8.0	92.0	100.0

Source: Chen, Y. (2001) 'Reproductive Health of Floating Women in Fourth District in Pudong New Area in Shanghai', *South China Population*, vol. 3: 53–9.

co-workers and urban friends. Recent female migrants, in gaining a more comprehensive notion of health, including RH, pay greater attention to their health status. According to the survey mentioned above, 25 per cent of migrated women have voluntarily asked for gynaecological examinations, 5 per cent more than those who had never migrated. And among those who were ill with colitis, 51 per cent of the migrant women afflicted were treated by medical services and cured, while just 43 per cent of rural inhabitants were treated and cured. The proportion of migrants among those who refused medical treatment was also lower than that of the rural residents (about 22 per cent of resident women interviewed refused medical treatment, 4 per cent higher than migrant women).

A study by Xie et al. (2001) shows that migrant women have different ideas about their RH and activity than village women. RH knowledge and attitudes towards marriage and sexuality changed after migration, including knowledge of contraceptives, the expected number of children, knowledge of AIDS and STDs, and knowledge about reproductive physiology in the processes of contraception and abortion.

This research also shows that migrant women have lower expected number of children than local village women (Figure 5.3), and the average number of children they eventually have (1.26) is lower than the latter (1.37). Women who had migrated were not only more aware of contraception and safe sex, they were also more likely to know about self-administered methods such as the pill and condoms. In this survey, 61 per cent of migrant women had heard of contraceptive pills versus 48 per cent of village women, and 51 per cent of migrant women had knowledge of condoms versus 44 per cent of the never-migrated women. Migrant women were substantially more likely to have heard of

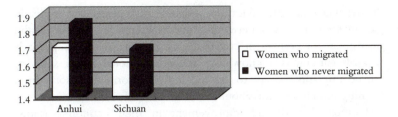

Figure 5.3 Difference between the expected number of children for migrant and non-migrant women (*N* = 3,186).

AIDS or STDs and to have the knowledge to defend themselves from these diseases. In the survey, a number of questions about AIDS and STDs were asked. In response to the simple question, 'Do you know about AIDS (STDs)?', less than half the sample answered 'yes', with migrant women substantially more likely to answer yes (about 90 per cent of migrated women versus 70 per cent of the never-migrated women). Of the women who had migrated, those who had migrated longer were more likely to answer yes.

Attitudes towards marriage change significantly when women leave the village. Migrant women are more likely to make their own decisions about marriage and to ask for decision-making rights in their families. They are also more likely to consider divorce as a way of solving a marital crisis. In the survey, there were questions such as 'Who should decide about who should marry whom?'; 'Is it alright for a couple that does not get along to get divorced?'; 'Is it alright for a wife to refuse her husband's desire to have sexual intercourse?' When answering the last two questions, migrant women were significantly more likely to say yes compared with those who had never migrated (32.8 per cent of migrant women agreed that a couple that does not get along well could get divorced, while only 28.8 per cent of resident women agreed; 64.1 per cent of migrant women agreed that a woman could refuse her husband's sexual desire, 7.4 per cent higher than resident women). They were also more likely to think that couples should make their own decisions about marriage (31.7 per cent of migrant women agreed to decide marriage by themselves, 5 per cent higher than resident women).

These changes in attitudes and concepts about RH better equip female migrants to protect their health. However, due to the disadvantages of little education, isolated work places and relatively narrow communication networks, migrant women are still outside the mainstream of permanent city residents. Lacking a formal approach towards gaining RH knowledge and conventional family support, female migrants are apt to get incomplete information, sometimes forming inaccurate ideas about sexuality and RH.

Compared with the improvement in their economic status, migrant women's knowledge of RH is sorely lacking and compromises their abilities to protect themselves from potential risks. The above survey, which was conducted in Shanghai City, also found that many of the interviewees had not heard of RH, and did not know about emergency contraception; some had even not heard of STDs. A number of interviewees were indifferent towards gynaecological examinations and ignored gynaecological discomfort.

From this analysis, urban life appears to exert complicated effects on migrant women from rural areas. Employment in urban areas improves personal hygiene, enriches RH cognition, and equips women with some degree of caution and capability to deal with potential RH problems. However, being marginalized from the urban mainstream can lead to incorrect ideas about RH, and more risky sexual activity.

Urban family planning control and RH services for migrants

People in different environments have different needs for RH services. In the highly variable context of China's economic reforms, rural–urban migrant women have very specific RH service demands. This section reviews the sources of demand and supply for RH services among unmarried and married women, focusing on how their work and social lives affect their need and demand for RH services and the extent to which these are being met.

Unmarried female migrants

According to Zheng (2002), considerable evidence suggests that while premarital sexual activity is not widespread among unmarried female migrant workers, it is certainly not a rare event. Compared with their peers in their home villages, young migrant women are more likely to have engaged in sexual activity. Usually, sexual debut occurs in migration. However, risky sexual activity is considerably more prevalent among migrant women than among non-migrants in urban areas: unmarried young migrants are observed to be less likely to practice contraception, and more likely to experience unwanted pregnancy and induced abortion (Wang 1999).

RH/family planning services in China are provided in two different ways. In rural areas, family planning service centres are available at county and township levels, and family planning workers and service offices are available in each village. A special feature of the rural system is its wide outreach and the capacity to provide services at a client's home. The urban health system functions differently. Services are provided in a variety of ways. Hospitals are formally responsible for the provision of RH and family planning services. Family Planning Commissions are responsible for contraception management and education and distribution of contraceptives; department stores and drug stores sell contraceptives. Urban residents can also obtain related information, educational material, contraceptive supplies and even counselling services from community family planning service posts. In addition, family planning workers are available in all work units (usually female doctors of the unit's clinic) to supply contraceptives.

Although family planning services are widely available in China, they have traditionally been accessible only to registered resident married couples. Unmarried youth and unmarried migrant youth have been effectively excluded from this array of services. The situation changed in the late 1990s with the introduction of RH hotlines and community mailboxes for RH counselling in several urban sites. At the same time, increased attention was being paid to the development of youth-friendly programmes and curricula for RH education at the high school level (Lou et al. 2002), and several counselling clinics became accessible to adolescents (Beijing Youth 2002). However, few RH/family planning workers are equipped with the skills necessary to provide sensitive counselling to youth, or have been trained in the provision of non-judgemental and confidential services to young people; unmarried young women attending gynaecological clinics reported embarrassment in their interactions with providers.

Compared with local urban residents, unmarried young migrants have very different characteristics that ultimately affect their access to RH services. They are not in schools or educational establishments, as is the case with most urban youth. They tend to be employed, yet lack social welfare support such as medical insurance. They tend to reside in independent living arrangements away from adult family members and have less social or family support than their non-migrant peers. They perceive themselves as outsiders in the city and are often treated as such. When they become sexually active, they remain out of the reach, in practice, of the available service network. Their positions as migrant workers make them a marginalized group, with greater exposure to sexual and reproductive risk, while being underserved by contraceptive and other RH services.

Data from Zheng's (2002) qualitative research, which included focus group discussions and in-depth interviews on the reproductive and sexual health status and related service needs of young female migrant workers in Beijing, Shanghai, Guangzhou (capital of Guangdong Province), Guiyang (capital of Guizhou Province) and Taiyuan (capital of Shanxi Province) between 1997 and 1999, show that there are a number of obstacles for young female migrants in accessing RH services. For most sexually active young women, sexual activity is risky and unprotected. Many are too embarrassed to ask for contraception at such a young age and fear that buying contraceptives in public places risks exposure, even if they know where to obtain contraceptive supplies.

Incomplete awareness of contraception and other safe sex behaviours is another barrier to contraceptive use among young migrants. Some unmarried workers agreed that unmarried women are not supposed to ask for contraception information. And most young unmarried workers reported little knowledge of these matters, and 'did not know where to ask'. Those who were aware of contraception and safe sex tended to be better educated, more likely to be involved with a steady partner, and more likely to work in the service and entertainment sectors than other young women. Even here, sources of information were limited to books, magazines and peers. Other options were effectively closed to the unmarried, even among those expressing interest and a willingness to seek out this sort of information.

Indeed, there is a general perception that government services are not available to unmarried youth or to migrants. While government facilities have done little to dispel this misperception, private facilities have tried to fill the gap by promoting their own services among these young women through aggressive public information campaigns (advertisements and flyers). Unmarried focus group discussion participants in all five cities reported exposure to private clinic advertisements on the street and were aware of the services these facilities offered (ranging from induced abortion to treatment of STDs).

Fear of a service provider's unfriendly attitude posed yet another obstacle to seeking contraceptive services. In the above survey, a few unmarried migrants who had undergone induced abortions reported that they had received contraceptives from the treatment facility. However, by and large, participants agreed that hospitals and other facilities were unwelcoming, required complicated procedures, did not ensure confidentiality or privacy, and necessitated long waiting times and high costs.

Finally, partner attitudes posed an additional obstacle to contraceptive use. Although some unmarried workers reported that their boyfriends brought and used condoms, the majority reported that the partner refused to use a condom, even though they were generally aware of how to obtain supplies.

Induced abortion is a serious reproductive problem among young, unmarried female migrants. Given the likelihood of engaging in unprotected sex, it was not surprising that sexually active participants had either personally experienced unwanted pregnancy or were acquainted with someone who had done so. Unwanted pregnancy was almost always resolved by induced abortion, and represented a situation in which young women were forced to seek care from a government or private sector facility. Findings from the above survey suggest that young unmarried migrants were about as likely to seek abortion services from private as from government facilities. For example, among abortion seekers in Guangzhou, those residing in the metropolitan area opted for abortion in government hospitals, while those who lived or worked in the outskirts of the city were more likely to opt for private clinics. Even though private clinics were usually small and poorly equipped, and providers at these facilities often had limited technical skills and sometimes not even licenses to perform abortions, they were preferred by many unmarried migrants for reasons centring largely on perceived quality of care, cost and confidentiality. Many reported that these services were not only more affordable but also more convenient and private.

Inconvenient procedures and scheduling posed another obstacle to public sector services. Most workers acknowledge that they require their managers' permission to obtain leave for an induced abortion, and they fear having to disclose the reason if repeated visits or long periods away from work are required. Others fear the loss of wages associated with procedures at government facilities, as migrant workers are rarely eligible for sick leave. Private facilities are perceived to be more convenient: they did not have limited schedules, abortions were provided throughout the day and even after working hours. Government facilities, in contrast, were perceived to be less flexible.

Married female migrants

Generally speaking, women who are married are less likely to migrate alone, but according to all the surveys mentioned above, those married women whose husbands have migrated were also more likely to have migrated themselves. This may indicate couples migrating together, or that incentives that lead one to migrate also drive one to marry someone who would migrate. Thus, women of childbearing age in migratory families are a target for urban family planning administrations for fear that they will exceed fertility limits. The Family Planning Offices in most cities now strictly investigate and register fertility information for married migratory women, offering free contraceptive services for these women, including free contraceptive surgical procedures, counselling and supplies, such as condoms. These help ensure that married migrants practice safe sex and protect their health.

However, these government-provided services focus on population control, not the RH needs of migrants. As a result, there is still a significant gap between demand and supply for official RH services among married female migrants. Due to low levels of education and bad working and living conditions, married migrants require more information and services than just technical contraception, including enough knowledge of contraceptive methods, safe sexual life and safe pregnancy, the provision of which by government services is still weak.

The scarcity of RH services worsens the RH of married migrants, as illustrated by the high rate of reproductive tract infections (RTI). A survey among married migrant women in Fengtai District in Beijing (Lijie 2003) found that migrant women were more likely to get an RTI than local rural residents (among migrant women, 30.26 per cent got one or more kinds of RTI, 7 per cent higher than local rural women residents), and most of them did not take it seriously, refusing to seek treatment. Half of the sufferers were unaware of the RTIs they were suffering from.

Government financing of RH services has also lagged behind the increase in the number of married migrant women, partly because financing decisions about services like those provided by the City Family Planning Administration are allocated based on the number of registered, local female residents. This situation is gradually improving as a result of a special fund for the protection of married migrant women's RH. But much more needs to be done to achieve an adequate level of services for migrant married women.

Conclusion

In summary, trade liberalization has greatly expanded the private sector, which in turn spurred large-scale rural–urban migration in China. For female migrants attracted by new opportunities in urban labour-intensive industries, these shifts impacted their RH via the mediating factors of changes in lifestyles, income, hygiene habits, the availability of sanitary facilities and RH service resources. The effects on RH were both positive and negative.

Our analysis of published survey data leads us to conclude that trade-related migration has certainly been of some benefit to the RH status of female migrants, especially as a result of the changes in lifestyle and RH awareness that is linked with urban residence, as well as the improvements in hygiene and the availability of sanitary facilities.

But there are significant limits to these benefits. The lack of enforceable and enforced labour protection within private sector labour-intensive enterprises can pose a direct threat to the female migrants who work there. The limits imposed by the household registration system mean that migrant women will continue to be a marginalized workforce, unable to garner the benefits of sustained access to urban work opportunities or the urban social welfare system. Moreover, the insufficiency of official RH services, and their tendency to focus on population control, inhibits the capacity of female migrants to translate the potential benefits of urban residence and employment into real improvements in RH.

Notes

1. This data is taken from the Economic Information Daily Publishing House (2004).
2. This figure is derived from the National Statistics Bureau (2000).
3. The statistics in this paragraph are all derived from the National Statistics Bureau (2003).

References

Beijing Youth (2002) 'Teenager Clinic', 8 March: 23.

Cai, F. (ed.) (2002) *Employment in Rural and Urban China: Issues and Options*, Beijing: Social Sciences Documentation Publishing House.

Chen, Y. (2001) 'Reproductive Health of Floating Women in Fourth District in Pudong New Area in Shanghai', *South China Population*, vol. 3: 53–9.

China Statistics Yearbook 2000, National Statistics Bureau, 2000.

China Statistics Yearbook 2003, National Statistics Bureau, 2003.

Cui, N., M. Li and E. Gao (2001) 'Views of Chinese Parents on the Provision of Contraception Services to Unmarried Youth', *Reproductive Health Matters*, vol. 9, no. 17: 137–45.

Economic Information Daily Publishing House (2004) *Economic Information Daily*, Beijing, 24 September 2004.

Jiang, Y. and Y. Zhang (1997) 'Surviving and Development of Working Women in the Non-State Owned Enterprises', *Collection of Women Studies*, vol. 3: 22.

Lijie, Z. (2003) 'A Survey of RTI among Married Floating Women in Fengtai District in Beijing-Relevant knowledge and their Treatment Behavior', *China Epidemic Studies*, vol. 8: 23–8.

Population Census Office under the State Council and Department of Population, Social, Science and Technology Statistics National Bureau of Statistics of China (2002), 'Tabulation on the 2000 Population Census of the People's Republic of China', China Statistics Press.

Sun, S. (1996) 'Market Economy and Female Floating Population', *Southern China Population*, vol. 4: 41–4.

Tan (1998) 'Gender Difference in the Migration of Rural Labor', *Social Science in China*, vol. 2: 70–7.

Wang, J. (1999) 'Sexual Behavior, Contraceptive Use and Choice of Gestation Results for the Unmarried Pregnant Immigrant Women in Shanghai', *Population Research*, vol. 1: 50–5.

Zheng, Z. (2001) 'Unsafe Sex among Unmarried Young Female Migratory Workers', Draft prepared for Analysis Workshop on Adolescent Sexual and Reproductive Health, Bangkok.

Zheng, Z. (2002) 'Reproductive Health Service Use among Unmarried Young Female Migratory Workers in Urban China', Draft prepared for APSSAM Conference, China.

6

Local Response to Global Development: An Emerging Culture of Health among Pregnant Women in Mexican *Maquiladoras*

Catalina A. Denman

Introduction

I would go to work regardless of how I felt, for my little girl, because I had to send her money.

Marina[1], age 30, operator and line inspector at Plant X, separated from her first child so she could support her family through work in the *maquiladoras*[2]

In the 1970s and 1980s, many countries adopted an export-led model of economic development based on a neo-liberal strategy of economic growth. According to this model, corporations from more industrialized regions or countries invested capital in developing host countries where specialized export processing zones (EPZs) offered attractive environments for investors: low wages, reduced export tariffs and more relaxed environmental standards than those in the country or region of origin. Host countries pursued the promise of increased employment, stronger domestic markets, and increased demand for national industries that would provide materials and infrastructure for the factories in the export zones. The industrialized regions produced under this model profoundly altered population demographics and cultural norms in the host countries. EPZs were often created in proximity to easy export routes, thus promoting mass migration into the factory-rich regions. New neighbourhoods arose while traditional family networks crumbled. Women flocked to work on assembly lines, thereby changing family structures and gender-based role expectations.

Mexico's implementation of an export-led development strategy, and its establishment of *maquiladora* zones, or regions of assembly-line factories built mostly, but not always, by foreign investors are one such example. Although the precise nature of an EPZ depends on the world region, the time period and the type of foreign investment involved, the *maquiladora* industry in Mexico has particular significance as a global example. The border between the United States and Mexico, which is the longest world border between an industrialized nation and a developing country, raises a broad range of issues that have emerged in processing zones worldwide.

One of these issues is the development of localized cultures as workers cope with their new environments. One manifestation of this new culture reflects the needs of women who work in export plants: balancing work and family, accessing health care, and providing for health needs brought about by the reproductive cycle, the subject of this chapter.

This chapter presents a medical anthropological study of fourteen women who became pregnant and delivered their infants while working at an American-owned *maquiladora* in Nogales, Sonora, Mexico. They were followed through pregnancy, birth and the post-partum period as they negotiated with their partners and managed the resources available to them to ensure a healthy birth. Their decisions and behaviours occurred within the context of their own gender identities and their relationships with their partners, family members, physicians, friends and other workers, all of whom held varying degrees of control over the women's decisions, resources and actions. Uprooted from their native homes and isolated from traditional family support, these women created a new 'culture of health' that includes a combination of traditional remedies, family knowledge and Western medicine.

This new culture of health counterbalances some of the negative impacts that *maquiladora* employment has on women's reproductive health. There is a complex relationship between the benefits that women derive from access to paid labour and the costs or limitations that arise from these same opportunities. Work outside the home provides economic independence, greater access to formal health care and the ability to leave an abusive or neglectful partner. Yet it can also lead to greater exposure to factory hazards and increased fatigue. Inevitably, this work also makes women responsible for a double shift: their full-time work hours, plus the full extent of domestic duties at home. The privilege of economic self-sufficiency and job-related medical benefits is paid for with fatigue, exposure to factory hazards and social isolation due to the long hours of manual labour still required at home.

In addition to revealing the complexities and contradictions of *maquiladora* work for women's health, studying the health of young female workers aids the identification of risks for other workers. The 'healthy worker effect' suggests that workers who choose to labour under difficult factory conditions are likely to start out with a level of health that enables them to withstand the occupational hazards and strain of such work. Observations made during pregnancy, a period characterized by rapid growth and increased vulnerability for otherwise healthy individuals, have widespread implications about the unforeseen impact of industrial labour on factory workers of both sexes.

This chapter begins by providing the background for the study. The next section describes the history of the *maquiladora* industry in Mexico, noting its strong dependence on women workers. It then reviews the linkages between reproductive health and *maquiladora* work and provides details of the study. The chapter concludes with some global implications of the findings, and recommendations for future research and implementation of international public policy.

Background

The Mexican *maquiladora* industry

Mexico initiated its *maquiladora* industry in 1965, when agricultural labourers who had been working in the United States under the *bracero* programme returned to Mexico. The newly instituted Border Industrialization Program (BIP) responded to these workers' need for employment by creating the *maquiladora* EPZ along the northern border with the United States, in an area initially restricted to a 20-km wide industrial strip. The factories were meant only as a transitory solution, quickly to be converted into national industry and to increase Mexico's presence in the industrialized world, but the rapid transition to a national industry did not occur as planned. Under primarily foreign ownership, the *maquiladora* zones continued to expand, eventually becoming one of the most vital export industries in Mexico. Yet foreign-owned factories repatriated most of the profits to their home countries.

In 1994, Mexico signed the North American Free Trade Agreement (NAFTA) with the United States and Canada, an agreement that reduced tariffs and market barriers among the three nations. NAFTA contained even greater benefits and reduced costs for US companies willing to invest in industrial plants in the *maquiladora* zones, and the *maquiladora* industry grew substantially. By 1999, the *maquiladora* industry was a central part of Mexico's economy, producing 23 per cent of all Mexican exports, third only to petroleum and agriculture. By the year 2001, over 3,600 *maquiladora* factories employed about 1.3 million workers in small towns and cities throughout Mexico (Biles 2004), with the majority dotting the northern border with the United States. The fragility of the *maquiladora* industry and the devastating impact of *maquila* instability on employment became evident after 2001, when investors responded to emerging markets in Asia by moving their processing plants from Mexico to regions that offered cheaper labour and lower overheads. The number of *maquiladoras* in Mexico declined from more than 3,600 plants in 2001 to 2,800 in 2004, resulting in a net loss of over 100,000 jobs.

As in EPZs worldwide, young women have played a crucial role in the creation and success of the Mexican *maquiladora* plants. In some industries, women represented 100 per cent of a factory's workforce (De la O 1995). Though the percentage of women workers declined from 78 per cent of the *maquiladora* workforce in 1975 to 56 per cent in 1999, the overall number of women workers in Mexico's export industry has continued to increase. Despite these gains, the nature and terms of this employment are of concern. Though women have, on average, more years of education then their male counterparts, they receive less pay (Grijalva 1996) and are passed over for promotions and raises more often than male employees (Carrillo 1992).

The pay and position discrepancies between men and women workers stem from the paradox that working mothers face. Women are seen as a liability by shift supervisors, who are ultimately responsible for maintaining high efficiency on the factory floor and ensuring a certain number of working hours per shift. Bathroom breaks, physician visits and paid maternity leave all negatively impact worker efficiency and incur benefit costs the factory must absorb. Factory administrators often work under the impression that pregnant women use *maquiladora* work as a way to access maternity leave and the IMSS (the Mexican Institute of Social Security), which provides access to physicians and hospital care.

The importance of reproductive health

Lerner and Szaz (2003: 309–10) have defined the following elements of reproductive health: (1) the ability of an individual to have sexual relations free of the fear of contracting sexually transmitted diseases or unwanted pregnancy, (2) the ability to reproduce and to decide whether and when this will occur (including knowledge of and access to contraceptive methods), (3) access to safe pregnancies and births and (4) safeguarding the survival and wellbeing of both mother and infant, meaning protection from harm and access to quality health services. This definition can be expanded to include other psychological and social factors: questions of gender identities and roles, sexual satisfaction and a healthy balance of power between reproductive partners. Freedom from domestic violence is also an issue of reproductive health and rights.

The right of women to bear children free of discrimination in the workplace has earned international attention. In 1994, the International Conference on Population and Development (ICPD) declared the importance of protecting an individual's reproductive rights in an increasingly globalized economy. In 1995, the Fourth World Conference on Women, in Beijing, proclaimed its commitment to breaking down traditional gender roles, promoting 'sexual rights', and improving a woman's control of her own fertility. And in October 2004, international leaders reaffirmed the declarations made by the ICPD a decade earlier, indicating that progress had been made but much work remained. While these conferences demonstrated a general international consensus regarding reproductive rights and reproductive health, the reality for women working in EPZs continues to lag behind the ideals embodied in these accords.

Reproductive health in *maquiladora* zones

> Yes, work is dangerous … for me, the risk lies in the area where they cut cables … because the material often falls to the floor and one has to continually bend down to pick it up … I had already seen with Nicolas (Teresa's first son) that when I bent down I started bleeding. This is when the doctor put me on bed rest because he was afraid I would lose the baby.
>
> Teresa

Among countries that have turned to export-led development strategies, Mexico has the largest body of published research on the health impacts of working in export factories (Denman et al. 2003: 249).

Approximately twenty studies, published or unpublished, have been produced since the early 1980s (see ibid. for a review). Findings indicate that time spent in factories greatly affects workers' health due to exposure to toxic substances, poor ventilation and lighting, hazardous equipment and ergonomic stress associated with repetitive assembly-line motions and body positions (Gambrill 1981; Fernández-Kelly 1983; Carrillo and Hernández 1985; Iglesias 1985; Arenal 1986). Safety training to minimize risks for workers also has been found to be inadequate or non-existent (Moure-Eraso et al. 1997). Researchers who have examined the living conditions of the *maquiladora* workers (Fernández-Kelly 1983; Iglesias 1985) have identified inadequate housing, lack of standard services (drinking water, sewage, transportation) and domestic problems (violence, alcoholism, substance abuse and unequal domestic workloads) as issues, which the workers face in their lives outside the factory. Numerous studies have focused specifically on reproductive health in the *maquiladoras* (Kamel and Hoffman 1999). To date, many scholars have documented health problems that pregnant women face in *maquiladora* factories: low birth weight rates greater than those of women in service industries (Denman 1994), risk factors associated with pregnancy problems (Guendelman and Jasis 1993), prematurity (Eskenazi et al. 1993), complications during pregnancy (González Block 1996) or deficiencies in prenatal care (Ojeda 1995). Women in the factories report exposure to excessive noise, heat, vibrations, poor ventilation, radiation, toxic chemicals and long hours spent in uncomfortable postures (Cedillo et al. 1997).

These exposures are significant, but if any symptoms, reproductive or otherwise, are to be declared factory-related, they must be isolated from the health conditions of workers employed in other industries, or from unemployed residents living in the same region. One study of female workers found the rate of low birth weight babies among Nogales *maquiladora* workers to be 2.8 times greater than the rate among women who worked in retail positions or the service industry (Denman 1990). *Maquiladora* mothers reported longer working hours and exposure to toxic substances, hazards absent in the occupational environments of the retail and service industries (Denman 1991). These findings are supported by González Block's (1996) study, which found a higher rate of premature births among *maquiladora* workers in Tijuana than among workers of other industries.

Outside the *maquiladora* industry, low birth weight in Mexican women has been associated with the lack of a tangible means of support and working more than fifty hours a week outside the home (Cerón-Mireles et al. 1996). A study by Eskenazi et al. in 1993 suggests the type of work that women perform can also affect birth weight. Eskenazi et al. re-examined the birth weight data collected by Guendelman and Jasis (1993) of women working in garment *maquiladoras*, electronics *maquiladoras* and the service industry. They found that the best predictor of birth weight was occupation, more so than number of pregnancies, smoking habits or age. Garment *maquiladora* workers gave birth to the lightest babies, followed by workers in an electronics *maquiladora*. Women working in the service sector delivered the healthiest babies, thereby suggesting that *maquiladora* work negatively affects the health of the developing child, and that specific *maquiladoras* have a more damaging effect than others.

Another earlier study on women in a *maquiladora* plant in Nogales, Sonora, examined the infant birth weights of 406 women: 143 *maquiladora* workers, 38 workers in the service industry or retail and 143 homemakers (Denman 1991). Concordant with other studies, the rate of low birth weight infants among women in the service sector was 4 per cent, compared with a rate of 9 per cent among *maquiladora* workers. Surprisingly, the rate of low birth weight babies among homemakers was 10 per cent, statistically equivalent to that of the *maquiladora* workers. Though the healthy worker effect may account for the high occurrence of low birth weight babies among unemployed homemakers, the numbers underscore the necessity of a more holistic approach to worker health.

The studies reviewed here are important in identifying the risks for pregnant women working in the *maquiladoras* and in specifying particular exposures from which these women should be protected. Yet these studies have limited their focus to only one aspect of reproductive health, that of the birth of a healthy child. Reproductive health must be examined in the context of the relationships between women and their partners, doctors, supervisors, friends, co-workers, family members and society at large. For instance, the way in which workers negotiate their domestic environment ultimately affects their health. Home is where self-care takes place, medical prescriptions are interpreted and domestic remedies are applied.

Previous studies on worker health have tended to focus on cases of 'negative' health, or specific instances of injury and illness. This approach overlooks the concept of 'positive' health, or the actions an individual takes to maintain and improve health. The concept of positive health includes two types of actions: actions of 'self-care', and actions of 'self-treatment'. Aspects of self-care include questions of hygiene, diet, exercise and other self-maintenance behaviours aimed at maintaining a level of health. Self-treatment, when a patient acts to cure an illness or injury without the use of biomedicine, involves the use of remedies, ethno-medicine or other therapeutic behaviours to treat certain maladies once they have occurred. In EPZs, where access to health care or prescribed medications can be minimal or non-existent, examining a worker's self-care and self-treatment is important for understanding worker health.

The Study

Methodology

Pregnancy is a time in the lives of women workers when health care needs are urgent and continually evolving. This period offers the opportunity to examine how workers act in their own behalf to negotiate their health care, how they maintain their health through self-care and self-treatment and how they manage stresses and hazards at work and at home. This study (Denman 2001) employs a holistic, medical anthropology approach to consider how women in a *maquiladora* plant in Nogales, Mexico use the range of resources available to them – public, private, traditional, friends, family, doctors and partners – in order to care for themselves and promote positive health during pregnancy and the post-partum period.

Plant X was the site for identification and selection of study participants. The factory has been in operation since the early 1970s and employs more than 2,300 workers in the production of automatic garage door openers that are primarily intended for sale in the United States. Plant X complies with legal requirements for workers, providing legal wages, regular breaks and access to IMSS doctors and hospital care. Plant X also provides free childcare for children under the age of five, and a cafeteria with inexpensive meal options. Like most *maquiladoras*, Plant X employs a greater percentage of women than men, and most are between fifteen and thirty years of age. Most of these women are migrants, 80 per cent of whom moved from outside Nogales to work in the plant.

The fourteen women workers in the study were observed over the course of a three-year period to construct a life history covering the period prior to their employment in Plant X, during their employment, pregnancy and delivery, and included a period after the birth of their child. Five of the women (Martha, Patricia, Marina, Alicia and Elizabeth) participated in extensive, long-term interviews, while the other nine (Magdalena, Ceclia, Teresa, Delfina, Isela, Mireya, Gloria, Lorenia and Claudia) participated to a lesser degree. Subsequent to the interviews, 473 take-home surveys were collected from other workers in the plant to gain a broader perspective on the work environment and services available. The interviews focused on issues of gender and the negotiation of reproductive rights before, during and after their pregnancy. The study also looked at the various health care practices, whether traditional or biomedical, available to working women and the way in which the women combined and used them. Details on contraception, sexual relations, first menstruation and partner relations were included as contextual information. Key actors in the lives of the women, including husbands or partners, relatives, friends, health care providers, managers and supervisors at Plant X were interviewed in order to understand their perceptions of their role in the lives of the women.

Findings

Without exception, the fourteen women in this study shared the dual burden of paid and unpaid work responsibilities experienced by working women worldwide. The women carried out an extensive range of domestic duties, which included carrying water, preparing meals, shopping, building homes, caring for their own children and those of others, monitoring schoolwork, negotiating childcare with their partners, paying debts, providing medical care for their family, and dealing with local bureaucratic institutions for legal property rights. In addition, the women in this study worked ten-hour days at Plant X with a total of three breaks: two ten-minute rest periods plus a thirty-minute meal break at mid-shift. The domestic duties were often the most exhausting. Many women stated that they longed to get to work so they could 'sit down and rest' after fulfilling their arduous domestic obligations at home.

> When I get to work it's to rest, because I get to sit down here. At home I never sit.
>
> Elizabeth, age 26, universal operator

Beyond granting relief from domestic burdens, employment helped the women escape abusive, neglectful or non-supportive spouses or partners, gave them access to health care services and offered them the ability to improve their living conditions and send their children to school.

Despite these benefits, the women workers' dual burden has led to increased social isolation (Oliviera and Ariza 2000). Limited time and energy to socialize and interrupted family networks both augment this isolation. For the women at Plant X, migration was both the cause of disruption in family networks in their home communities and the inspiration for new networks that developed. Relationships with other factory workers became the basis for the social network that provided access to knowledge, resources and support. Friendships grew out of extended contact with other women and the ability to converse while engaged in the repetitive motions associated with assembly line production. Many of the women in Plant X shared similar living conditions and lived near each other. These commonalities formed the basis for a network of mutual support that partially replaced the functions formerly provided by traditional family networks.

> I never saw my mother pregnant, I never noticed. And my sisters, I have never been around when they were pregnant. We never talk about it ... in the factory we talk about how we care for ourselves, which pills you can take ... how certain things can help you avoid pregnancy. We always talk about these things among ourselves.
>
> Gloria, age 28, machine operator at Plant X

Co-workers proved to be an invaluable source of information, while relationships between worker and supervisor were carefully cultivated. An amicable relationship with the shift leader could mean the difference between receiving or not receiving small loans, an extra bathroom break, permission to leave early, or other important benefits.

The women in this study considered motherhood to be their greatest achievements. These women existed, worked and endured difficulties in order to support their families. They reported a mixture of pain and satisfaction with their pregnancy and motherhood, and their status as mothers endowed them with a sense of self-importance. Motherhood represents a step towards empowerment for women in Mexico (Ortíz Ortega 1999). For the women of Plant X, their status increased as they negotiated with other actors during the course of their pregnancy. The majority of the women in Plant X stated that their primary goal in coming to work was to provide better living conditions and a brighter future for their children. Only when the women became pregnant did their own well-being become important,

at which point the women began using their pregnant status to negotiate the responsibilities of domestic chores, questions of family planning
and special needs in the work environment with their partners, families, co-workers and supervisors.

The evolution of women's negotiating power and the strategies they
applied to exercise this power formed a central focus of the study. Five
distinct stages of pregnancy were identified based on the experiences of
these women. Each stage was associated with a distinct set of actors,
resources and actions to promote their health within the opportunities
and limitations in their environment. The first stage involved verifying
the pregnancy and then negotiating the terms of this new status with a
husband or partner. The second phase involved hiding the pregnancy
from the employer for as long as possible, using practices based on
household wisdom and traditional medicine to treat any discomforts.
The third stage began once the woman's pregnancy could no longer
be hidden from the employer. This stage included initiation of prenatal care at IMSS. The fourth stage was childbirth, which normally
occurred in the IMSS hospital. The fifth stage encompassed the post-
partum period after leaving the hospital. In this period, women used
traditional domestic remedies to heal the body.

Notwithstanding the exalted status of motherhood, most of the
pregnancies in this study were unplanned and stemmed from complications with the method of contraception. Commonly cited problems
with contraception included the failure of an intrauterine device (IUD),
their partner's refusal to use condoms and/or unwillingness to let the
women use contraceptive pills, or the inability to find a contraceptive
method that did not produce unwanted side effects. Most contraceptive methods used were modern methods, although one woman consulted an indigenous *sobadora* (masseuse).

During the first stage, women negotiated the terms of their pregnancy
with their partners. The negotiation phase for each woman differed,
depending on the support, security and longevity of the relationship
with their partner. The knowledge of this new pregnancy also inspired
all women to consider their financial stability and capacity to care for
their new child. Negotiations with parents and other family members
also began to take place during this time.

> I thought I might be pregnant, but I couldn't believe it and at the same time
> didn't want to accept it because of the relationship I had with Thomás ... I
> went home. I told Thomás what had happened. He asked me what I was
> going to do. I said, you tell me what to do in these cases. You know, you

already have kids. I also have a little girl ... tell me what we are going to do. He said, we'll do what one has to do in these cases ... I didn't say anything more. I imagined that he meant that he wanted to abort ... I thought the worst. But then he hugged me and he told me that it was no problem for him, that if I wanted to have the baby, that I should have it, because he wanted to have another boy.

Marina (Thomás is married, with other children)

The second phase of pregnancy represented the period of secrecy. This stage consisted of modifying their diets to minimize nausea. The women practiced self-care related specifically to their pregnancy, concentrating on hygiene more carefully than when not pregnant, and resting at home. This additional rest often meant neglecting duties around the home, or negotiating with partners, spouses or other family members to complete the tasks. The women also practiced self-treatment, using home remedies that they learnt about from family members, neighbours or co-workers to treat nausea. All of the women continued to work their regular shifts, hiding rice crackers or bread in their clothing since food was not permitted on the factory floor. Factory smells became more bothersome during this stage, and the need for comfortable seats increasingly critical. None of the women were particularly concerned about prenatal care during the first months, stating they did not believe that it would provide any additional benefits to themselves or the child. All of the women kept their pregnancies secret for as long as possible to avoid losing their jobs or having to change to a new position in the factory.

> I cared for both my pregnancies at the IMSS. With my daughter, I started going in the second month, and with my son I did not go until the fifth month because I didn't have a contract at the factory. I didn't want them to realize I was pregnant and fire me.

Gloria

The third stage of pregnancy began when the women could no longer hide their shape from the supervisor. At this stage, the women requested permission from their employers to go to IMSS for prenatal care. The IMSS ran laboratory analyses, provided the women with iron supplements and performed a clinical review of their health. Despite a vocalized appreciation of the IMSS, most of the women complained about the service offered, stating the doctors did not spend enough time with them, provide adequate information or answer their questions. Alicia, a thirty-three-year-old Universal Operator, noted that, 'in the IMSS they don't pay any attention to you. They treat you whenever they feel like it'. No specific transportation or waiting system was provided for pregnant women. They walked, negotiated rides or took public buses, sometimes waiting in a combination of lines for three to four hours before seeing their physician. Women usually attempted to see a physician to whom a friend or family member referred them but this was not always possible. Some sought private physicians or visited a favourite IMSS physician after hours. However, in order to use the IMSS hospital during childbirth, these women needed a certain number of prenatal visits to IMSS physicians, and most saw doctors in the IMSS.

Physical discomfort increased greatly during the third stage of pregnancy, and women used a variety of self-treatment strategies to reduce the symptoms. Elizabeth ate plain rice to help her heartburn, while Marta converted to a diet of fruit and vegetables. Others asked their daughters to massage their feet, continued to neglect regular housework so they could rest, took herbal teas and other remedies to reduce swelling, and modified their eating habits. Older women bore these symptoms without complaint, while younger women were more vocal about their discomforts.

The most common complaints made by pregnant women about the environment in the *maquiladora* were uncomfortable chairs, cramped body positions and the inability freely to access the bathroom. Social networks became crucial as the pregnancy advanced and the women negotiated with their co-workers and supervisors for bathroom breaks, the least uncomfortable chair and permission to go to IMSS. Co-workers and supervisors also provided pregnancy information, recommending medications, herbal treatments, alternatives for medical care and physicians. The personal relationship the pregnant women had with their immediate supervisor was critical in these negotiations. Their immediate supervisor had the ultimate say in their access to benefits during their pregnancies. Female supervisors often adopted a motherly role, expressing a genuine concern for their workers. In some cases, the supervisors were working mothers themselves, such as Martha (age 40, day shift inspector), who brought medication and snacks to share with 'her girls' and Patricia, who kept a careful eye out for fatigue or injury and brought hand-made gifts to the workers she supervised.

The plant physicians saw the women for gastrointestinal problems, respiratory illnesses and other complaints. The physicians had no training in prenatal care, and generally offered the women pills to treat some of the symptoms. Women generally returned to work after these complaints, reporting to the IMSS only in case of emergency. Physicians both at the plant and the IMSS tended to treat the patients with a certain amount of contempt, reprimanding them for not taking their medications or vitamins as directed, and expressing frustration that the women did not follow their medical instructions. The women, however, viewed the doctors' prescriptions as one option among many.[3] The women also voiced frustration with a system that made them wait for hours, yet did not provide adequate time to discuss their health concerns fully with the physician. At the same time, they were also anxious about the anticipated reprimands from their physicians.

In spite of this conflict, women's relationships with their physicians were crucial for negotiating the terms of their maternity leave. Plant X complies with Mexican law, providing forty-two days of maternity leave before birth and forty-two days after, but most women tried to work up to the last possible moment of their pregnancy to increase the number of days they could stay home with their newborn child. In order for this to happen, the physician needed to be flexible about the due date. Working until the last possible day meant women worked full shifts until very far along in their pregnancy, with continued exposure to occupational hazards, chemical toxins and increased fatigue.

Labour pains announced the arrival of the fourth stage, birth, which occurred at the IMSS hospital in thirteen out of the fourteen cases in this study. Most women remained in Nogales or moved to another city in Sonora to be close to their mothers. Women in the IMSS hospital found little support and were told just to *aguantar* (endure) the pain and discomfort. Some reported reprimands or harassment by the nurses, and many complained that the epidural injections caused long-lasting back pain. Other complaints included a lack of privacy, not being listened to by nurses and doctors, insufficient bed space and hygiene concerns in the hospital. Women greatly appreciated little gestures of kindness: a nurse's hand on their forehead, or a physician coaching them during labour. After birth, the women received very little attention. Because of the isolation and lack of support, and IMSS policy, most women in this study entered the hospital, gave birth and left in less than twenty-four hours.

Although the IMSS provides initial assistance in lactation and infant care, it does not provide support in stage five, the post-partum period. The women in this study relied on female family members or companions for support and recommendations for self-treatment. They turned to domestic remedies to heal and restore their bodies, including teas, douches, specialized diets and rest. Apples, star anis and chicura leaves were part of the recommended diet during the post-partum period, while beans and pork were commonly listed as foods to be avoided.

The key actors in the reproductive cycle of these women were their partners, physicians, factory supervisors and managers, friends, family and co-workers. Within this network, women used the power position allocated to working mothers to promote their own positive health and negotiate their reproductive health care. Power relations were concentrated into two groups. Partners, physicians, factory supervisors and managers all claimed varying degrees of control over the women's bodies and their access to resources. Friends, family and co-workers tended to play a more supportive role as the women progressed through the stages of their pregnancies. Because the needs of the women were different in each stage, a new negotiation would begin with the particular actors who would help them meet their needs at that stage.

Gender roles, and relationships between women and their partners, particularly impacted women's experiences at all stages of pregnancy. For instance, all women combined paid employment and domestic work, which contributed greatly to their fatigue during pregnancy. Others faced challenges from unsupportive spouses. Alicia related:

> My husband was never with me ... once I became pregnant he detested me ... when I gave birth to my daughter, he was not at the hospital. I didn't even know if I had given birth to a boy or a girl because nobody was there to tell me. I was alone the whole pregnancy, struggling the whole time because the baby was very small

Teresa said,

> This pregnancy was problematic, because I started having problems with my partner. There was the threat of miscarriage, and I was working. I was either on bed rest at the IMSS or at home, fighting with him. We fought a lot, argued too much. I kicked him out of the house, and then I felt terrible. My health suffered. So many times he hadn't listened to me or paid attention to me, then he left, and left me pregnant, with no money, with the rent due, and he left ... I suffered many relapses because we fought so much.

For both Alicia and Teresa, instability and violence in the home had a direct impact on the health of their children and themselves during the course of their pregnancies.

The networks, options available and decisions made by the employees formed a common 'culture of health' for the working mothers at Plant X. Within this culture, women sought desirable physicians, found treatment for certain complaints, accepted or rejected physician recommendations, negotiated domestic roles, enjoyed increased leverage due to their status as expectant mothers and expressed their own interpretation of the purported 'normalcy' of the aches and pains associated with their pregnancies. They also gained the status of being a working mother at Plant X, a status that will allow them to pass on the culture of health to the next generation of expectant women.

Conclusion

This study identifies an emerging culture of health within and among women workers at Plant X as they strive to improve their health during pregnancy. The common core of the culture of health consists of: (1) the combination of various specific practices of self-care, including positive health practices, physician-prescribed medicine, or the use of traditional medicines; and (2) the right to access the IMSS, even though the quality of service is questioned and pregnancies are hidden in the workplace for as long as possible. These practices are negotiated with key actors in the women's lives, in negotiations guided by gender identities and relationships.

The centrality of the reproductive-age woman worker in EPZs makes it imperative to raise questions about the policies and structures that permit workers to exercise their reproductive rights. Further research is necessary to understand more fully the complex relationship between the benefits women obtain by earning a salary and gaining access to the IMSS versus the hazards they face in their work and home environments. Specific environmental hazards need to be categorized in an attempt to understand how specific toxins, stresses or hazards present dangers to pregnant women. Better controls must also be developed for these studies, such as, for example, controlling for the healthy worker effect and isolating cause and effect as much as possible. A 'closest siblings' study across work environments might help better define some of the hazards unique to specific conditions in *maquila* factories, more successfully isolating them from other factors. More studies also need to examine the joint impact of exposures in the domestic and work environments by considering family dynamics as a potential hazard exposure. The positive and negative health impact of family relationships in the *maquiladora* industries need to be explored, especially in light of the profound societal transformations the *maquiladora* zones have brought about in Mexico.

Cultural conceptions of a woman's biological health in the work and home environments also should be explored. Researchers might look into the specific mechanisms to combine different health care practices, comparing and contrasting the practices observed in this study with combinations of practices in other environments. Additionally, the relationship between patient and provider could be explored more fully in order to increase satisfaction with the health care practices.

Nonetheless, some immediate improvements can be made in policy and practice. The IMSS should train their physicians and medical personnel to provide more and higher quality attention to their patients and to treat them with dignity and respect. Relaxing bureaucratic limitations on the amount of time providers can spend with patients and the number of visits patients could facilitate higher quality service. Reproductive health could also improve significantly by increasing the types of care available to pregnant women working in factories.

At the factory level, measures should be implemented to ensure that women do not lose their jobs, seniority or pay because they require health care. Greater awareness of the risks of factory work on reproductive health and pregnancy is necessary, and plant physicians and health care providers should communicate this information to women workers. Additionally, more ergonomic equipment and improved safety devices would also reduce the stress, fatigue and hazards of the work environment. Finally, additional support after childbirth, both in the post-partum stage and in terms of childcare, would reduce the burden on the mother and improve her overall health.

On a national scale, Mexico could support a policy that provides greater protections for pregnant women and benefits that extend beyond maternity leave and access to the IMSS. Public health campaigns directed towards the health of women workers could help raise awareness and increase support. Additionally, Mexico could set specific research priorities and make resources available for further study of reproductive health.

Of course, the cost of such programmes to business and national industry runs counter to the neo-liberal economic model, as factories are built and maintained where production is cheapest.

International policies geared towards limiting factory movement or creating a mandatory global worker wage and benefits minimum would protect workers from the current situation where they have little leverage.

Global economic models ultimately affect the individual. Yet, individuals who migrate into EPZs are not passive victims. The individual worker in an EPZ is an active agent within a social, cultural and economic model that has changed rapidly in the past half century. The response of the worker to this changing reality is to form new relationships and behaviours. The culture that emerges guides the worker in her new workplace or neighbourhood. This culture is clearly apparent in the study discussed in this chapter.

This study has focused on the working and living conditions of women workers in a single plant in Nogales, Sonora, Mexico. Yet, workers in EPZs worldwide have comparable demographics and experience working and living conditions similar to workers in Mexico. Women workers in other zones are confronting rapidly changing social and economic structures and must also fend for the health and safety of themselves and their unborn children during pregnancy. Research into the health culture of women in global EPZs would add important insights into debates on international policy and reproductive rights for workers, and provide a basis on which realistic policy can be structured.

Global regulations on worker rights, heightened consumer awareness (which has led to successful boycotts, such as the cases of Nestlé and Infant Mil), and limitations on the factories' ability to relocate to countries with less 'demanding' workforces would grant more leverage to factory employees and give them legal recourse to fight substandard health care and working environments. In turn, this would help contain the 'race to the bottom', maintaining a balance between human rights and the interest of international corporations. Examining the movement of export factories reveals that the reasons for factory movement are diverse, and not all factories move as a result of labour pressure (Lee 1999). More thorough understanding of the reason behind factory mobility could help policy-makers generate stabilization policies that minimize impacts on export producers. Global regulations of the type described here in combination with greater factory stability would result in a healthier environment for all, representing the interests of multinational corporations, the importance of ensuring humane working conditions and the health of a factory worker's unborn child.

Notes

The author is grateful to Kelley Merriam Castro, Jane Rubin Kurtzman, Elissa Braunstein and Caren Grown for their support in the writing of this chapter.

1. All names are pseudonyms.
2. Translation of quotations from workers and family members by Kelley Merriam Castro.
3. Because prescribed medication was often expensive, workers modified the regimen. For instance, Patricia decided to take a pill prescribed every six hours only once a day so they would last longer.

References

Arenal, S. (1986) *Sangre Joven: Las Maquiladoras por Dentro*, México, DF Editorial Nuestro Tiempo.

Biles, J. (2004) 'Export-Oriented Industrialization and Regional Development: A Case Study of Maquiladora Production in Yucatán, Mexico', *Regional Studies*, vol. 38, no. 5: 519–34.

Carrillo, J. (1992) *Mujeres en la Industria Automotriz, Cuadernos de Colef.* Tijuana, BC, México: Colegio de la Frontera Norte.

Carillo, J.V., and A. Hernández (1985) *Mujeres Fronterizas en la Industria Maquiladora*, México, DF: Secretaría de Educación Pública (SEP) and Centro de Estudios Fronterizos del Noroeste de México (CEFNOMEX).

Cedillo, L., S.D. Harlow, A.R. Sánchez and M.D. Sánchez (1997) 'Establishing Priorities for Occupational Health Research among Women Working in the Maquiladora Industry', *International Journal of Occupational Environmental Health*, vol. III, no. 3: 221–230.

Cerón-Mireles, P., S.D. Harlow and C.I. Sanchez-Carrillo (1996) 'The Risk of Pre-Maturity and Small-for-Gestational-Age Birth in Mexico City: The Effects of Working Conditions and Antenatal Leave', *American Journal of Public Health*, vol. 86, no. 6: 825–31.

De la O, M. (1995) 'Maquila, mujer y cambios productivos: Estudio de caso en la industria maquiladora de Ciudad Juárez', in S. González, O. Ruíz, L. Velasco and O. Woo (eds), *Mujeres, Migración y Maquila en la Frontera Norte*, México: El Colegio de México y el Colegio de la Frontera Norte, pp. 241–70.

Denman, C. (1990) 'Industrialización y maternidad en el noroeste de México', Cuadernos de Trabajo No. 2. [Working Papers No. 2], Hermosillo, México: El Colegio de Sonora.

Denman, C. (1991) *Las Repercusiones de la Industria Maquiladora de Exportación en la Salud: El Peso al Nacer de Hijos Obreras en Nogales*, Hermosillo, México: El Colegio de Sonora.

Denman, C. (1994) 'Madres y maquiladoras en Nogales, Sonora', in V. Salles and E. McPhail (eds), *Nuevos Textos y Renovados Pretextos*, México: El Colegio de México, pp. 277–316.

Denman, C. (2001) *Prácticas de Atención al Embarazo de Madres-Trabajadoras de una Maquiladora en Nogales, Sonora, México*, Dissertation for Doctorate in Social Sciences, El Colegio de Michoacán.

Denman, C., L. Cedillo and S. Harlow (2003) 'Work and Health in Export Industries at National Borders', in J. Heymann (ed.), *Global Inequalities at Work: Work's Impact on the Health of Individuals, Families, and Societies*, Oxford: Oxford University Press, pp. 247–77.

Eskenazi, B., S. Guendelman and E.P. Elkin (1993) 'A Preliminary Study of Reproductive Outcomes of Female Maquiladora Workers in Tijuana, México', *American Journal of Industrial Medicine*, vol. 24, no. 6 (December): 667–76.

Fernández-Kelly, M.P. (1983) *For We Are Sold, I and My People*, Albany, NY: State University of New York Press.

Gambrill, M.C. (1981) *La Fuerza de Trabajo en las Maquiladoras. Resultados de una Encuesta y Algunas Hipótesis Interpretativas: Maquiladoras*, México, DF: Centro de Estudios Económicos y Sociales del Tercer Mundo.

González Block, M.A. (1996) *La Salud Reproductiva de las Trabajadoras de la Maquiladora de Exportación en Tijuana, Baja California, Diagnóstico y Retos Para las Políticas de Salud*, Investigative report presented to the Instituto Nacional de Salud Pública, El Colegio de la Frontera Norte and the Fundación Mexicana para la Salud, November.

Grijalva, G. (1996) Empleo femenino: Análisis de la Encuesta Estatal de Empleo en Sonora, 1995, Hermosillo, México: El Colegio de Sonora, Draft.

Guendelman, S., and M. Jasis (1993) 'The Health Consequences of Maquiladora Work: Women on the U.S.–Mexican Border', *American Journal of Public Health*, vol. 83: 37–44.

Iglesias, N. (1985) *La Flor Más Bella de la Maquiladora*, México: SEP and CEFNOMEX.

Kamel R., and A. Hoffman (eds) (1999) *The Maquiladora Reader: Cross-border Organizing since NAFTA*, Philadelphia, PA: American Friends Committee.

Lee, Y.S. (1999) 'Labor Shock and the Diversity of Transnational Corporate Strategy in Export Processing Zones', *Growth and Change*, vol. 30, no. 3: 337–65.

Lerner, S., and I. Szaz (2003) 'La investigación sociodemográfica en salud reproductiva y su aporte para la acción', *Estudios Demográficos y Urbanos*, vol. 18, no. 2 (May–August): 299–352.

Moure-Eraso, R., M. Wilcox, L. Punnett, L. MacDonand and C. Levenstein (1997) 'Back to the Future: Sweatshop Conditions on the Mexico–U.S. Border. Part 2: Occupational Health Impact of Maquiladora Industrial Activity', *American Journal of Industrial Medicine*, vol. 31: 587–99.

Ojeda, N. (1995) 'Salud materno-infantil entre la población trabajadora en Tijuana: Un estudio de caso', *Estudios Demográficos y Urbanos*, vol. 10, no. 3: 651–86.

Oliviera, O., and M. Ariza (2000) 'Género, trabajo y exclusión social en México', *Estudios Demográficos y Urbanos*, vol. 15, no. 1: 11–33.

Ortiz Ortega, A. (ed.) (1999) *Derechos Reproductivos de las Mujeres: Un Debate Sobre Justicia Social en México*, México: Edamex and Universidad Autónoma Metropolitana-Xochimilco.

7

Runaway Knowledge: Trade Liberalization and Reproductive Practices among Sri Lanka's Garment Factory Workers

Sandya Hewamanne

Introduction

> These big fat women (middle class women's organization members) think that we are ignorant fools. We know all about contraceptives and sexual health. Let them come and learn from us.
>
> A free trade zone (FTZ) worker at a boarding house in 2000

> Why do we need to know about contraceptive methods or safe sex behaviour? We are unmarried women.
>
> An FTZ worker responding to a study done on HIV/AIDS vulnerability in 2004

> Appearing to be worldly or being stubborn achieves nothing; that is if you want to get married to a boy friend or through a proposal. ... If you blurt out all you know you become the fool, if you act ignorant he becomes the fool.
>
> An FTZ worker at a boarding house in 2000

These quotations paint a contradictory picture of FTZ workers' knowledge and attitudes regarding sexual and reproductive health. This chapter focuses on the development of new knowledge and attitudes on sexuality and reproductive health among Sri Lanka's garment factory workers in the Katunayake FTZ. It argues that the contradiction in the expressed knowledge and actual practices of reproductive health by FTZ workers reflects the way in which they negotiate the cultural meanings attached to acquiring and practising certain knowledge. As industrial workers at transnational factories and innocent daughters of patriarchal villages, FTZ workers straddle varied cultural discourses. I argue that their constant movement within a continuum of knowledge on sexuality and reproductive health is a conscious strategy of stigma management that helps them when they leave their temporary employment in the urban transnational space of the FTZ.

A woman's ability to decide for herself whether, when, if and with whom to have sex and children is a fundamental right. However, studies in different localities show that this notion of individual freedom does not always translate into local practice, and women's ability to make reproductive choices is deeply affected by patriarchal power relations (Ginsburg and Rapp 1991, 1995; Blanc 2001; Mullings and Wali 2001; Tremayne 2001). It has also been stressed that reproductive health should not be studied in isolation from the broader social, economic and political contexts that shape reproductive behaviour (Ginsburg and Rapp 1995; Ali 2002). This chapter explores FTZ women workers' reproductive knowledge and practices in the global context of trade liberalization, migration and employment. It asserts that Sri Lanka's female factory workers' reproductive woes occur not because of lack of knowledge but because of cultural barriers to practicing their newly acquired knowledge.

The chapter first focuses on new sources of knowledge that women are exposed to within the FTZ, including NGO workshops and tabloid magazines, and then analyses reading sessions in these workers' boarding houses, in which they read and discuss a pornographic magazine. They expressed new ideas and knowledge on sexuality and reproductive health during these sessions. Thereafter, by focusing on unwanted pregnancies and abortions among the FTZ workers, the chapter explores why such knowledge seems to abandon women workers at crucial moments.

The chapter also showcases how, in a survey on reproductive health and a later study on HIV/AIDS, women denied practical knowledge of sexual and reproductive health (except for scientific knowledge gained through 'legitimate' means) and instead expressed allegiance to Sinhala-Buddhist cultural ideals of innocent women (virgins who are sexually naïve) with shame or fear. This response contrasted with their open discussions on sexual activities during a year of ethnographic research. By focusing on the post-FTZ lives of seven former workers, I also show how their public denial of acquired knowledge is a conscious tactic that helps to ease the tensions stemming from the stigma associated with FTZ work. This work will show that we need to focus not only on knowledge acquisition or practice but also on the nexus of power shaping the reproductive experiences of women who have been affected by trade liberalization policies.

The bulk of the data for this study was collected during one year of ethnographic fieldwork conducted in 1999–2000. During this period, I worked in a garment factory for seven months and stayed in a boarding house with about seventy other FTZ workers. This living and working situation allowed me to interact closely with the factory workers. The discussions on sexuality and reproductive health usually occurred within boarding houses, at night-time discussions or reading sessions. In addition to discussions and interviews with the workers I also interviewed factory managers, supervisors, boarding house owners, neighbours and workers' relatives and boyfriends, and conducted a survey on reproductive health knowledge among 300 garment factory workers. I also volunteered my time at Dabindu and associated myself with several other NGOs active in Katunayake and conducted interviews with staff members. In 2004, I conducted a study of HIV/AIDS vulnerability among the FTZ workers, and data from both these studies is mentioned throughout this chapter to strengthen my claims regarding workers' reproductive health knowledge. Finally, in 2003–04 I visited several former FTZ workers' village homes to investigate the way they negotiate village culture with the new knowledge they acquired within the FTZ.

Lack of knowledge?

The effects of gendered power imbalances and socio-economic marginalization on local reproductive practices have been well documented (Mason 1994; Riley 1997; Mason and Smith 1999; Blanc 2001). Many such studies suggest that inequality within relationships hamper discussion of reproductive choices. They also suggest that education and women's socio-economic status can improve communication between couples and consequently improve decisions regarding reproductive health (Hogan et al. 1999; Blanc 2001; Singh et al. 2001).

Some writings on the links between power relations and reproductive health focus on how cultural perceptions of virginity, sexual passivity and other sexual mores can affect reproductive decision-making (Gupta and Weiss 1993; Blanc et al. 1996). These accounts, in the main, underline the effects of cultural perceptions on women's ability to acquire reproductive health information and stress the need for service programmes to address the power relations that can be an obstacle for women acquiring such information (Gupta and Weiss 1993; Mason and Smith 2000; Blanc 2001).

Work on Sri Lanka also focuses on lack of knowledge and access to information and services in explaining reproductive problems (De Silva et al. 2000; Wickramagamage 2000; Gunaratne and Goonewardena 2001; Bujawansa 2002; Ratnayake 2002). A baseline survey conducted among 2,214 secondary school students by the Family Planning Association of Sri Lanka (FPASL 1999) revealed that the level of knowledge on reproductive health was low. Another study on sexual health education carried out among 1,350 students and 1,000 parents concluded that the respondents did not understand certain reproductive health topics (FPASL 1997). Many such studies stress the need for more educational programmes and counselling to minimize reproductive health problems (Hewage 1999; Fernando 2000; Hettiarachchi and Schensul 2001; Wickramasinge et al. 2002). Studies of other countries in South Asia also emphasize the lack of access to information and the need for more educational programmes (Chaudhury 2001; Gubhaju 2002).

None of these studies focus on the cultural aspects that may hinder communication and reproductive practices, even when the group studied has more than average awareness of all aspects of reproductive health. In her essay on abortion discourses in Sri Lanka, Wickramagamage (2000: 11) points out that while information on contraceptives is freely available, culture-induced inhibitions may nevertheless prevent women approaching institutions providing such information and support. She further notes that the cultural ideals of marriage and taboos on premarital sex increase the vulnerability of women in patriarchal societies and may hinder their ability to exercise free choice in reproductive matters. However, her observations are not based on empirical research, and she does not delve into this point further.

Hettiarachchi and Schensul's (2001: 137–8) work on reproductive health among Sri Lanka's FTZ workers concludes that FTZ reproductive dilemmas stem from the limited knowledge of poor rural women who work in the FTZs, and they emphasize the need for more health education programmes and counselling services for FTZ workers. My work, on the contrary, demonstrates new knowledge that women workers acquire within the FTZs, and explores the conditions that prevent women from applying such knowledge in their daily lives.

Trade Liberalization, the FTZ and the
'Respectable Woman'

The United National Party, which came to power in 1977, adopted open economic policies, and this initiated changes that affected people's lived experiences in significant ways. When the first Sri Lankan FTZ in Katunayake (near the capital city of Colombo) was established in 1978 as part of the government's structural adjustment programmes, thousands of unmarried rural women migrated to the area.[1] This was not surprising, as the government, in order to attract investors, had touted the availability of 'well disciplined and obedient women workers who can produce more in a short time' (Dabindu Collective 1997: 17).

In the predominantly Sinhala-Buddhist Sri Lankan rural villages, women's purity is closely tied to the honour of the family. Women are expected to be virgins at the time of marriage and without any knowledge of sexual activities. Ideally, mothers, aunts or older cousins educate them on sexual and reproductive issues at the time of marriage. Knowledge of traditional contraceptive methods is kept secret from young women, and there are strict zones of silence surrounding these matters. Girls are presumed to glean fragmentary information through peer contact, yet a public expression of this knowledge will affect the reputation of the girl and her family since possessing such knowledge is usually interpreted as having engaged in premarital sex. The taboo on premarital sex also keeps young women under the control of male kin. The social and economic basis of these ideals was challenged by Sir Lanka's economic liberalization programme, which replaced the hitherto socialist, state-controlled economic system of 1977. Even though the moral code was maintained, if not intensified, rural women eagerly sought employment in the newly established FTZ.

The Katunayake FTZ houses around one hundred multinational industries that practise a distinctive form of gendered working relations. Garment factories comprise the majority of all the industries within the FTZ and large numbers of young, unmarried, rural women join these factories to work as machine operators. Although they belong to economically and socially marginalized families, the free public education system in Sri Lanka has ensured that they are well educated, often with eight to twelve years of schooling (Rosa 1990; Fine and Howard 1995). The vast majority of these young women are ethnically Sinhala and Buddhist by religion.[2] Poor living conditions, coupled with physically and mentally arduous working conditions, make life difficult in the FTZ (Dabindu Collective 1989, 1997; Stiftung 1997; Hewamanne and Brow 1999).

It is, however, their status as young women living alone and without male protection that receives the most public attention. Sri Lankan women have engaged in paid employment such as teaching, nursing and clerical work for a long time. While poor rural women sometimes worked as agricultural labourers, urban women from working class families have long engaged in low-paid industrial work and participated in the informal economy. But rarely did women leave their families for work.[3] Women who work in the formal sector (teaching, nursing and clerical work) sometimes get transferred to different regions of the country, and they usually find residence with relatives or family friends living in the new area. Such arrangements protect women's reputations, and these relocations do not result in the massive congregation of women as enabled by the FTZs. The female university students who temporarily migrate to urban areas for their education do congregate in female-only university hostels for at least their first year of education. But the system of female wardens, twenty-four-hour guarded gates and curfew times promote different dynamics from that experienced by FTZ workers who live in barely protected rooms and often engage in night work.

The concentration of vast numbers of young women has attracted many men looking for easy sexual conquest to the FTZ area. Newspapers report women being cheated by married men, date rapes, unwanted pregnancies, death or sickness due to unsanitary abortions and suicide attempts. Their neighbours in the FTZ area also liken the 'free living women' amidst them to a great (cultural) disaster. Such fear derives from an ideal image of the Sinhala-Buddhist woman that was constructed in the late nineteenth and early twentieth centuries. Primarily constructed as a response to colonial discourses on women and culture, this ideal projected women as passive and subordinate beings who should be protected within the confines of their homes.[4] As a result, women leaving their parental homes to live alone in urban, modernized spaces arouse intense anxieties about cultural degradation and female morality. Protestant Buddhist traditions and discipline[5] constructed 'decent and correct' manners and morals, as well as a proper attitude towards sexuality for middle-class women. Men who dominated the early twentieth-century nationalist movement believed that instilling virtues of Victorian femininity, domesticity, discipline and restraint were essential for transforming Sinhala-Buddhist women into a symbol of national greatness (Guruge 1965; De Alwis 1998). Laced with anti-imperialist rhetoric, these codes of gendered behaviour were enthusiastically embraced by many sections of society.

According to Obeyesekere (1984: 504–5), Sinhala children are socialized from a young age into practices of shame-fear (*lajja-baya*) – to be ashamed to subvert norms of sexual modesty and proper behaviour and to fear the social ridicule that result from such subversion. When women started migrating to the cities for FTZ work, it was the impact on their *lajja-baya* that the middle-class and males feared the most. Romanticized notions of superior morals and undisturbed traditions in Sri Lankan villages were superimposed on women, initiating expectations that village women are naïve, innocent (in the sense of being sexually ignorant) and timid and that they are the unadulterated bearers of Sinhala-Buddhist culture.

However, in the FTZ, rural women encountered new global cultural flows and acquired new knowledge. They consequently developed strong community feelings and actively engaged in a transgressive sub-culture, which centred on fashions, language and the creation of new tastes in leisure activities such as dance and music (Hewamanne 2003). As they migrated from rural agricultural communities and became subject to the discipline of capitalist industrial production, young women underwent a change in their cognitive, social, emotional and moral dispositions. The sense of self they developed in the new environment, however, coexisted with deeply internalized notions of ideal Sinhala-Buddhist womanly behaviour, and while they collectively performed unrespectable behaviour, they tried individually to express allegiance to cultural norms (Hewamanne 2002, 2003). The articulation of these apparently incompatible positions of being urban industrial workers and young unmarried daughters from patriarchal villages enabled viable spaces for creativity, tactics and strategies.

What knowledge, who has it and when to own it

In the FTZ, rural women acquired knowledge on reproductive matters from several sources. NGOs working among Katunayake FTZ workers were one source. The two major NGOs active within the FTZ, Dabindu and Mithurusevene, both conducted educational programmes for workers that included health, nutrition and reproductive health as components. These programmes are foreign-funded, receiving money to conduct awareness and prevention programmes on HIV/AIDS.

Therefore the component on reproductive health focused heavily on safe sex behaviour and did not delve into attitudes on love, trust, intimacy and sexuality.

According to an NGO staff member, only about 1 per cent of the total worker population is knowledgeable about safe sex, contraceptives and general reproductive health matters. When I asked why, after so many years of NGO-provided educational programmes, a vast majority of workers are not yet knowledgeable about such issues, the staff member said it is usually the same socially oriented group of women who attend their workshops, and the women who actually engage in risky activities deliberately avoid attending workshops or associating with NGOs. About 2,000 workers attended their 2003 camp, but most of the women who participated had attended prior workshops and were already knowledgeable about the issues.

The workers vehemently contradicted this general attitude, claiming that they are adequately knowledgeable about sexuality and reproductive health issues and that the reason they do not attend these programmes is that they are fed up with hearing old facts. These rhetorical assertions were confirmed by two studies done later in which the respondents displayed a sound knowledge of reproductive health. In the first survey, conducted among 300 FTZ workers in 2000, almost all respondents provided detailed information on the questions designed to garner information regarding their 'scientific knowledge' on reproductive health.[6]

In another study on migrant workers' vulnerability to HIV/AIDS, all the workers interviewed (fifteen in-depth interviews and sixty focus group participants) conveyed an excellent level of awareness.[7] Unlike the other three groups of migrant workers (construction and transport workers and Middle Eastern migrants) studied, none of the FTZ workers held myths about HIV/AIDS, and they knew the importance of taking measures to protect themselves. It has to be noted that during this study the NGO officials reiterated the same low opinion of FTZ workers' knowledge on the AIDS epidemic and safe sex behaviour (Hewamanne 2004).

Though the FTZ workers displayed an above average knowledge of scientific information of reproduction and sexual health, their responses showed a lack of awareness regarding traditional knowledge on reproductive health. In fact, many respondents in the second study said that acquiring and displaying western, scientific knowledge made one more urban and modern. For these workers, displaying such knowledge was symbolic of leaving the village and traditional ways of thinking behind and becoming urban and modern women.

Having observed workers negotiating health and reproductive matters when I lived among them in 2000, I was surprised when they denied knowledge of even the rhythm method for preventing unwanted pregnancies in 2004. In contrast to their enthusiastic display of scientific knowledge, they seemed to perform 'innocence' for each other and for me. As one woman said, there is no need for them to know about contraceptive methods or safe sex behaviour since they are unmarried women. She did not elaborate further, but it was clear that she was alluding to the dominant cultural ideals of young unmarried women being innocent of sexual matters and worldly ways. Scientific knowledge is sanitized through its association with the respectable spaces of secondary schools, state institutions, such as the family planning association, mainstream media, and the legitimate authority of doctors and other experts. Therefore, displaying such knowledge makes one modern and educated. Scientific knowledge is privileged knowledge, and acknowledging it does not necessarily indicate that the unmarried women were concerned about methods to prevent pregnancies or to induce abortions. But traditional knowledge is kept secret from unmarried women and held by rural midwives and older female relatives. Thus association with this body of knowledge puts an unmarried woman's reputation at serious risk, leading them to pretend that they are ignorant of such knowledge.

In fact, in my ethnographic field research in 2000, I learnt that workers know a lot more about these traditional methods than they acknowledge in public, especially in the presence of a person that they had met recently. I had many occasions to witness spontaneous discussions on health and sexuality and to participate in community reading sessions where workers discussed stories published in a pornographic magazine. These boarding room discussions and several workers' narratives showed that they daily negotiated both scientific and traditional information on reproductive health as they manoeuvred through lives characterized by social and sexual stigma and political and cultural marginalization.

Reading pornography and fantasizing choice

Women workers claimed that scientific knowledge obtained from schools, tabloid magazines, mainstream newspapers and NGO workshops, in that order, were the sources of their knowledge on reproductive and sexual health. But in everyday life they seemed to be mostly influenced by several colourful weekly magazines that they claimed were their favourite reading materials. Workers asserted that these magazines provided them with knowledge on sexuality, reproductive health and life in general. They read these magazines, especially the one titled *Priyadari*, in groups in their boarding houses. The workers usually discussed the sexually explicit stories after one of them had read them aloud. It is through these discussions that they expressed their knowledge, wishes, and hopes about sexual and reproductive experiences.

Priyadari *reading community*

While all the other tabloids belong to the pulp category, *Priyadari* can be considered a pornographic magazine because it contains sexually explicit material designed for sexual arousal and is sold for a profit (Nead 1993). Tabloids usually target young people, but *Priyadari* especially caters to FTZ workers. *Priyadari* publishes articles authored by its readers about their relationships and contains lurid sexual material and articles translated from sex advice books published in Western and East Asian countries. Among the readers' contributions, some were about FTZ women workers, while some were authored by the workers and based on their personal experiences with men. *Priyadari*'s acceptance of any article, regardless of the language used, has made it a popular forum for marginalized groups, especially garment factory workers and soldiers. The magazine gives these groups a space to write about their relationships and to release pent up emotions of anger, hatred and unrequited love as well as to boast about their casual attitude towards love and sex. Pages are devoted to various topics, with titles such as 'Scattered Flower Petals' (how I lost my virginity before marriage), 'My Wedding Night', 'The Experience of My Child Birth', 'What We Did Before Marriage', 'How We Eloped from Home', 'A Secret I Can't Tell Anybody' (on adulterous relationships) and the like.

FTZ workers admit that they read *Priyadari* for juicy sexual accounts (*pani keli*). Studies show that reading romances fulfils very real emotional needs while representing a resistance, however limited, to patriarchal values (Modleski 1982; Radway 1984). *Priyadari* also gave women information on sexuality and reproductive experiences, which in turn generated discussions that further enhanced their knowledge on such matters.

Usually the reading sessions were lively and interactive, and as the reading went on, women expressed their opinions on a particular story or its characters. The magazine carried other features dealing with sex advice and personal advertisements that were of interest to young women. But the readers admitted it was the sex stories that made them re-read the magazines.

The FTZ experience gave them a chance to escape some of the social codes surrounding sexual behaviour. Rather than getting married right after high school they now experienced difficult but relatively free lives in a vibrant urban social space that allowed more room for expressing physical desires. In comments made during reading sessions women expressed frustrations, fears and hopes for their own lives. For instance, *Priyadari* published numerous stories of incest, child molestation and rape. Although these also emphasized sexual aspects, such stories made women workers angry about the social structures that let women and children suffer at the hands of people holding power over them. They talked about their hopes for better social conditions in which women and children could exercise free choice over when, where and with whom to have sex. They also critiqued the police and the justice system for being lenient with the culprits and not providing better social and physical security for women and children.

Workers talked about modern and traditional contraceptive methods when they read stories about women who were forced to stay with abusive men because they suddenly found themselves pregnant while contemplating escape routes. They question how the authors could be so ignorant of contraceptive methods and discussed how they should have protected themselves from getting pregnant by using whatever methods available. This led to a discussion about traditional methods that a woman could easily employ, which in turn led to discussions about the relative merits of traditional contraceptive methods and to their hopes and wishes for a world in which reliable, modern contraceptives could be made easily available in any part of the country. Despite disagreeing on strategies, workers at such sessions agreed that while male support is important, ultimately women are responsible for their choices.

Many women blamed the FTZ workers who got pregnant before marriage, not for breaking cultural taboos on premarital sex but for not using contraceptive methods that are more freely available in the modern space of the FTZ. On several occasions I heard women referring to women who ended up with unwanted pregnancies as stupid cows (*eladennu/harakiyo*) or donkey cubs (*buru pataw*) whose stupid behaviour make all FTZ workers hang their heads in shame. Women usually agreed that abortions, especially those performed in illegal health centres, were dangerous, and discussed possible long-term consequences, such as permanent infertility and the damage to reproductive organs.

Women workers also discussed where they could obtain free advice and services, criticizing the FPASL's local offices for ineffective service and for the discourteous and paternalistic manner in which they provided it. These very reasons seemed to prompt them to rely more on private outlets to obtain contraceptives, and in these discussions, they focused on strategies to fulfil these basic needs while safeguarding whatever dignity they were allowed as FTZ workers. Some strategies included asking a friend's boyfriend to buy pills and condoms from area pharmacies. They also thought that if they had to go to a doctor they could inquire about contraceptive methods or reproductive health by pretending they were seeking advice for a friend who was too ashamed to come to the doctor's office. While talking about these practical solutions they lamented that they could not obtain reproductive services without employing such means. Several women knew through NGO workshops and by reading translated material published in tabloid magazines that women in other countries obtained contraceptives and legal, sanitized abortions without trouble or cultural concerns. They also talked about the cultural consequences of making such services easily available.

FTZ: an enabling and empowering space?

State institutions and NGOs easily reach FTZ workers given the large number of unmarried women living in a relatively small area. There are many educational programmes conducted by these organizations, and most workers more or less get exposed to their ideas. NGOs have monthly publications and also distribute leaflets and booklets that focus on workers' experiences.

Moreover, as described above, it is in the FTZ that women read the tabloids and engage in thought-provoking discussions with peers about sexual and reproductive health. Once, urging a relatively new worker to start a relationship with an admirer, one woman said, 'otherwise you will have to live your life reading *Priyadari*'. The specific use of the language conveyed how *Priyadari* provides sexual contentment and knowledge about life. This knowledge acquisition remains a transgressive act, since unmarried women were not supposed to obtain sexual knowledge except the limited scientific knowledge provided in secondary schools. The role played by the transnational space of the FTZ becomes more evident when we consider how difficult it is to access tabloid magazines, like *Priyadari*, in typical villages. Workers recounted how, when they first came to the FTZ, they felt embarrassed to go to a shop and ask for such magazines. But they soon overcame the fear by going to the shops in groups. By providing a space where young unmarried women can buy pornographic weeklies and an environment where they can share their experiences, hopes and fears of their reproductive futures, the FTZ had initiated a process that undermined dominant cultural values. This is more salient when we consider that FTZ workers enjoyed smuggling *Priyadari* home and sharing it with younger, unmarried women who have never migrated to urban areas. So trade liberalization and transnational production made FTZ workers into agents who channelled global cultural flows to the romanticized village and its symbol of honour – the rural women. However, whether the workers themselves were enabled to practice this newly acquired knowledge depended on many factors.

Knowledge versus Practice – Unwanted Pregnancies and Abortions

During my research in 2000 and 2004, NGO officials, area civic leaders and neighbours presented a bleak picture of women's reproductive behaviour. As indicated above, the congregation of so many single women in a small area attracted many men. An extraordinary number of young couples could be seen around the FTZ area at any given time, as they walked hand in hand and stole kisses by the roadside, railway tracks and overgrown spaces between boarding houses. Neighbours and others agreed that harsh work and living conditions propelled them towards romantic relationships.

NGO activists and civic leaders agreed that women were vulnerable for many reasons to sexually transmitted diseases (STDs). One of the common reasons they cited was their fascination with military personnel who often started casual relationships with FTZ workers while their wives lived in their villages. Military men, according to NGO activists, are prone to associate with sex workers and this increased the risk of spreading STDs. They also commented on the number of illegal abortion clinics that had sprung up around the FTZ, saying that approximately twenty to thirty abortions were being conducted in the vicinity every day.[8] One doctor I talked to said that at least two to three women a day came to him for urine pregnancy tests. He also said that about 75 per cent of the FTZ workers must have gone through an abortion at least once. This number seems highly exaggerated and prompts one to consider that health care providers in Sri Lanka are generally influenced by hegemonic cultural norms; most do not approve of providing contraceptives to unmarried women (Hewage 1999) and are divided regarding abortion on religious and moral grounds (Ministry of Plan Implementation 1983; Sirisena 1996). Still, the incidence of abortion seems alarmingly high, indicating that a significant portion of the workers who engage in premarital sex do not protect themselves against unwanted pregnancies, let alone STDs.

The three physicians I interviewed unequivocally held that the workers are ignorant of STDs and HIV/AIDS. Their observations are based on occurrences such as women coming for urine tests after they missed their periods consecutively for three to four months. But most women wait a couple of months more before deciding on an abortion, and do not seem to care about the complications involved in such late-term abortions. Most illegal clinics perform operations if their fees are paid, and women have died owing to such abortions. All the doctors complained that women were extremely shy of talking about these situations, and the secrecy and reluctance to talk complicated matters further.

Even allowing for exaggeration, the situation seems bleak. The discussions at their boarding house reading sessions and their responses to the study on HIV/AIDS showed a sound knowledge of safe sex behaviour and other preventive measures – such as the need for blood tests before starting a sexual relationship and checking whether syringes are fresh before health workers use them. It is important to see why there is such a gap between the workers' expressed knowledge on correct reproductive health behaviour and their everyday practice of such knowledge. How is it possible that area physicians and other people see them as ignorant of reproductive health when they apparently know much, sharing their experiences in their boarding houses and, to a lesser extent, even on the shop floor?

In 2000, and in 2004, I presented these facts to the workers and asked what they thought about the general situation regarding unwanted pregnancies and public attitudes towards their lack of knowledge on reproductive health. On both occasions they got angry over the allegations that they lacked knowledge, but nevertheless agreed that many FTZ workers experienced unwanted pregnancies and that they had no other choice but to use the abortion clinics around the FTZ. When asked how it was possible that women workers who seemed to know so much about contraceptives and safe sex behaviour got pregnant or contracted STDs,[9] workers in their varied ways blamed socio-economic structures and state institutions (including military and law enforcement agencies) for the current situation.

According to the workers, almost all women got involved with men they thought were honest and truly loved them, believing this would lead to marriage. Yet the stories they told me and the ones published in tabloid magazines showed how men very skilfully enticed women to trust them by promising that they would engage in physical intimacy only when legally married. But after a month or two some incident ensued, such as the couple visiting friends in a distant area and finding it too late to return home as buses had stopped running. The couple then spends the night together, and women more often than not find themselves unprepared, becoming party to unprotected sex.

While workers first blamed the men for deceiving women and not taking precautions themselves (such as wearing condoms), they also blamed the cultural values that forced both men and women to act as hypocrites by never acknowledging sexual desires and the need for sexual intimacy. Idealist sexual norms dictate that premarital sex is evil. Especially for a woman, associating with a man before marriage poses a serious threat to her reputation. This pressures women into hanging on to men even if they know that the men have deceived them into sexual activities. This situation makes it easy for men to persuade women to have repeated sexual encounters.

While there are numerous such stories of women being manipulated into sexual activities, there are as many anonymously published stories of FTZ workers having consensual sex with men and then being abandoned after the women conceive.[10] Workers also provided reasons as to why women who consented to sexual intercourse would not take precautions to prevent pregnancies and STDs. They claimed the rhythm method was out of the question because the men wanted sex whenever they visited the women. In such instances, most women had sex because they feared their boyfriends would leave them if they did not provide sexual services when needed.[11] In fact, one soldier I talked to reiterated this by saying that he would find another woman if his current girlfriend refused to provide him sexual satisfaction.

The workers indicated that there are acute cultural constraints that prevent women from starting on the pill or asking men to wear condoms. As explained earlier, even though FTZ workers gained new knowledge and attitudes, they still had to live within the Sinhala-Buddhist society that expected them to conform to the ideals of Sinhala-Buddhist womanhood.[12] Starting on the pill would indicate that the woman desired sexual intercourse, and if discovered, most people would consider her promiscuous and not worthy to become a wife. With eight to ten women sharing small boarding rooms, it is almost impossible to keep secrets from other residents sharing the room. Being found with contraceptive pills will seriously jeopardize a woman's reputation, and the rumours will soon reach her village through other workers from the same area. Given the particular structure of their urban employment, in which they are forced to leave after five to six years, it becomes very important for women to strategize their lives in a way that would allow for easy re-integration into patriarchal village life. The villages did not offer much space to find a fulfilling life as single women, and workers looked forward to getting married to either their current boyfriends or, failing that, to village men their parents found them. In both these circumstances it is important for women to pretend to be innocent village women who have not been corrupted by urban knowledge flows.[13]

As the Cart that Follows the Bull

In 2003–04, I collected narratives of former FTZ workers with whom I had continued to stay in touch even after they left the FTZ. Here, I focus on seven former workers' experiences. During my research I visited their village homes (most had by now moved to their husbands' villages) and spent time talking to them, their husbands, in-laws and their new neighbours. Three of the seven women married their village boyfriends, two had arranged marriages and two remained unmarried. Four of the seven women had belonged to a politically conscious, rebellious FTZ factory group that expressed rudimentary forms of proletarian and feminist consciousness.[14] Now, all four were housewives and mothers. Even though development planners, BOI and other government officials claimed that FTZ employment is an avenue for rural women to earn their dowry, these women wanted to keep working after marriage. However, employers' reluctance and other socio-psychological reasons prevented them from doing so, and these rebellious workers had to accept the role of traditional village wives. It is through a display of acquiescence to such ideal gender roles that all of them have obtained their in-laws' approval.

I have explained how women acted as naïve, shy and timid women when they visited their villages on vacations so that they would be included in the category of the 'small number of innocent women' in the FTZ, and not identified with the transgressive FTZ workers who have no shame-fear. When I talked to some of the same women about their post-FTZ lives, they said it helped them to get married to their boyfriends without his family making objections or to get into 'respectable' proposed marriages.[15]

However, their pretences to be naïve women with shame-fear has had adverse consequences in that three women, including one who married her long-time boyfriend, found it difficult to talk to their future husbands about family planning before they got married. As such, they did not use contraception and four married women now have small children.[16] One woman, Vinitha, who perhaps most strongly expressed her need to be financially independent and started her own village shop, had a baby in the tenth month of her marriage. She talked to her boyfriend about not getting pregnant for a year or two so they could develop their shop with her spending more time there. But he desired a baby and expressed concern over becoming permanently infertile due to use of contraception. She knew this was a myth but did not have the courage to appear too worldly by arguing about the relative merits of contraception methods. While she dotes on her child she regrets that her shop is closed more often than it is open.

Vasanthi has not conceived despite being married for two-and-a-half years. She fears that people will soon insinuate that her immoral lifestyle while at the FTZ (wada varadha gaththa) is responsible for her infertility. Once, when watching a TV programme with other members of her husband's family, she found herself squirming when the doctor talked about infertility caused by abortions. Another day someone asked her about the sex and abortion stories coming out of the FTZ, and she pretended she did not associate with women who had casual sexual relationships. In fact, during many conversations on mundane health matters she feigned ignorance to prevent people from thinking that she led a fast life while in the FTZ.

While having babies thwarted their attempts to start income-generating activities and burdened them with heavy responsibilities at a young age, these FTZ workers seem to use biological reproduction as a means of cultural image management. All of them found the intense scrutiny of their behaviour for transgressions had lessened since they became pregnant. With a child or two in tow they did not look much different from a woman who had never migrated, and this less scrutinized social space allowed them more freedom to exercise choice over movement and even biological reproduction.

These narratives show that it is important for village women who have to integrated themselves back into patriarchal families to disavow new knowledge acquired within modern, transnational spaces. I contend that when FTZ workers recant the reproductive knowledge previously displayed within their boarding houses, when an unfamiliar researcher or an official questions them, they are hoping to minimize the collective stigma accrued due to FTZ employment. As one former FTZ worker said, 'As the cart follows the bull, the shame of spending time in the FTZ comes after us.' Creating and performing a completely contradictory picture to the worldly FTZ worker is a strategy that helps them stay clear of accusations regarding cultural transgressions. Therefore, I assert that their public denial of knowledge of actual reproductive health practices is a part of this effort at stigma management, which helps them ease into post-FTZ lives. Their narratives, however, show that the success of their efforts depends on the context, and while this strategy makes their village lives easier, it does not totally absolve them from the stigma of being FTZ workers or protect them from widely publicized reports of FTZ workers' reproductive dilemmas.

Conclusion

This discussion shows that FTZ workers are exposed to cultural flows peculiar to such transnational spaces and acquire knowledge on modern practices of reproductive health. However, it also makes clear that they are not empowered to use their knowledge when the situation demands it. The discouraging picture of illegal abortions around the FTZ area, and the former FTZ workers' inability to realize their reproductive choices within marriage, confirm this situation.

The workers' own ideas showed that the normalized dominant cultural expectations of innocence, virginity and norms of shame-fear discourage workers from practising their newly acquired knowledge on reproductive health. State institutions, media representations and NGOs, for varying reasons and in varying degrees, also contribute to this environment, an environment that effectively marginalizes workers' own ideas about their reproductive health.[17]

Reproductive health is not just about women and their bodies but includes communities, networks, and the socio-cultural and political structures within which sexuality is negotiated. In order to become agents shaping their own reproductive futures, women need a different kind of knowledge – one that helps them overcome cultural constraints and allows them to pursue choices that matter to them. They need ways to apply their knowledge of modern reproductive technologies as they negotiate activities enmeshed in issues of love, intimacy, respect and trust. Educational programmes should focus on talking about these latter issues, enabling workers to bring in their own perspectives that eventually might lead to discussions of local strategies to overcome barriers to exercising reproductive choices. Developing women's negotiation skills and promoting better self-esteem and assertiveness are important to help them manoeuvre through relationships characterized by patriarchal norms. Including young men in at least some of these educational programmes is also necessary.

Trade liberalization resulted in employment of migrant rural women in transnational industrial work and their subsequent exposure to varied transnational cultural flows. However, FTZ employment is temporary, and women are forced to negotiate disparate cultural discourses as urban, industrial workers who eventually have to settle in rural villages. Their constant attempts at stigma management, especially with regard to reproductive choices, sometimes lead them to grave and even fatal consequences. The temporary nature of FTZ work ensures that the empowerment women gained by acquiring knowledge and developing new urban cultural practices is short-lived. While they are different from other village women, former FTZ workers' new sense of self more or less contracts and adjusts to the different circumstances extant in their villages. In this vein trade liberalization's effects on women's employment and their subsequent exposure to new ideas and resources, especially regarding reproductive health, rarely lead towards agency in shaping their own reproductive futures.

Yet FTZ workers stand out among their non-migrant peers in the ways they strategize their lives and become critical, even if cautiously, of the patriarchal power relations in which they are enmeshed. This leads me to conclude that state officials, activists and scholars should address issues of women's empowerment holistically. The temporary nature of FTZ employment appears to be the biggest setback in achieving women's aspirations. If they must leave after a certain number of years, then rural industrialization, agricultural development, improving infrastructure, networking facilities and law enforcement could contribute towards addressing their employment and personal security problems in their villages. Changes in the rural economy and infrastructure will facilitate changes in cultural perceptions, which women workers cited as the main obstacle to achieving long-term empowerment.

Notes

1. The then UNP government relied heavily on financial assistance from the World Bank and the International Monetary Fund (IMF) to implement their promises of economic prosperity through trade liberalization. The assistance from the two agencies was provided under the condition that Sri Lanka would implement structural adjustment policies. The establishment of the Katunayake FTZ was a major component of this new development programme.
2. The majority of Sri Lankans are Sinhala (74 per cent). While 7 per cent of the Sinhala are Christians (principally Catholic), most are Buddhist (93 per cent). The Tamil minority (18 per cent of Sri Lankans) is mostly Hindu (83 per cent) with some Christians (17 per cent). Muslims (7 per cent of Sri Lankans) and small communities of other ethnic groups, such as Burghers and Chinese, also live in the country (Mann 1993: 59).
3. Older, married women from poor, marginalized families migrate temporarily to Middle Eastern countries to work as housemaids. The effects of this form of migratory work on women themselves, their families and the society have been the focus of many studies (Brochman 1993; Hewamanne 2000; Gamburd 2002).
4. Christian missionaries, educationists and colonial government officials in their writings described Sinhala-Buddhist women as unrestrained, disobedient and uncivilized in manner (De Alwis 1997). Men belonging to the early twentieth century nationalist movement were shamed by this image, and saw instilling virtues of Victorian femininity, domesticity, discipline and restraint as essential to transforming Sinhala-Buddhist women into a symbol of national greatness.
5. Gananath Obeyesekere uses the term 'protestant Buddhism' to refer to new traditions of Sinhala Buddhism that were configured by incorporating

Victorian and Protestant ethical ideas, and notes that sexual morality, monogamous marriage ideals and divorce rules are several such ideas adopted from Protestantism (see Obeyesekere 1970).

6. However, they showed extreme reluctance to respond to questions about their own reproductive experience or their ideas on love, intimacy and sexuality. This shows the ineffectiveness of survey methods in gathering data on sensitive matters that have traditionally been shrouded in secrecy. This point was made clearer when I was able to contrast this reluctance with the enthusiasm with which they talked about such matters during my ethnographic research when I shared a boarding house with them and worked in a FTZ factory.

7. This study was carried out with UNDP funding. The earlier survey of 300 workers was conducted as part of a Population Council-funded research project and was a part of my one-year ethnographic research among the workers.

8. According to the penal code of Sri Lanka, an abortion can only be performed to save the life of the woman (Section 303). An abortion carried out for any other reason would result in imprisonment or fine or both for the woman and the person who carried out the abortion.

9. NGO officials and the doctors agreed that they had not dealt with that many STD cases even though the workers seemed vulnerable to contracting them.

10. It is important to note that it is very rare that women confess to consensual sexual activities in face-to-face conversations. In my research since 1995, I met only four women who themselves reported that they had consensual sex because they desired it. However, many workers reported on other women who got involved in consensual sex, and their anonymous writings to *Priyadari* also talked about the way men aroused sexual desires and how they enjoyed the act until the man betrayed them.

11. The increased militarization of Sri Lankan society, in the context of the continuing civil war raging in 2000, also had a profound influence in the way women treated their military brothers/boyfriends. They publicly acknowledged that it was a national duty to provide services such as cooking, laundry and affectionate comforts to the war-weary soldiers when they were on vacation. The militarized ideology also resulted in women willingly giving in to soldiers' demands for sexual favours, thus becoming part of a series of informal welfare services provided for soldiers with the consent of powerful segments of society – including the military hierarchy and the media.

12. I have elsewhere explicated how FTZ workers collectively performed oppositional identities in public and how as individuals they strategize FTZ knowledge and traditional expectation according to the specific contexts in which they were in (Hewamanne 2002, 2003).

13. It is necessary to note here that there indeed were women who seemingly did not fear such consequences and used different types of contraceptives.

While they did not claim this in public discussions, they reported their experiences with contraceptives and details of sexual experiences in private conversations with me. The women who used contraceptives also tried to make sure that their men did not know about these precautions.

14. See Hewamanne (2002) for more details on this group and its activities within their FTZ factory and in the area.

15. One of the women who belonged to the same factory group expressly challenged the village sensitivities by not making that many changes to her FTZ ways while in the village, and also not making any effort to stem the rumours that reached the village. When she left the employment, her village boyfriend married her despite serious objections from his family and was banished from attending any family functions. Even though his family has softened their attitude over time, the husband now uses these past rumours in arguments, and the couple quarrel often.

16. I have heard workers talking about a few former FTZ workers who had discussions with their husbands and came mutually to agree upon reproductive decisions. My efforts to interview one of them were not successful.

17. Veiled cultural ideals are intertwined with the reproductive knowledge given to workers through most NGO workshops. State and NGO personnel are also deeply conflicted over their role in educating unmarried women on reproductive technology, and these conflicts convey themselves to the workers.

References

Ali, K. (2002) *Planning the Family in Egypt: New Bodies, New Selves*, Austin, TX: University of Texas Press.

Blanc, A. (2001) 'The Effect of Power in Sexual Relationships on Sexual and Reproductive Health: An Examination of the Evidence', *Studies in Family Planning*, vol. 32, no. 3 (September): 189–213.

Blanc, A., B. Wolff, A. Gage, A. Ezeh, S. Neemaand and J. Ssekamatte-Ssebuliba (1996) *Negotiating Reproductive Outcomes in Uganda*, Claverton, MD: Institute of Statistics and Applied Economics (Uganda) and Macro International.

Brochman, G. (1993) *Middle East Avenue: Female Migration from Sri Lanka to the Gulf*, Boulder, CO: West View Press.

Bujawansa, B. (2002) 'An Analysis of Fifty Cases of Unintended Pregnancy', *Sri Lanka Family Physician*, vol. 24, no. 1: 37–9.

Chaudhury, R. (2001) 'Unmet Need for Contraception in South Asia: Levels, Trends and Determinants', *Asia-Pacific Population Journal*, vol. 16, no. 3: 3–22.

Dabindu Collective (1989) *Prathiba*, Boralesgamuwa: CRC Press.

Dabindu Collective (1997) *A Review of Free Trade Zones in Sri Lanka*, Boralesgamuwa: CRC Press.

De Alwis, M. (1997) 'The Production and Embodiment of Respectability: Gendered Demeanors in Colonial Ceylon', Manuscript.

De Alwis, M. (1998) 'Maternalistic Politics in Sri Lanka: A Historical Anthropology of its Conditions of Possibility', PhD Dissertation, Department of Anthropology, University of Chicago.

De Silva, I., L. Rankapuge and R. Perera (2000) 'Induced Abortion in Sri Lanka: Who Goes to Providers for Pregnancy Termination?', *Demography of Sri Lanka: Issues and Challenges*, Colombo: Department of Demography, University of Colombo, pp. 182–96.

Family Planning Association of Sri Lanka (1997) 'Needs Assessment Study on Sexual Health Education and Services for Adolescents and Youth in Sri Lanka', Colombo: FPASL.

Family Planning Association of Sri Lanka (1999) 'Baseline KAP Survey', Colombo: FPASL.

Fernando, A. (2000) 'Promotion of Reproductive Health among Rural Women through Education and Awareness Building: Lanka Mahila Samithi', Seventh National Convention on Women's Studies, 23–26 March, Colombo: Center for Women's Research.

Fine, J., and M. Howard (1995) 'Women in the Free Trade Zones of Sri Lanka', *Dollars and Sense*, November/December: 26–27 and 39–40.

Gamburd, M. (2000) *The Kitchen Spoon's Handle: Transnationalism and Sri Lanka's Migrant Housemaids*, Ithaca: Cornell University Press.

Ginsburg, F., and R. Rapp (1991) 'The Politics of Reproduction', *Annual Review of Anthropology*, vol. 20: 311–43.

Ginsburg, F., and R. Rapp (eds) (1995) *Conceiving the New World Order: The Global Politics of Reproduction*, Berkeley, CA: University of California Press.

Gubhaju, B. (2002) 'Adolescent Reproductive Health in Asia', *Asia-Pacific Population Journal*, vol. 17, no. 4: 97–119.

Gunaratne, K.A., and M. Goonewardena (2001) 'Teenage Pregnancy and Contraception', *Sri Lanka Journal of Obstetrics and Gynecology*, vol. 23: 15–19.

Gupta, G.R., and E. Weiss (1993) 'Women's Lives and Sex: Implications for AIDS Prevention', *Culture, Medicine and Psychiatry*, vol. 17: 399–412.

Guruge, A. (1965) *Anagarika Dharmapala: Return to Righteousness*, Colombo: Government Press.

Hettiarachchi, T., and S. Schensul (2001) 'The Risks of Pregnancy and the Consequences among Young Unmarried Women Working in a Free Trade Zone in Sri Lanka', *Asia-Pacific Population Journal*, vol. 16, no. 2: 125–40.

Hewage, P. (1999) 'Induced Abortion in Sri Lanka: Opinions of Reproductive Health Care Providers', in A. Mundigo and C. Indriso (eds), *Abortion in the Developing World*, New Delhi: Vistaar Publications.

Hewamanne, S. (2000) 'Making Histories within: Resistance, contradictions and "Agency" among Sri Lanka's Migrant Housemaids', *Asian Women*, vol. 11: 109–36.

Hewamanne, S. (2002) 'Stitching Identities: Work, Play and Politics among Sri Lanka's Free Trade Zone Garment Factory Workers', PhD Dissertation, Department of Anthropology, University of Texas, Austin, TX.

Hewamanne, S. (2003) 'Performing Dis-respectability: New Tastes, Cultural Practices and Identity Performances by Sri Lanka's Free Trade Zone garment-factory workers', *Cultural Dynamics*, vol. 15, no. 1 (March): 71–101.

Hewamanne, S. (2004) 'Migrant Workers and HIV-AIDS Vulnerability: Sri Lanka', unpublished report on UNDP sponsored study on South Asian region.

Hewamanne, S., and J. Brow (1999) 'If they Allow us we will Fight: Strains of Consciousness among Women Workers in the Katunayake Free Trade Zone', *Anthropology of Work Review*, vol. 19, no. 3 (Spring): 8–13.

Hogan, D., B. Berhanu and A. Hailemariam (1999) 'Household Organization, Women's Autonomy and Contraceptive Behavior in Southern Ethiopia', *Studies of Family Planning*, vol. 30, no. 4: 302–14.

Mann, R. (1993) *International Investor Guide to Sri Lanka*, Ontario: Gateway.

Mason, K. (1994) 'HIV Transmission and the Balance of Power between Men and Women: A Global View', *Health Transition Review*, vol. 4: 217–40.

Mason, K., and H. Smith (1999) 'Female Autonomy and Fertility in Five Asian countries', Paper presented at the annual meeting of the Population Association of America, New York, USA, 25–27 March.

Mason, K., and H. Smith (2000) 'Husbands' versus Wives' Fertility Goals and the Use of Contraception: The Influence of Gender Context in Five Asian countries', *Demography*, vol. 37, no. 3: 299–311.

Ministry of Plan Implementation (1983) *Perspectives on Abortion in Sri Lanka*, Colombo: Ministry of Plan Implementation.

Modleski, T. (1982) *Loving with a Vengeance: Mass Produced Fantasies for Women*, Connecticut: Archon Books.

Mullings, L., and A. Wali (2001) *Stress and Resilience: The Social Context of Reproduction in Central Harlem*, New York: Kluwer Academic/Plenum Publishers.

Nead, L. (1993) 'Above the Pulpline: The Cultural Significance of Erotic Art', in P. Gibson and R. Gibson (eds), *Dirty Looks: Women, Pornography, Power*, London: BFI, pp. 144–55.

Obeyesekere, G. (1970) 'Religious Symbolism and Political Change in Ceylon', *Modern Ceylon Studies*, vol. 1, no. 1: 46.

Obeyesekere, G. (1984) *The Cult of the Goddess Pattini*, Chicago: University of Chicago Press.

Radway, J. (1984) *Reading the Romance: Women, Patriarchy and Popular Literature*, Chapel Hill, NC: The University of North Carolina Press.

Ratnayake, K. (2002) 'Youth at Risk? Knowledge, Attitudes and Behavior Relating to Reproductive Health Including STDs and HIV-AIDS among Bachelors in Sri Lanka', *Journal of Population Studies*, vol. 5: 1–20.

Riley, N. (1997) 'Gender, Power and Population Change', *Population Bulletin*, vol. 52, no. 1, Washington, DC: Population Reference Bureau.

Rosa, K. (1990) 'Women Workers' Strategies of Organizing and Resistance in the Sri Lankan Free Trade Zone (FTZ)', *South Asia Bulletin*, vol. 10, no. 1: 33–43.

Singh, S., J. Darroch, J. Frost and the Study Team (2001) 'Socioeconomic Disadvantage and Adolescent Women's Sexual and Reproductive Behavior: The Case of Five Developed Countries', *Family Planning Perspectives*, vol. 33, no. 66: 251–8 and 289.

Sirisena, J. (1996) 'Gynecologists' Opinion on Induced Abortion', *Proceedings of the Kandy Society of Medicine Annual Sessions*, 18.

Stiftung, F. (1997) *Diriya Diyaniyo*, Colombo: Fedric Ebert Stiftung.

Tremayne, S. (ed.) (2001) *Managing Reproductive Life: Cross Cultural Themes in Fertility and Sexuality*, New York: Berghahn Books.

Wickramagamage, C. (2000) 'Her Body, her Right?: Interrogating the Discourse on Abortion Rights in Sri Lanka', Paper presented at the Seventh National Convention on Women's Studies, Center for Women's studies, Sri Lanka, 23–26 March.

Wickramasinge, V.P., P.P.C. Prageeth, D.S. Pullaperuma and K.S.R. Pushpakumara (2002) 'Pre-Conceptual Care: Are we doing Enough?', in *Proceedings of the Sri Lanka College of Pediatricians 6th Annual Scientific Congress*, Colombo, Sri Lanka, 18–22 September.

Trade Liberalization and Government Capacity
to Deliver Reproductive Health Supplies and
Services

PART III

Trade Liberalization and Government Capacity
to Deliver Reproductive Health Supplies and
Services

8

I Would Pay, if I Could Pay in Maize: Trade Liberalization, User Fees in Health and Women's Health Seeking in Tanzania

Priya Nanda

Introduction

An interdisciplinary effort to understand the direct and indirect effects of trade liberalization on women's reproductive health and rights traverses through a globalized landscape exploring many conceptual links, be it women's occupational health in export processing zones in Mexico, the effects of migration of nurses on women's access to health in Jamaica or advocacy to change trade restrictions for the use of more affordable generic antiretrovirals in Brazil. A less obvious though important link explored in this chapter is the effect of trade liberalization on government resources for the health sector, through revenue from trade, and the consequent effects of health sector resources on user fees in health and women's utilization of reproductive health care services.

In many countries with poor taxation norms, taxes on trade or tariffs are an important source of government revenue and spending for its social sectors including health. In a resource-poor economy with an underdeveloped health system, the distribution of public health goods, such as preventive and promotive health care, is contingent on government spending on health care. The private sector, where it exists, cannot guarantee a minimum essential health care package to all, which includes preventive services such as immunization and antenatal care, and is a basic human right of every individual, irrespective of their ability to pay for health care. The role of the state is hence paramount in fostering the values of rights and equity in health care delivery through the provision of universal and comprehensive health care services.

However, the role of the state in health care in many of the less developed countries has been declining and that of the private sector is increasing in the last few decades. Since the early 1980s, many less developed countries that have undergone debt crises or economic recession have inevitably turned to the IMF and the World Bank for loans. These loans come with certain conditions that are premised on the singular assumption that governments are inefficient, and that the private sector can play a more effective role in areas where governments have been wasteful or unsuccessful in achieving the desired outcomes, including health and education. Loan conditions, articulated as structural adjustment packages, typically involve cuts in government expenditure for social sectors, and privatization of government-provided health services, including cost recovery strategies, such as user fees, health insurance and prepayment schemes (Abel-Smith and Rawall 1992). The conditions set through structural adjustment policies have created norms and language around health sector reforms, which governments have been urged to carry out as a part of adjustment. One of the objectives of health sector reforms is to improve efficiency of public health services through increased private spending for health care, such as user fees, based on the assumption that the private sector is more efficient. User fees for health care have thus become a natural corollary of health sector reforms.

In this chapter, I consider the linkages between trade liberalization, the decline in trade tax revenues and the consequent decline in resources for the government health sector, which have led to the implementation of user fees in health care. Due to a decline in government resources, Tanzania's health sector has been deteriorating since the early 1980s and user fees in health care have been implemented since the early 1990s. During the same period, its revenue from trade tariffs has declined. With the explicit aim of understanding the effects of trade liberalization on women's access to reproductive health care, in this chapter I juxtapose the situation of declining trade revenue, health reforms and user fees with the microreality of women's agency and poverty. Given that women's reproductive health needs are largely unmet due to their own impoverishment and disempowerment, as well as low quality and scope of public health care services, I argue that user fees further constrain women's ability to seek reproductive health care services. I look at user fees in health care as a conceptual lens to understand these hypothesized links between trade liberalization, declining revenue for the public health sector and women's ability to access health care for themselves. This chapter draws upon qualitative primary data from Tanzania collected for a study on the implications of health sector reforms for women's reproductive health. The premise underlying this analysis is that broad macroeconomic policies do affect women's ability to seek better health care or livelihoods, and their experiences need to be given recognition when policies of trade or health reforms are formulated and implemented.

Trade, an Ailing Economy and Resources for Health Care

Since its independence over four decades ago, Tanzania has been struggling to raise its standard of living (Richey 2004). In the last decade or so, real growth has been stagnant, and poverty is highly pervasive with almost half of its population classified as living below the poverty line (UNDP 2001). Its current gross national product (GNP) of US$265 per capita is much lower than some of the other neighbouring sub-Saharan countries like Kenya and Zambia. The economy, and most of the population, is heavily dependent on agriculture, which accounts for some 50 per cent of the GDP and provides 85 per cent of exports (UNDP 2001). Average life expectancy, at 48 years, is also below the sub-Saharan African average of 52.5 years. Other vital statistics show that the infant mortality rate is 99 per 1,000 live births, and the total fertility rate is 5.5 children per woman. Thirty-two per cent of Tanzania's population aged 15 years and above are illiterate (UNDP 2001). Although the ratio of gross enrolment (those who enter at level 1 regardless of age) in primary school to the total eligible population is officially estimated at 76 per cent, the ratio for net enrolment (those who are enrolled in school at the official school age as defined by the national education system) is 56.7 per cent (UNDP 2001). The gross enrolment ratio in secondary schools is only 5 per cent. Table 8.1 presents the selected indicators for Tanzania.

With an external debt to GDP ratio of almost 100 per cent, as of 1999, Tanzania was classified as a highly indebted poor country. As in other low-income countries, Tanzania's debt problems are due to a

Table 8.1   Broad indicators of Tanzania's development

	1992	1995	2001	2002
Gross national income (GNI; billion $)	4.8	4.9	9.0	9.6
GDP per capita (1995 US$)	182.0	177.0	199.0	207.0*
Adult literacy rate (percentage of people aged 15 years and over)	62.9	69.2	76.0	77.1
Total fertility rate (births per woman)	6.3	5.8	5.2	5.0
Life expectancy at birth (years)	50.1	48.5	43.7	43.1
Aid (percentage of GNI)	28.8	17.1	13.3	–
External debt (percentage of GNI)	158.5	144.5	71.9	–
Investment (percentage of GDP)	26.1	19.8	17.0	17.4
Trade (percentage of GDP)	50.1	59.3	39.9	40.0

*Despite its high rate of indebtedness, the GDP per capita has increased at the average annual rate of 1.3 per cent over the ten years from 1992 to 2002. However, over the same time period the life expectancy has decreased at the average annual rate of 1.4 per cent. So, in fact, adjusting for mortality decline the annual average rate of GDP per capita seems to be stagnant.

Source: Tanzania's Millennium Development Goals and World Development (1995).

combination of faulty domestic policies and adverse external shocks. The first and second oil price shocks in the early 1980s, which contributed to serious budget and balance of payments deficits, created the need to borrow not only from external, but also from domestic sources to finance its deficits (World Bank 2002).

For more than a decade, Tanzania has been trying to reduce its outstanding debt through various debt reduction programmes in collaboration with donors and international financial institutions (World Bank 2002). Since 1986 the government has implemented several programmes aimed at revamping the economy, with support from the World Bank, the IMF, and other multilateral and bilateral agencies. Between 1986 and 1998, total external debt stock grew by about 62.2 per cent, with the aggregate ratio of debt service to exports estimated at 27.4 per cent at the end of 1998. This implied that more than 20 per cent of Tanzania's export earnings were required just to service its foreign debt (World Bank 2002). A high proportion, close to 30 per cent in the years 1998–2001, of government revenue goes towards servicing debt. Specifically, the effect on the health sector has been to lower government resources available for health (World Bank 2002).

The WHO's commission on macroeconomics and health suggests that low-income countries need to spend at least 12 per cent of their GNP for health in order to cover essential health care effectively (WHO 2001). This is far more than can be, or is currently being, mobilized in Tanzania or any of the other poorer countries of Africa. The allocation to health has increased only slowly over recent years, from 7.5 per cent in fiscal year (FY) 2000 to 8.7 per cent in FY02, which is low in relation to projections in the Poverty Reduction Strategy (PRS) and the Abuja commitment of 15 per cent. Again, despite the PRS commitments, the absolute budgetary increase year-to-year has declined from a high of 41.1 per cent in FY02 down to a 5.6 per cent increase in FY04. The FY05 budget ceilings indicate that the health sector will actually have fewer resources in real terms than in FY04.

The commission has correspondingly examined the extent to which domestic resources can be increased for health in low-income countries. Their findings suggest that low-income countries mobilize an average of 14 per cent of their GNP through taxes. Since income taxes are limited, given the low-income population base, the majority of taxes come from international trade and taxes on specific commodities (WHO 2001). Given that trade taxes are an important component of government revenue, it is therefore important to understand what effect trade liberalization has on the revenue from these taxes.

Khatry and Rao (2002) in an analysis of eighty countries suggest that efforts to liberalize trade result in revenue losses in most cases, unless the liberalizing countries successfully replace the forgone revenue from trade by revenue from domestic sources. Most low-income countries have faced declining tax revenue/GDP ratios in the wake of trade reform. As low-income countries have become more open and increasingly integrated with the international economy, the tax revenue/GDP ratio has declined by approximately 3 per cent (from 14.5 to 14.1) between 1980–84 and 1995–98 (Khatry and Rao 2002). This has had the effect of reducing public spending on physical and social capital and these effects are evident in Tanzania.

Rationalizing User Fees: Deficit in the Health Sector Revenue

At the time of its independence, Tanzania was committed to being a socialist democracy, popularly referred to as the principles of

Ujamma, based on communal production and distribution. The period from independence to the mid-1970s saw an expansion in the role of the state. Under Ujamma, the government provided free social services financed primarily by foreign aid. Some critics state that people were reduced to being passive recipients of the development process (Rwebangira and Liljestrom 1998). In the 1960s and 1970s, Tanzania had a balance of payments surplus and foreign aid flowed freely (Richey 2004). However, foreign aid declined in the 1980s, owing to a growing current account deficit, which increased the donor dependence to finance this deficit (Richey 2004). The economy remained dependent on a few cash crops (coffee, cotton, sisal, tobacco, tea, cashew nuts) with very little growth in industrial capacity. The decline of aid, deteriorating terms of trade and a consequent low competitiveness in the world market for its exports (coffee, cotton, tobacco, tea, cashew nuts), along with a decline in tax revenue and growing government deficits, led Tanzania to take its first structural adjustment loan (ESAP) from the IMF in the mid-1980s (Richey 2004). Structural adjustment, coupled with a deteriorating national economy, led to greater market orientation and a reduced role for the state in social sectors such as education and health services.

The first wave of health sector reform initiatives started in the post-independence era in the early 1960s, when efforts were directed towards orienting the health sector away from curative to preventive and promotive health services. The country achieved milestones in implementing its primary health care strategy that saw expanded health facilities in rural areas, improvements in trained human resources for health and concrete steps to achieve equity in health services (Makundi et al. 2004). During this period, the country experienced rapid development not only in health services, but also in the provision of education, water and other social services to the rural areas, where the majority of the people live.

The economic downturn in the 1980s, along with declining overall governmental revenue, began to reverse some of the gains of the previous decade. Despite an extensive network of hospitals, health centres and dispensaries across the country, the quality of services deteriorated. There were no funds for staff, drugs or maintenance of facilities. The health system started to experience frequent drug shortages and inadequate services. Compounding these problems were issues of mismanagement of health services and the lack of clarity on power and responsibility, all of which seemed to arrest the growth of a health system geared at providing equitable health services (Makundi et al. 2004). The greatest impact of this on the health sector is stated to have been the low salaries in the health sector, leading to a drop in real incomes of health sector staff (Richey 2004).

In 1985, as a part of the new recovery programme, the government resolved to reform all sectors in order to improve efficiency and accessibility of services to the communities. Structural adjustment provided the impetus for implementing alternative sources of financing the health system through a policy of cost-recovery introduced in the early 1990s, leading to the introduction of user fees for health care services and rising school fees. User fees are generally considered complementary to tax-based financing for government health services, even for countries that previously provided free public health care (Gilson 1997). In most scenarios, user fees have been introduced as a cost-recovery measure to compensate for the cutbacks in government health expenditure. The rationale for introducing user fees in Tanzania was to generate additional revenues, improve the availability and quality of health services, strengthen the referral system and rationalize utilization of health services, and improve equity and access to health services (Makundi et al. 2004). Charges were introduced in four stages: at referral, regional and district hospitals in 1993, and by 1994 at the district level. Fees have also been introduced in some health centres and dispensaries in some districts but will be disbanded formally in 2004 (Mamdani and Bangser 2004). The government introduced cost sharing starting with user fees at tertiary and referral hospitals in July 1993, although it became operational in 1994 (Makundi et al. 2004). In Tanzania, exemptions are granted to children aged five years and under, for maternal and child health (MCH) services, to those with specific chronic diseases and for people with long-term mental disorders. Waivers are also granted to some who are unable to pay, but do not fall into the exempt categories. While an exempt individual can identify herself based on her knowledge about the exemptions, a waiver is based on an evaluation from the district social board.

Our study district was the first and only district in the Kagera region of Tanzania that has implemented cost sharing at the dispensary level. The implementation of fees began in 2001, with a slight variation from the national policy on cost sharing. At a national level, children under the age of five years are exempted from cost sharing. However, in the study district, a decision was made at the council level that children under the age of five years have to pay for health services. The implementation of cost sharing nationally was meant to go hand-in-hand with the formation of district and facility health boards that were to oversee the implementation and management of funds collected through cost sharing. However, in the study district cost sharing was introduced before health boards were formed. The district is also in the final stages of initiating a Community Health Fund to which each participating household (maximum of six members) will have to contribute Tsh 10,000 per year.

Women's 'Unmet' Reproductive Health Needs

The poor state of the public health system and the neglect in health service delivery is mirrored in women's reproductive health indicators. Overall the situation is abysmal with maternal mortality rates estimated as high as 530 per 100,000 live births. Although the total fertility rate has dropped from 5.8 per woman in the period 1994–96, it remains high at 5.6 births for the period 1997–99. Abortion alone accounts for 20 per cent of maternal deaths (MOH 1997). Unsafe abortion is reported to be a contributing factor to high maternal mortality, though legal restrictions mean that the actual magnitude of abortion in Tanzania remains largely unknown. It is also noted that women suffer long-term health problems as a result of abortion complications. Because law restricts abortion, the national family planning programme offers post-abortion and post-coital contraceptive measures, though these services are available only in 50 per cent of the hospitals.

Statistics indicate that only 36 per cent of births are attended by skilled personnel, such as doctors, nurses and midwives, 20 per cent of the deliveries are assisted by birth attendants (trained and untrained) and 29 per cent by relatives or friends (Bureau of Statistics and Macro International 1999). The proportion of births delivered in health facilities has been declining steadily over time, from 53 per cent in 1991–92, to 47 per cent in 1996 and 44 per cent in 1999 (ibid.). In the rural areas only 34.5 per cent of births are delivered in health facilities. This is very different from urban areas, where 82.8 per cent of births are delivered in health facilities. While as many as 98 per cent of women receive antenatal care, the number of deliveries at health facilities is still very low, highlighting constraints in access and resources that affect women's ability to deliver at a health facility (ibid.).

Maternal deaths also occur due to complications of pregnancy related to lack of emergency obstetric care, violence against women, practices like female genital mutilation (FGM), inadequate post-natal care attendance and unsafe abortions. HIV/AIDS has recently become an important cause of maternal morbidity and mortality (MOH 1997). From a health system perspective, the major contributing factors for the high maternal mortality ratio are noted to be inadequate medical supplies and services, inadequate birth preparedness (birth plans, funds, transport) and the inadequate number of skilled attendants in public health facilities (MOH 1997).

The contraceptive prevalence rate in Tanzania remains low, although it has increased from 7 per cent in 1984 to 25 per cent in 1996 (Bureau of Statistics and Macro International 1999). The demand for family planning is 40 per cent, with 17 per cent of all women who were pregnant three years prior to the study reporting unplanned pregnancies (Bureau of Statistics and Macro International 1999). The unmet demand for family planning among married women is 24 per cent (Bureau of Statistics and Macro International 1999). The 1999 reproductive and child health survey showed that 39.5 per cent of all women were in need of family planning services. Two-thirds of the unmet need comprised women who wanted to space their next birth, while one-third was for women who did not want any more children. Currently, only 56 per cent of this 'total demand' for family planning is being met.

It is estimated that about 1.7 million people are infected with HIV, out of whom about 600,000 have already developed AIDS. A situational analysis undertaken in Tanzania in 1997 shows alarming increases in HIV transmission, especially in the rural areas; in some areas the prevalence rate is reported to be more than 10 per cent (United Republic of Tanzania 2000). Recent data suggest that the prevalence rate among pregnant women ranged from 4.2 per cent in Mwanza to 32 per cent in Iringa (United Republic of Tanzania 2000). Prevalence among males was noted to be lower than females (9.2 and 13.3 per cent, respectively). Statistics indicate that women are infected at an earlier age than men.

Overall, these statistics reflect the poor status of women's health and suggest that the health system is both underprovided and underutilized. Although we do not have data for Bukoba, the district where we conducted this study, the status of women, as noted by our health system respondents, is very similar to the national figures reported above.

Data and Methodology

The study was conducted in the Bukoba rural district, one of the districts in the Kagera region, which is located in the extreme northwestern corner of Tanzania. The 2002 census shows that the Kagera region has a population of approximately 2 million people, with an average annual growth rate of 5.2 per cent. The people of Kagera are relatively homogenous in that they are of Bantu origin with few exceptions, with the Wahaya forming the largest tribe. The major economic activity in the region is agriculture, mainly for subsistence, engaging about 90 per cent of the regional population, with women contributing 70 per cent of labour. The most important food crops are banana and beans. Coffee, cotton and tea are the main cash crops although they are grown at a subsistence level.

The Bukoba rural district has two hospitals, five health centres, fifty-three dispensaries and forty-four MCH clinics. Figures from the 1998 regional profile report shows that the district has a population per hospital of 193,861; the population per bed is 2,041; the population per doctor is 96,930 and the population per dispensary is 7,314. The number of hospitals in the region has not increased since 1985, and there has been a very small increase in the number of health centres from thirteen in 1985 to fifteen in 1996 (*Kagera Region Socio-economic Profile* 1998). In 1996, Kagera reported the highest rate of home deliveries with 67.7 per cent of all deliveries taking place at home, compared with a national average of 47 per cent recorded in the same year (Bureau of Statistics and Macro International 1997). Malaria is the primary cause of death in the region. In 1996, malaria was reported to account for 43 per cent of all deaths. AIDS is reported as the second most important cause of death after malaria, accounting for 12 per cent of all deaths. Kagera was the first region in Tanzania where the first case of AIDS was reported. In 1996, the cumulative number of AIDS cases was 7,429. By 1998 the epidemic had left behind 100,000 orphans (*Kagera Region Socio-economic Profile* 1998). Proceedings from the Kagera Health Sector Reform first annual conference in 2001 report HIV prevalence of 9.5 per cent among pregnant women in the region, and 26 per cent HIV prevalence among blood donors in the rural areas.

For the study, we purposely selected four health facilities in the district on consultation with the DMO, based on criteria of geographical spread, utilization and available health services. Four villages were then selected based on the location of health facilities. Two villages

Table 8.2 Data and methods

Method	Type of respondent	Number of respondents
FGDs	Community leaders	33 (4 FGDs)
	Men	34 (4 FGDs)
	Women	61 (8 FGDs)
Semi-structured interviews (in depth interviews)	Women of reproductive age	100
Key informant interviews	CHMT member	4
	DED's office	2
	Health staff	19
	Community elders	4
	National stakeholders	5
Facility exit interviews	Women attending ANC and STI services	80

ANC, antenatal care; FGDs, focus group discussions; STI, sexually transmitted infection.

were close to a health facility (Bunazi and Kikomelo) and the other two villages were located far from the health facilities (Msira and Igaluagati). From the selected villages, 100 women were sampled for the interviews, twenty-five per village. We interviewed key informants in the Community Health Management Team (CHMT) and in the district administrative office. At the health facility level, all heads of wards and sections at the district hospital and health centres were interviewed. Other individuals interviewed included district executive director (DED), district planning officer (DPO), heads of existing health projects and district administrative secretary (DAS). At the national level, interviews were carried out with different stakeholders, including MoH and donors (the data and methods are also shown in Table 8.2).

Living on the Margins and a Gender Dimension of User Fees

Any analysis of how user fees in health care can affect women's decisions to seek care for themselves has to note that user fees are charges to the individual for health care at the time of utilization. Unlike other forms of financing health care, such as prepayment or insurance, it prescribes the timing of the payment that coincides with the need for health care (Abel-Smith and Rawall 1992). There are three main arguments to support user fees. One is that fees are nominal and an amount that even poor people can pay since they are already paying for private health care; revenue from user fees will lead to improvement in quality of services including availability of drugs; and finally, there are exemptions in place to protect the poor who are unable to pay. In reality, the experience of user fees has been very different.

Recent reviews of user fees in Africa suggest that user fees are in fact regressive, that is, they hurt the poor proportionately more than those who are better off unless there are effective safety nets in place (Nanda 2002). Studies from Tanzania, Ghana, Swaziland, Zaire and Uganda suggest that the introduction of user fees is often followed by a subsequent decrease in service utilization. The magnitude of this drop in utilization is often greater and occurs over a longer period for the poorer population (Nanda 2002). A study from Swaziland suggests that those most affected by fee increases are patients who have low incomes, who need to make multiple visits or who decide that their ailment is not serious enough to justify costs (Yoder 1989).

The studies that specifically look at women's health care services validate that women's demand for health care is price-sensitive, and that their utilization has tended to drop when fees have been charged. Evidence from several African countries suggests that use of maternal health care services is affected when fees are introduced or revoked. A study from Zimbabwe noted a decline in prenatal use in the early 1990s when user fees were strongly enforced. Another study of the impact of user fees for antenatal care in government hospitals in three districts of Tanzania showed a 53.4 per cent decline in utilization after fees were introduced (Hussein and Mujinja 1997). A study from Nigeria reports that when user fees were introduced, maternal deaths in the Zaria region rose by 56 per cent along with a decline of 46 per cent in the number of deliveries in the main hospital (Ekwempu et al. 1990). In contrast, in South Africa antenatal care attendance improved after charges were revoked (Schneider and Gilson 2000).

One of the main arguments in support of user fees rests on the assumption that fees are nominal and that people do pay for health care, so in effect there is ability to pay for fee-dependent health care. Women's ability to pay user fees, however, needs to be reconsidered from a gender perspective, taking into account their access to and control over cash resources within their household and decision-making about health. Women in subsistence economies may not have access to or control over cash income. Where women are struggling to make ends meet, either through loans from microcredit programmes or from their subsistence of informal employment, they have little to save for contingencies, which include health and sickness.

Furthermore, because illness necessitates reallocation of time and resources within a household, a person's status in the household will determine the reallocations made towards that person's health care. In a qualitative household study in Uganda on coping strategies to pay for health care, women were found to have the primary responsibility towards their own and their children's health, while it is frequently men who have available cash, particularly that derived from the sale of cash crops (Lucas and Nuwagaba 1999). The burden of taking care of the sick falls on women, which not only increases their workload but also makes less time available for earning an income, creating a vicious cycle of 'inability to pay'.

Illness is often unpredictable and cannot be anticipated; therefore fee-based health care systems presume that poor households have an inbuilt insurance against such income shocks. For the rural poor, this would be from savings or community funds that would allow them to borrow against their future stream of income. In reality, we find that health and illness are the major reasons for poor households going into debt, precisely because of a lack of savings or any other safety nets (Breman and Shelton 2001).

In Tanzania, the fees at 1,000–2,000 Tsh (50 cents–1 dollar) indeed do seem nominal. The total cost for in-patient services may range from Tsh 1,800 to 8,000, including 500 Tsh for a registration card and 1,000 Tsh for a bed. However, poor women on average may earn no more than 500 Tsh a day from rural work or selling a handful of coffee beans; that is, they live below the poverty line of $1 or 2,000 Tsh a day. An average household earns about 5,000–15,000 Tsh a month. A woman's ability to pay has to be viewed within the context of her ability to earn an income, her control over that income and the prices of other commodities that she needs to buy for the survival of her household.

Of the 100 women interviewed, forty-seven were involved in some income-generating activities. The main income generation projects were agricultural. Women sell beans and groundnuts as their main source of income. Some women were also involved in hiring out their labour seasonally for clearing farms, and others in selling food products, such as buns (sweet bread). Overall, women are involved in lower paying income-generating projects relative to men. Agricultural crops are gender stratified by who controls their production. The non-food income crops, such as coffee and a special kind of banana, commonly referred to as 'strong banana', used for making local brew, are principally men's crops. Women are mainly involved in the production of food crops, such as beans, groundnuts and bananas that are used for household consumption. Even when these crops are sold in the market the prices are not very high. Despite their low income, women contribute significantly to family expenses.

In all of the sixteen group discussions done in the four study villages with community leaders, men and women, there were repeated accounts of people's inability to pay fees and other costs of seeking health care. The major explanation of people's inability to pay was stated to be the collapse of the local coffee economy. Coffee is the main cash crop in the district, but in the past five years coffee has performed very poorly. Our respondents reported that they faced difficulties in selling their harvest, and hence many families had little cash to pay for different services, including education and health services.

> The disease does not inform you as to when will it come so that you start saving. In fact, there is no need to hide, this is a big problem because those who do not have money they have not been able to go to the hospital once they fall sick – go to traditional healers or wait at home to die.
>
> An elderly woman aged 66, FGD – Msira Village

> The costs are too high for the ordinary people because when some one gets treatment from the government health facility like Rubale Dispensary and being asked to pay Tsh 15,000 or Tsh 20,000 within a week, it is too expensive – we don't have money nowadays – coffee prices nowadays are so low. Worse still we don't know where to sell our coffee – private buyers have been barred from buying coffee in the region.
>
> Male participant, FGD community leaders, Kikomelo village

Of the forty-seven women engaged in income-generating activities, forty reported to have some savings from their income. Some women have also organized themselves into savings groups that have monthly or weekly contributions ranging from Tsh 500 to 2,000. Most of these savings are so small that they get spent on ongoing daily household expenses. Moreover, not all women have control over the income they earn. Of the forty-seven women, five reported that they have limited control over the money they earn, because they hand over the money to their husbands. While the opportunity to earn an income for some women can assure them access to user fee-dependent health services, for others, participating in income-generating projects only adds to their workload.

> I have a small garden that I grow beans ... my husband is the one who decides how the money should be spent ... I can not refuse, he will take the money by force.
>
> Married, 27 years, four children, Bunazi village

> I did not have much say as to where I will have my baby, it was my husband who decided that a TBA will assist me ... he had his own reasons, it was only after there were complications that he decided to take me to the hospital ... I lost the baby.
>
> Divorced, 20 years, no children, Msira village

One of the public health arguments against user fees is the effect on an individual's ability to seek health care in a timely manner. This is especially relevant in a context where maternal mortality and morbidity is high often for reasons that are mostly preventable. We observe this with greater clarity through women's narratives as they specifically talk about lack of income as a constraint to access fee-dependent health care. For example, of the forty women who had their deliveries with a skilled attendant at a health facility, thirty-three were involved in income-generating activities, whereas only seventeen out of the sixty women who had their deliveries at home were involved in any income-generation activity. However, it is important to note that access to income is not the sole factor that is likely to influence whether a woman delivers in a health facility or not. Despite having the cash, women may need to make trade-offs between seeking health care and using the money for other things, such as food, fuel, child's health or education.

> We may try to find money but still you may not get. I have been suffering for three weeks and when I now get Tsh 500, I have come and got the treatment for this baby and I am leaving without my treatment because the money was not enough, I was told to pay Tsh 1,100 that I don't have.
>
> Married, 32-year-old woman suffering from a reproductive tract infection, Bunazi Health Centre

> I attended clinic throughout my pregnancy ... initially I had thought that I will have collected enough money, but other things [expenses] keep coming up that by the time I went into labour I did not have money so I had to ask the assistance of a traditional birth attendant ...
>
> Married, 32 years, four children, Bunazi village

Women's ability to pay is affected not only by user fees but by other informal or hidden costs in addition to fees. Several studies have reported other out-of-pocket costs for maternity care such as gloves, syringes and drugs. The effective decision for the very poor may be not to seek care at all, or to go to traditional healers or resort to partial treatment. However, there are likely to be further costs if care is sought only after an illness is severe, or from partial or ineffective treatment been sought earlier.

> The nurses informed me during the clinic that I need to buy and prepare for all these things, plastic sheet Tsh 750, gloves Tsh 500 and wash basin Tsh 800. I told my husband and kept some money. They say delivery services are free – but the facilities are not there. In addition, if you need a safe delivery, give 5,000 to a nurse (informal payments) – then you will be okay. Now we are used to paying.
> Married, 34 years, six children, Facility Exit, Bunazi Health Centre

> Sometimes you may need the drugs but they will want you to pay Tsh 200. This is a lot of money … when you are being admitted they will want you to pay Tsh 1,000 for a hospital bed. In addition to this, we pay money for kerosene, which is about Tsh 230; leave aside that we are supposed to prepare the food for the patient … can we afford it? And I have heard that the kerosene is used by the health workers for personal uses. That is why sometimes we decide to avoid using this facility and prefer to buy the drugs from the pharmacies because we know that with Tsh 800 you can get the drugs.
> Married, 37 years, five children, Facility Exit, Rubale Dispensary

There was unanimous agreement in all the focus group discussions that the availability of drugs has improved as a result of user fees. Even when essential medicines that are supposed to be free are 'officially unavailable', health staff may offer to make them available to those patients who are willing to pay a price (Mamdani and Bangser 2004). Once again, it is those who are the poorest who can easily be left out of the calculus. In interviews, women across the board report that even though drugs were available they were still unable to pay for them or for fee-dependent health care.

> In fact the drugs are available but in order to get them you must have the money and if you don't have then, you won't be able to get drugs … for people who don't have the money they don't come, they remain in the village …
> Married woman, 44 years, six children, FGD Bunazi

I was sick a few weeks ago but thinking of going to the hospital ... when you know you have no money and there is no way I can get the money for drugs from the hospital, I had Tsh 100 so I decided to go and buy some aspirin until when I get money.

Married, 32 years, three children, Rubale Dispensary

Slightly more than half of the women respondents from facility exit interviews stated that they have had to delay treatment because of lack of money to pay for medical costs. This was also resonated in interviews with health providers. Most providers agree that cost sharing has prevented the poor from accessing health services (decline in utilization of health services) or that people delay seeking treatment until conditions are critical, while others think that cost sharing has helped prevent misuse of drugs.

People (the patients) are staying at home because they lack money ... even if you will decide to move around, you will find some people are sick but they don't have money ... some go to traditional healers, while some wait at home to die. What will they do?

Health worker – Bugandika Dispensary

The impact of cost sharing on women's reproductive health illness came up at various levels of the research. Women reported having to wait longer before visiting a health facility because of lack of cash to cover indirect costs (hiring a bicycle, especially in villages far from a health facility) and direct costs (consultation fees and in some instances they had to pay for medication). Women's limited access to cash resources limits their access to health services. Out of the seventy-two women reporting chronic reproductive tract infections, thirty explained that they were discouraged from seeking health care from a modern health facility because of the user fees they were required to pay for consultation or for drugs. While, in theory, cost sharing in government facilities in the study area has exempted antenatal and post-natal care services, family planning services, and childbirth and STI services, in practice, women are forced to pay for treatment of reproductive morbidity and childbirth. Even if women are exempt from fees per se they are still asked to bring materials for deliveries, or pay for drugs or 'better' health care, which in some cases could mean any health care.

I have been having pains in the lower abdomen ... I have also been having heavy vaginal discharge, like sour milk with a bad smell ... I did not go to the hospital because of the costs, so I decided to use some traditional medicine.

Married, 29 years, three children, Bunazi village

I have been having serious back and abdomen pains for some time now. People say it is malaria, so I have just used some traditional medicine. It has not helped ... if I decide to go to the hospital, I think of the money I will have to pay. What if they say 20,000, will I afford that?

> Married, 34 years, five children, Igulugati village

Women have very limited knowledge about exemptions and most are unaware about who is exempt and for what services. Focus group discussions with community members revealed that many people at the community level are not aware of the exemptions for cost sharing. The exemptions are meant for the vulnerable groups such as pregnant women, poor families and the elderly. There has been inadequate planning to raise awareness of the exemptions prior to the implementation of cost sharing. For example, while pregnant mothers are exempt from paying user fees, they are asked to pay some costs during antenatal visits to clinics and buy gloves and a plastic sheet for delivery in a health facility.

When we were in the seminars with the District Medical Officer we were told each and everything but we had a different understanding ... so when they told us that the services for pregnant mothers and children would be free ... I did so and when I went to present the first returns I paid Tsh 9,000 from my own sources ... they said that every drug which is sent to us is being counted for.

> Health worker – name of facility withheld for
> confidentiality purposes

Conclusion

Growth and development has been slow in Tanzania and its primary export, coffee, has faced a decline in the world market. The lack of robustness of cash crops, such as coffee, and declining trade taxes has had direct implications for poor people in rural Tanzania. The consequent and dramatic shift in the role of the government with regard to public provision of health care has implied that people now have to pay nominally for their health care. It is well known that the poor face a highly elastic demand for health care, and increasing the price of health services does affect their utilization by either delaying or not seeking care. We see testimonies to this in women's narratives presented in this paper.

Unlike other forms of financing health care, such as prepayment or insurance, user fees can both prescribe the timing of the payment and coincide with the need for health care. These narratives underscore the fact that women's ability to pay fees is often conditioned by factors out of their control, such as lack of cash, lack of control over household income or dependence on seasonal income. They may be forced to make trade-offs between seeking health care, purchasing food or fuel or seeking traditional care that may not address their health needs adequately. User fees impose an added constraint on household budgets for women deciding whether to seek timely and quality health care. Given the unpredictability of illness and added constraints, women, as producers of health care for themselves and their children, have to negotiate both the household budget and their social circumstances to seek health care.

Women also face gender inequities, such as those restricting their mobility, economic autonomy and choice of employment. During their key productive years, which correspond with their reproductive life span, women have unequal reproductive and sexual health needs and opportunities compared with men. Over a lifetime women face chronic morbidities related to their gender vulnerabilities, such as coercive sex, HIV/AIDS or violence, necessitating repeated contact with their health care system. However, women often have low levels of entitlement within the health care system, often due to provider biases and attitudes, which again restrict their choice to seek health care.

To those dependent on agricultural income, access to cash is seasonal and restricts the ability to pay for health care. In addition, women often do not control earnings from cash crops even if they do the work on the farms. If a woman has a condition that needs regular care or treatment, she may not be able to afford this over a longer period even if she can pay the 'nominal' fees at any one point in time. We need to ensure that effective safety nets are in place, be it in exemptions or waivers, before user fees are actually applied, especially for services that are disproportionately used by poor women, such as primary and secondary health care. Women also need access to income and savings, and community insurance schemes. The millennium development goals, a new landmark for development in this decade, cannot be achieved if strategies for health reform neutralize the intended goals of reducing maternal mortality by a third or poverty by half.

Notes

The primary data used in this chapter is from the multi-site health sector reform studies carried out by The Centre for Health and Gender Equity and

its partner institutions in Tanzania. The author acknowledges her colleagues in Tanzania, Emanuel Makundi from the National Institute of Malaria Research and Joyce Nyoni from the University of Dar es Salaam, who are the partners and the principle investigators for this study in Tanzania. The report on the health sector reform study carried out in Tanzania is referred to in this chap-
The author also thanks her colleagues Anna Brit Coe, Anastasia Trudell and Shari Doi for their comments and suggestions on this chapter.

References

Abel-Smith, B., and P. Rawall (1992) 'Can the Poor Afford "Free" Health Services? A Case Study of Tanzania', *Health Policy and Planning*, vol. 7, : 329–41.

Bureau of Statistics (Tanzania) and Macro International Inc. (1997) *Tanzania Demographic and Health Survey 1996*, Calverton, MD: Bureau of Statistics and Macro International.

Bureau of Statistics (Tanzania) and Macro International Inc. (1999) *Tanzania Demographic and Health Survey 1999*, Calverton, MD: Bureau of Statistics and Macro International.

Breman, A., and C. Shelton (2001) 'Structural Adjustment and Health: A Literature Review of the Debate, its Role Players and Presented Empirical Evidence', CMH Working Papers Series WG6, Paper 6, Geneva: World Health Organization.

Ekwempu, G, *et al.* (1990) 'Structural Adjustment and Health in Africa', Letter to *The Lancet*, vol. 336, no. 7: 56–7.

Gilson, L. (1997) 'The Lessons of User Fee Experience in Africa', *Health Policy and Planning*, vol. 12, no. 4: 273–85.

Hussein, A.K., and P.G.M. Mujinja (1997) 'Impact of User Charges on Government Health Facilities in Tanzania', *East African Medical Journal*, 74, no. 12: 751–7.

Kagera Region Socio-economic Profile (1998) Dar es Salaam, Tanzania: Planning Commission and Regional Commissioner's Office.

Khattry, B., and J. Mohan Rao (2002) *Fiscal Faux Pas?: An Analysis of the Revenue Implications of Trade Liberalization*, Amherst, MA: Department of Economics, University of Massachusetts.

Lucas, H. and A. Nuwagaba (1999) 'A Household Coping Strategies in Response to the Introduction of User Charges for Social Service: A Case Study on Health in Uganda', IDS Working Paper 86, Brighton: Institute of Development Studies.

Makundi, E., J. Nyoni and P. Nanda (2005) 'The Implications of Health Sector Reforms on Reproductive Health Services, The Case of Bukoba District – Kagera Region, Tanzania Study', Center for Health and Gender

Mamdani, M., and M. Bangser (2004) *Poor People's Experiences of Health Services in Tanzania, a Literature Review*, Women's Dignity Project, Dar es Salaam: Tanzania.

Ministry of Health (1997) *Report of Health Sector Reform Programme of Work 1998/99–2000/01*, Dar es Salaam, Tanzania: MoH.

Nanda, P. (2002) 'Gender Dimensions of User Fees: Implications on their Utilization of Health Care', *Reproductive Health Matters*, vol. 10, no. 20: 127–34.

Richey, L. (2004) 'From the Policies to the Clinics: The Reproductive Health Paradox in Post-Adjustment Health Care', *World Development*, vol. 32, no. 6: 923–40.

Schneider, H., and L. Gilson (2000) 'The Impact of Free Maternal Health Care in South Africa', in M. Berer and T.K. Ravindran (eds), *Safe Motherhood Initiatives: Critical Issues*, London: Reproductive Health Matters.

United Republic of Tanzania; Ministry of Health; National AIDS Control Programme; HIV/AIDS/STI Surveillance Report January – December, 2000; Report Number 15.

UNDP (2001) The United Nations and the International/Millennium Declaration Development Goals (MDGs).

World Bank (2002) 'Tanzania at the Turn of the Century', Background Papers and Statistics 23738, February.

WHO (2001) 'Macroeconomics and Health: Investing in Health for Economic Development', Report of the Commission on Macroeconomics, Geneva: World Health Organization.

Yoder, R. (1989) 'Are People Willing and Able to Pay for Health Services?', *Social Science and Medicine*, vol. 29, no. 1: 35–42.

9

Tripping Up: AIDS, Pharmaceuticals and Intellectual Property in South Africa

Pranitha Maharaj and Benjamin Roberts

Introduction

AIDS is one of the most serious and urgent global health problems facing the world today. The United Nations Secretary General has declared the AIDS epidemic the most formidable development challenge to human life and dignity and the enjoyment of fundamental human rights (Declaration of Commitment on HIV/AIDS 2001). The disease has a strongly gendered dimension, with an estimated twelve to thirteen women infected for every ten men, and an average rate of infection that is five times higher for young girls than young boys in some countries in the region (UNAIDS 2000). The higher levels of HIV infection among women are a manifestation of gender inequalities, deeply rooted in patriarchal norms. In many societies, gender relations are characterized by an unequal balance of power, with women having less access than men to education, training and resources (Sivard 1995). As a result, not only are women rendered vulnerable to the sexual transmission of HIV infection, but their ability to access treatment, care and support is also affected (Rao Gupta 2000).

The discovery of antiretroviral (ARV) therapies has meant that tremendous progress has been made in the treatment of AIDS. Nevertheless, due to the exorbitant costs charged by pharmaceutical companies, these drugs are largely out of reach for the vast majority of the people living with HIV/AIDS. Consequently, men and women are dying prematurely because they cannot afford to purchase treatment.

Improving access to essential medicines in developing countries is therefore a pressing global health concern that could save innumerable lives. Over the last several years, there has been a growing recognition by the international community that concerted action is required for affordable prices and reliable health and supply systems, coupled with increased efforts to develop needed vaccines, drugs and other health technologies. This is reflected by the internationally agreed Millennium Development Goals (MDGs), which strongly prioritize health outcomes, specifically the need to improve maternal and child health outcomes, tackle the burden of HIV/AIDS and other major diseases, and provide access to affordable, essential drugs.

As discussed by White in Chapter 11, the global trade regime has resulted in the introduction of trade agreements that contain rules and commitments that have notable repercussions for, among other things, the availability and affordability of pharmaceuticals. For instance, concerns have been raised that the World Trade Organization's (WTO) Trade-Related Aspects of Intellectual Property Rights (TRIPS) Agreement, which provides 20 years of patent protection for pharmaceuticals, may perpetuate or even exacerbate the situation of unaffordable life-saving medication in many developing nations.

South Africa is by no means exceptional in this regard. The transformation of the health system in the country has been and remains an urgent priority for the democratic government. The right to have access to basic health care services, including reproductive health care, is also enshrined in the 1996 Constitution (Section 27.1a). The right to health implies that the government is responsible for prevention, treatment and control of diseases and the creation of conditions to ensure access to health facilities, goods and services required to be healthy (Braveman and Gruskin 2003). In an endeavour to make medicines more affordable and accessible to poor, AIDS-affected South Africans, the government introduced the *Medicines and Related Substances Control Amendment Act* in 1997. The measures contained in this legal framework became the focal point of one of the more notable trade-related legal disputes involving access to pharmaceuticals in developing countries.

This chapter focuses primarily on the gendered dimensions of access to HIV/AIDS treatment and examines the role of trade agreements in determining the supply of pharmaceuticals. In so doing, a number of themes are emphasised. The first of these relates to South Africa's use of the flexibilities in the TRIPS legal framework to defend a policy authorizing the implementation of affordable generic drugs to treat HIV/AIDS. This was done in defiance of threats of economic sanctions and legal action brought against the country by multinational drug companies for the infringement of patent rights. The outcome of the court case has played an important role in shaping debates on, and ultimately promoting access to, affordable essential medicines for developing countries within the parameters of the TRIPS Agreement.

The second theme focuses on the importance of strong political commitment and national leadership in ensuring the widespread availability of life-prolonging drugs for AIDS treatment. The South African government's vacillation on the introduction of ARV treatment has resulted in a situation where access to ARVs in the public sector is severely circumscribed and narrowly focused. The role of civil society in ensuring access to affordable drugs is equally vital. Third, while the South African government's recent commitment to provide treatment and its decision to introduce ARV treatment programmes is commendable, the process of implementing these is likely to be costly, complicated and hindered by infrastructural constraints.

Finally, despite the decision to begin rolling out nevirapine to HIV-positive pregnant women, the reality remains that women continue to be burdened by persisting gender inequalities in society. The complex relationship between HIV/AIDS and gender inequality signifies that responses to the pandemic need to extend far beyond affordable treatment and drugs. They must, as a matter of urgency, encompass wider political, economic and cultural issues. A particular emphasis needs to be placed on challenging the patriarchal values and norms that render women vulnerable to HIV infection and influence care-seeking behaviour.

The Status and Impact of the AIDS Epidemic

With estimates of between four and six million, South Africa has the largest number of people living with HIV/AIDS in the world (Ijumba et al. 2004). The results from antenatal sentinel surveillance surveys show that HIV prevalence increased from less than 1 per cent in 1990 to almost 27 per cent in 2002 (Doherty and Colvin 2004). The level of HIV prevalence varies sharply by age and sex. The level of HIV infection among women increases steadily and peaks among 25–29-year-olds, whereas it increases more slowly among men and peaks at a slightly older age group. As in other parts of the African continent, young women in South Africa are particularly at increased risk. The level of HIV prevalence among women aged 15–24 years was 12 per cent, compared with 6 per cent among young men (NM and HSRC 2002). Women often become infected earlier and at higher levels than their male counterparts (Harrison et al. 2001).

The greater risk of HIV infection among women is attributable to a complex mix of biological, social and economic factors. Although physiology has a significant bearing on this situation, it is arguably women's lack of control over their bodies and their sexual lives, reinforced by their social and economic inequality that increases their risk of HIV infection (Albertyn 2003: 597). Traditional views on the roles and responsibilities of women have meant that they continue to serve as primary caregivers, fulfilling reproductive and (unpaid) domestic functions, such as housework, fetching and heating water, cooking and caring for children, old people and sick people. This constrains their access to education, training, land and productive assets, as well as restricting the time available for paid productive work and the choice of income-earning activities (Budlender 2004). The temporal demands of this unpaid care work have also been shown to have a negative impact on women's mobility and hence utilization of health-care services, especially in rural localities (McCray 2004).

Gender and cultural norms, by skewing access to resources, have additionally served to exacerbate the feminization of poverty. The poverty rate among female-headed households in South Africa is considerably higher than male-headed households since they are more likely to be rural, have fewer adults of working age and reliant on remittances and state transfer income. Female unemployment rates are also higher and the wage gap between male and female earnings persists (Woolard and Leibbrandt 2001). The economic dependency of women severely constrains their ability to adopt risk-reducing strategies and contributes to their increased vulnerability to HIV infection. Changing patterns in sexual practices (the lowering of age at first sexual intercourse) and the age differentials between girls and their first male sex partners further increases the risk of HIV infection (Wood et al. 1998). For countries with high levels of violence against women, such as South Africa, the strong risk of HIV transmission during violent or forced sexual encounters is also of grave concern.

The nature of the epidemic in South Africa raises important questions about the extent to which the health system is responding to the increasing demands being imposed on it. In the absence of treatment, individuals can expect to experience prolonged periods of illness that are likely to multiply in frequency, intensity and duration (Barnett and Whiteside 2002). Loewenson and Whiteside (2001) estimate that the AIDS epidemic has increased the burden of disease up to sevenfold in highly affected African countries. As a result, the demand for and cost of public health care services has increased, crowding out other health conditions and doubling bed occupancy rates. In some provinces in South Africa, almost 46 per cent of hospital admissions are associated with AIDS-related illnesses (Shisana et al. 2003). Health services are also adversely impacted by the loss of staff due to factors such as the burden of increasing patient load, illness, absenteeism and low staff morale. The increase in the number of AIDS patients at health facilities has meant an increased workload for health workers, often without compensation. In some cases, they also have to deal with being HIV positive. A study of health workers in four provinces found that 16 per cent of health personnel in the public and private sectors were HIV positive (Shisana et al. 2003). Health workers are therefore faced with increasing emotional and physical strain and job dissatisfaction (Kober and Van Damme 2004). In such a situation, it is hardly surprising that large proportions of health workers are leaving the country. Between 1989 and 1997, more than 82,000 health workers are estimated to have emigrated (Padarath et al. 2003). The health situation is further exacerbated by the racially segregated and unequal health sector inherited from South Africa's apartheid past, which was characterized by unnecessary duplication and fragmentation aimed at strengthening government control rather than ensuring efficient and effective services (Buch 2001).

Intellectual Property and AIDS Treatment

Over the last decade, tremendous progress has been made in the treatment of AIDS. The discovery of ARV drugs has revolutionized the treatment of AIDS (Martinson et al. 2003). While there is no cure for AIDS, these drugs may slow the onset of the disease and also prevent the emergence of opportunistic infections, such as tuberculosis (POST 2001). The US Food and Drug Administration currently list over forty approved therapies that slow or interrupt viral replication or treat opportunistic infections (Bloom and River Path Associates 2000: 2171).

In some countries, AIDS has become a chronic illness because people can afford to pay for treatment to prolong their lives. In these countries, the number of AIDS deaths has declined dramatically over the last few years. In the United States, for example, deaths declined from 49,895 in 1995 to 17,171 in 1998 (Bloom and River Path Associates 2000: 2171). However, the situation in many developing countries remains bleak. Due to the exorbitant costs charged by pharmaceutical companies, often a consequence of strong intellectual property protection, these life-prolonging drugs are largely out of reach for the vast majority of people living with HIV/AIDS. Estimates suggest that up to 95 per cent of people living with HIV/AIDS in developing countries would report that they have no regular access to ARV treatment (Matowe 2004).

The global trade in medicine is governed by national laws and regulations and international rules such as those in the WTO's Agreement on TRIPS. The TRIPS Agreement, which came into force in 1995, provides the minimum standards in the field of intellectual property protection for WTO member states. A major provision requires member states to adopt US style patents, which apply both to any invention of a pharmaceutical product or process that fulfils established criteria and lasts for a minimum of 20 years. The deadline for implementing these TRIPS standards depends on the level of development of the country involved. Most developing countries have until the end of 2005, while certain less developed countries have until 2016. What is novel and distinct about TRIPS is that developing countries must alter existing national legislation to tighten up property rights and widen coverage to all areas including medicines and pharmaceuticals. Pharmaceutical products are not ordinarily articles of trade because consumers are not in a position to determine the quality of products. Also, pharmaceutical drugs play an integral part in the realization of a basic human right, namely the right to health. Prior to the TRIPS Agreement, a substantial number of developing countries did not adequately cover intellectual property rights for medicines and pharmaceutical products. In addition, patent coverage was highly inconsistent between some developing countries, ranging from as little as three years (Thailand) to as long as sixteen years (South Africa). These conditions generally favoured the local production of less expensive generic medicines where possible (Williams 2001).

For developing countries, perhaps one of the most critical issues emanating from the TRIPS Agreement is the impact of extending intellectual property protection on the price of patented drugs and, in turn, access to essential medicines for poor people (DFID 2004). In many developing countries, the poor often have to pay for their own drugs because state provision is usually selective and resource-constrained (CIPR 2002). While the importance of medicine prices for poor consumers in developing countries is self-evident, it is worth emphasizing that should TRIPS increase the amount a sick person has to pay for medication, she would have less income for basic necessities, such as food and shelter. Alternatively, forgoing the medicine because it is not available or affordable is likely to contribute to increased morbidity and mortality (CIPR 2002). The TRIPS Agreement is likely to impact negatively on the abilities of countries to protect their public health and also weaken the support systems of households and communities. It is to also likely adversely to affect women because they often have to care for the sick, and at the same time assume primary responsibility for providing food and maintaining other basic household needs, especially when the male head of the household falls ill.

Theoretically, the implementation of the TRIPS Agreement by most countries in 2005 signifies that pharmaceutical products will be afforded twenty years patent protection, making access to generic versions of patented medicines more difficult for poorer countries. Safeguards were included in the agreement as a means of enabling governments to overcome patent barriers when needed. While this does introduce some flexibility into TRIPS, it has also been the source of a number of vigorously contested political struggles in recent years. The TRIPS Agreement has raised intense international debate, due to concerns that its implementation may entail increases in the price of pharmaceuticals, which may reduce access to life-saving drugs, especially in developing countries. The concern that stronger patent protection may mean price increases has led certain critics to assert that the agreement supports the economic and technological domination of the West (Petchesky 2003). According to this view, the agreement severely constrains the trade of pharmaceuticals in order to protect the profit margins of western drug producers at the expense of the infected populations in developing countries (Petchesky 2003). It is further suggested that patent laws and parallel licensing should be reassessed to ensure greater assistance to those infected in the developing world and that through these revisions, those living in developing countries would be given wider access to life-saving ARVs. While the debate on the public health aspects of TRIPS deals primarily with the cost of medicines for diseases such as AIDS, malaria and tuberculosis, other public health issues also warrant attention. For instance, in developing countries, numerous women die from debilitating gender-specific illnesses for which the required medicines are prohibitively expensive and there may be no generic substitutes available. Unlike the AIDS pandemic, the numbers involved may be too small to call for a national emergency, so the problem may demand governmental intervention to secure cheaper drugs (Williams 2001).

Proponents of the TRIPS Agreement argue that patent protection is not the most important factor impeding access to AIDS drugs in developing countries. Instead, they tend to emphasize the lack of spending on health care and the absence of an adequate health infrastructure to administer medicines safely and effectively (IIPI 2000; CIPR 2002). Improper use may contribute to the development of drug resistance, apart from being ineffective. In the case of HIV, where the virus mutates readily, wide distribution of ARVs without the development of adequate infrastructure may contribute to the emergence of drug resistance (IIPI 2000; CIPR 2002). It is also argued that generic versions of patented drugs may be of substandard quality or even dangerous (IIPI 2000; CIPR 2002). This is largely because many developing countries do not have the technical, financial or human resources that are required to monitor the quality of drug products (IIPI 2000). In order to help dispel concerns about delivery mechanism for AIDS drugs, the WHO issued the first treatment guidelines for using ARVs in resource-constrained settings and a list of manufacturers of patented and generic products (including eleven ARVs) that meet WHO quality standards as suppliers to UN agencies (CIPR 2002).

The pharmaceutical industry has consistently argued that protecting intellectual property rights is fundamental for stimulating and sustaining further drug research and development (R&D). Innovations require considerable financial investment, and if an invention does not have patent protection, the inventor may not be able to recover his/her losses or profit from that investment. As a result, there is limited incentive for innovation and this is likely to impact negatively the availability of new drugs to treat diseases (Foreman 2002). The discovery and development of medicines targeted at parasitic and infectious diseases in developing countries has virtually halted, the reason being that pharmaceutical manufacturers in developed and developing countries cannot recover the cost of R&D for such products (T'Hoen 2003). According to the Pharmaceutical Research and Manufacturers of America (PhRMA), which represents the major research-based pharmaceutical and biotechnology companies in the United States, $32.2 billion was invested in discovering and developing new medicines in 2003 (PhRMA 2004). What they fail to indicate is that a large proportion of this investment is spent on advertising and marketing as well as benefits to the top executives of the company. A study by researchers at the Stanford Center for Research in Disease Prevention estimated that the industry spent $12.7 billion promoting its products in 1998 alone (Selis 2003). Some commentators have suggested that the costs will be substantially reduced if R&D is shifted to developing countries. For example, the senior vice-president of medicine manufacturer Ranbaxy Laboratories in India estimates that the costs of R&D in his country are approximately 30 per cent of those in the US (Foreman 2002: 9).

The global intellectual property rights (IPR) system is exceedingly inequitable, with almost 97 per cent of patents being held by developed countries possessing both the experience and expertise to undertake R&D (Matowe 2004: 719). Moreover, the exacting administrative processes associated with intellectual property rights tend to dissuade local-level research and efforts by people with limited resources, especially women (Fosse 2002). It has been argued that the enforcement of the TRIPS Agreement will adversely affect local manufacturing capacity in developing countries and ultimately eradicate an important source of generic quality drugs on which developing countries rely (Ford 2003). Thus the imposition of intellectual property rights at varying levels of development had the possibility of 'consolidating an international division of labour whereunder northern countries generate innovations and southern countries constitute the market for resulting products and services' (Correa 2000: 5). Some commentators also argue that lowering prices in developing countries is unlikely to make a significant financial dent in the pharmaceutical industry (Weissman 1999). The industry is concentrated in the north, with 80 per cent of sales and more than 80 per cent of profits originating mostly in the United States and Europe, but also Japan and other wealthier parts of Asia. In 2002, Africa accounted for only 1.3 per cent of the entire worldwide sales of pharmaceutical products while Southeast Asia and China accounted for 5 per cent (Berger 2001; Matowe 2004). Thus, such marginal markets are unlikely to have any significant impact on incentives to innovate. According to Berger (2001: 34), the major concern for drug companies is not the threat to intellectual property rights in Africa per se, 'but the impact on more lucrative markets in wealthier countries, accompanied by the fear that cheaper drugs may flood such markets' (Baker 2002). More specifically, they remain apprehensive about a situation whereby low manufacturing costs of generic drugs could fuel demands for the major pharmaceuticals to reduce their prices, and a situation whereby cheap generics are re-exported by developing countries to the north (Baker 2002).

Patently Defiant: South Africa versus the 'Big Pharma'

South Africa was the focal point of one of the more notable trade-related legal disputes involving access to pharmaceuticals in developing countries in recent years, triggered by the introduction of a supposedly WTO/TRIPS compliant law. The South African *Medicines and Related Substances Control Amendment Act* (No. 90 of 1997) aimed to provide a legal framework for national drugs policy and contained measures to make medicines more affordable and accessible.[1] The Act gave the government the power to override patent rights in the pharmaceutical sector on public health grounds. It seemed that this would enable the health minister to permit the use of parallel importing and the compulsory licensing of AIDS drugs. Both compulsory licensing and parallel imports can be used as mechanisms to lower prices for consumers and thus undercut multinational drug companies. Parallel importing involves the procurement of products from another country where they are sold at a lower price, and thus trading in parallel with the local seller of the same (often more expensive) drugs (Gray and Matsebula 2001). Compulsory licensing enables a government temporarily to override a patent and domestically produce generic copies of patented drugs, provided that safeguards are followed and a royalty is paid to the patent holder. For example, a government may issue a compulsory licence to a company to produce generics when faced with a public health emergency, which may reduce the price of a certain drug by up to 70 per cent (Weissman 1999).

South Africa's *Medicines Act* provisions are legitimate from the perspective of the global trade regime if ARV patent suspension is viewed as fitting within TRIPS exceptions (Gupta 2003). Parallel importing and compulsory licensing are permissible under international trade rules.

Compulsory licensing is governed by Article 31 of TRIPS, which is sufficiently vague to provide member nations with significant flexibility as to how and when compulsory licensing might be used. Therefore, as a WTO member and given the belief that the AIDS pandemic constituted a public health emergency, South Africa interpreted the TRIPS exemptions as a licence for it rightfully to access cheap generic ARV drugs. Nonetheless, the act evoked widespread opposition from the pharmaceutical industry. The Pharmaceutical Manufacturers' Association of South Africa (PMA) and thirty-nine pharmaceutical companies[2] challenged it in the High Court, claiming it had violated intellectual property rights, contradicted the South African Constitution[3] and contravened WTO patent rules (Bond 1999). South Africa was also threatened with sanctions for infringing drug patents. Since the pharmaceutical industry represents a powerful lobby in the United States, it was somewhat unsurprising when, in 1998, the Clinton administration, Congress and the United States Trade Representative campaigned to persuade the South African government to modify the *Medicines Act*. A complaint was filed against the South African government with the WTO, and the country was placed on the 301 Watch List.[4]

The pharmaceutical industry faced mounting public pressure among workers, activists and the media to reassess the TRIPS Agreement. In 1998, Médecins Sans Frontières (MSF) announced a global campaign to lobby for improved access to essential medicines for poor countries. An activist campaign opposing the United States' threat of sanctions against South Africa was also initiated. Arguably, these collective efforts met with some success, particularly in relation to the notable policy shift that emerged in the United States during 2000. Apart from initiating a special session of the United Nations Security Council that declared the AIDS pandemic a threat to world security, President Clinton issued an executive order stating that the United States would not continue pursuing its threat of sanctions against African countries seeking to access cheaper AIDS drugs. The emphasis shifted to ensuring that, within the TRIPS Agreement parameters, AIDS-related drugs and medical technologies become more accessible and affordable in sub-Saharan Africa. In 2000, the Treatment Action Campaign (TAC), an NGO, initiated a defiance campaign and imported generic HIV drugs from Brazil and Thailand in violation of South Africa's patent law (Gupta 2003; Petchesky 2003). By importing generics, market competition for ARVs was created, which has increased availability and reportedly lowered the cost of ARV drugs.

At the Thirteenth International AIDS Conference in Durban in 2000, the TAC organized the first global march for access to treatment. Following the conference, the PMA reopened its lawsuit. In March 2001, the PMA case against South Africa was heard in the Pretoria High Court, while thousands demonstrated in thirty cities worldwide. MSF launched an international petition in an attempt to get the pharmaceutical companies to withdraw the lawsuit (Kasper 2001).[5] In April, following appeals from Kofi Annan and Nelson Mandela, the pharmaceutical companies suing the South African government announced the decision unconditionally to suspend their lawsuit. The PMA called this a 'negotiated settlement', whereby the South African government agreed to recommit to complying with TRIPS and all the involved parties agreed to work together to implement the legislation.

This resolution to the legal challenge against South Africa's *Medicines Act* prompted an acrimonious international debate between developing and developed countries over the implications of the TRIPS Agreement for access to essential medicines. The conflict focused in particular on the interpretation and scope of TRIPS flexibilities and how they could be used to meet public health needs in developing countries. These tensions ultimately informed the agenda of the Fourth WTO Ministerial Conference in Doha in November 2001. During this conference, the Declaration on TRIPS and Public Health was adopted, thereby signalling a final agreement between these two blocs of countries.

The Doha Declaration reconfirms the legal basis for member states to take appropriate measures to ensure that their TRIPS obligations do not frustrate the promotion of public health. This represents an important victory for developing countries, in that it strengthens the position of countries wanting to take advantage of the TRIPS flexibility (Cullet 2003). This milestone was followed by a 2003 WTO decision on the implementation of paragraph 6 of the Doha Declaration on the TRIPS Agreement and Public Health. This tasked the TRIPS Council with the development of a solution to the difficulties that WTO member governments that are unable to produce pharmaceuticals domestically could potentially face in making effective use of compulsory licensing under the TRIPS Agreement. However, Article 31(f) of the TRIPS Agreement limits the amount that countries manufacturing drugs can export when the drug is made under compulsory licence. This, in turn, affects countries unable to make medicines and wanting to import generics. Such countries would struggle to find countries able to supply them with drugs made under compulsory licensing. The 2003 Decision allows countries producing generic copies of patented products under compulsory licences to export the medicines to eligible importing poor countries.

Therefore, the outcome of the South African court case played a salient role in helping to clarify the margin for manoeuvre developing countries have in relation to the flexibilities contained in the TRIPS Agreement. By acting as a catalyst for the 2001 Doha Declaration and the 2003 Decision, the country has helped prevent recurrences of the situation in which a country is challenged if the measures adopted reflect a broad interpretation of TRIPS in the ongoing struggle to respond to health crises such as AIDS, malaria and tuberculosis.

Contested Realities: South Africa and the TAC

In the past few years, the global response to the AIDS epidemic has intensified. A number of donor organizations have committed funds to fighting the AIDS epidemic globally and in the most affected countries in southern Africa. Following the suspension of the court case against the South African government, five pharmaceutical companies made their drugs available at markedly reduced prices largely in response to pressure from social movements, and also potential competition from generic manufacturers (CIPR 2002: 37). For example, Table 9.1 shows that between October 2001 and January 2004, the cost of selected ARVs declined steadily but was still not competitive with the best priced generic drugs. As a result, these drugs remain out of reach for the bulk of the population living with HIV in developing countries. The suspension of the court case by the pharmaceutical industry paved the way for South Africa to import cheaper AIDS drugs, even if international companies possess the rights to manufacture and market the drugs in South Africa. However, at a press conference held immediately after the court cases, the Minister of Health was quick to caution that these drugs would not be immediately available in the public health sector.

In the past few years, the policies of the South African government have become the subject of widespread criticism, both nationally and internationally. The government has been frequently criticized for moving slowly against the epidemic. To date, high profile leadership

Table 9.1 Prices of selected ARVs between October 2001 and January 2004 (US$)

US$ cost per patient/year	Oct-01	Jun-02	Apr-03	Jan-04
Zidovudine (ZDV or AZT) 300 mg (GlaxoSmithKline)	584	584	274	212
Best priced generic	193	140	140	140
Nevirapine 200 mg (Boehringer Ingelheim)	438	438	438	438
Best priced generic	150	112	105	80
Combavir: 300 mg zidovudine + 150 mg lamivudine (GlaxoSmithKline)	730	730	329	237
Best priced generic	270	204	204	197

Source: Joint Health and Treasury Task Team (2004); Médecins Sans Frontières (2004).

in attacking the AIDS pandemic has been sorely lacking in South Africa. Instead, the President of South Africa, Thabo Mbeki, and Minister of Health, Dr Manto Tshabalala-Msimang, have become embroiled in a debate about the causal link between HIV and AIDS in the face of overwhelming and convincing evidence provided by the global scientific community. The government has shown widespread reluctance in introducing ARV treatment and has on occasion criticized researchers and activists for 'presenting drugs (or treatment) as the solution, rather than addressing poverty as a cause' (Schneider 2002: 94). In addition, researchers and activists who have called for ARV treatment have been accused by the government of being manipulated by the multinational pharmaceutical industry, motivated by profit (Mankahlana 2000).

In August 2001, the TAC brought an application against the South African government for failing to implement the prevention of mother-to-child transmission of HIV and held the government responsible for jeopardizing the lives of mothers and children.[6] At the Pretoria court hearing, the TAC argued that the government was violating the right to life, dignity and equality of HIV-positive pregnant women and their children, guaranteed by the constitution of South Africa, by failing to provide sufficient ARVs at affordable prices (Annas 2003). In the midst of the debate, the producer of nevirapine, Boehringer Ingelheim, announced its offer to provide the drug free of charge for a period of five years. In December 2001, the TAC won a lawsuit against the South African Minister of Health and nine provincial health ministers, compelling the government to provide nevirapine through the public health care system for the prevention of mother-to-child transmission. In July 2002, the Constitutional Court of South Africa, the country's highest court, affirmed the ruling stating that limiting nevirapine to a few pilot sites in the public sector violated the health care rights of women and newborns, and was unreasonable and thus unconstitutional. Although it recognized that health services in South Africa are under increasing pressure and that HIV is just one of the many illnesses that deserve attention, the HIV epidemic is of such a grave nature that the government has a constitutional duty to act.

Towards Comprehensive HIV Prevention: A Directional Shift

In South Africa, as in many other developing countries, access to ARVs in the public sector is severely limited. Of the almost 500,000 South Africans who could immediately benefit from highly active antiretroviral therapy (HAART), fewer than 8 per cent are currently receiving this treatment (Doherty and Colvin 2004: 206). The provision of ARVs in the public sector has been limited to the prevention of mother-to-child transmission and post-exposure prophylaxis. However, the situation has changed somewhat. In November 2003, the Cabinet publicly declared its approval of the Operational Plan for Comprehensive HIV and AIDS Care and Treatment, which included, first, the recognition that ARV medicines play a key role in the treatment of people living with HIV, and second, the provision of ARV medicines at health facilities for the treatment of people living with HIV/AIDS who cannot afford medicines easily accessible in the private health sector (Hassan 2004). The plan was to provide care within five years to 1.4 million South Africans and permanent residents who require it. As of January 2004, efforts were under way to assess facility preparedness for providing treatment services and also to identify the potential infrastructural constraints that may serve as barriers to the provision of this service (Doherty and Colvin 2004).

The introduction of ARVs is likely to have a huge impact on AIDS mortality, reducing considerably the number of deaths. The Joint

Health and Treasury Task Team (2004), established in South Africa to determine the feasibility of providing ARVs through the public sector, estimated that between 2003 and 2010, assuming a 20 per cent ARV coverage scenario, an estimated 293,000 deaths would be avoided until after 2010. If a 50 per cent coverage model is applied, 733,000 deaths would be avoided while a 100 per cent coverage model would avoid up to 1,712,000 deaths over the same period. However, the costs of providing comprehensive treatment for AIDS are quite considerable. In South Africa, there have been several studies modelling the cost of providing HAART. A model published in 2000 reported that if 25 per cent of the HIV-infected adult population received triple combination treatment from 2000 to 2005, life expectancy at birth is likely to increase by 3.1 years by 2005 at a cost of US$15,000 per life year gained. The total cost to the country estimated over the five-year period was US$19 billion (Wood et al. 2000). The costs of ARVs have steadily declined in the last few years but it still constitutes a substantial proportion of total costs of any HAART programme. As the price of ARVs goes down, other associated costs, such as CD4 and viral load tests and equipment contribute to overall costs (Stewart et al. 2004). In the long term, the simultaneous expansion of both prevention and treatment is critical. Unless the incidence of HIV infections is dramatically reduced, HIV treatment will not be able to keep pace with all those who need ARVs. Also, there is a great deal of variability in capacity at the district, provincial and national levels. At this stage, it seems unlikely that the government will be able to reach its original targets.

Access to treatment is strongly influenced by gender norms in society. In many societies, men are more likely than women to exercise control over sexual interactions and decision-making, which is likely to have direct implications for women's sexual and reproductive health and their access to treatment (Du Guerny and Sjoberg 1993). Sometimes women may be afraid to access or use services and treatment for fear of their partner's reaction, thus prolonging and perhaps intensifying their health problems. Moreover, women who are financially dependent on their husbands may not be able to seek treatment immediately because their husbands may refuse to assist them to access services. Learning their HIV-positive status may have severe repercussions for women, including stigma and discrimination, violence against women blamed for infecting partners, shame, anxiety and other psychological consequences (Hankins 2000). Hence, interventions are necessary to challenge traditional 'gender-biased attitudes of sexual shame and stigma, otherwise women will reject ARVs and the testing they require' (Petchesky 2003: 437).

Conclusion

This chapter has examined the relationship between international trade policy and access to life-saving ARV drugs, using South Africa as an example. The HIV/AIDS crisis and the high prices of pharmaceuticals to alleviate the disease have produced situations where developing countries have sought to explore specific interpretations of the TRIPS provisions or acted on the margin of TRIPS (Cullet 2003). From an international perspective, the legal challenge to South Africa's 1997 Medicines and Related Substances Control Amendment Act represents a notable case study in this regard. It has served to expose the tension that exists between intellectual property rights and human rights, as well as between the desire of multinational pharmaceutical companies to use patent law to protect profit margins and the moral imperative for national governments to address health inequalities.

On the national front, the victorious outcome of the court case presented an opportune moment for the government to make the global trade in pharmaceuticals work for the South African citizenry by scaling up access to ARV drugs. Nonetheless, the government's commitment came under question, not least because of assertions that HIV does not cause AIDS and the questioning of the effectiveness of ARVs. This resulted not only in global criticism and condemnation, but a protracted legal dispute between the government and the TAC over the provision of nevirapine to HIV-positive pregnant women at all state facilities. The subsequent judgement in favour of the TAC and the November 2003 Cabinet approval of a national HIV/AIDS treatment programme represent major landmarks in the endeavour to widen access to ARV treatment, especially to those with the fewest resources.

Despite the progress made in the international and national domains in ensuring that international trade agreements and the globalization of public health do not adversely affect women, salient concerns remain. While the cost of pharmaceuticals, especially ARV medicines, has fallen dramatically, the reality is that these cheaper drugs remain beyond the reach of those in need. At the end of 2003, only 400,000 out of an estimated five to six million people in low- and middle-income countries had access to ARV treatment, signifying that at least 90 per cent of those requiring life-saving treatment are not being reached (UNAIDS 2004: 101). While women outnumber men in terms of access to treatment services in South Africa, they are at the same time likely to be over-represented among those remaining without access for a number of reasons. Given that the high prices of potentially beneficial drugs most adversely affects those with the fewest resources and the lowest social status, the impact on women might be especially severe (Doyal 2002). Women are more susceptible to HIV infection than men, with the risk of infection being exacerbated by gender inequalities emanating from socio-cultural beliefs and practices that influence sexual behaviour.

The TAC's emphasis on access to ARV treatment for pregnant women in an effort to prevent mother-to-child transmission, while commendable, may also serve to perpetuate inequalities. It is imperative that treatment extends beyond a narrow focus on pregnant women. Adolescent girls and non-pregnant women in particular should also be target beneficiaries of such services. There also needs to be recognition of the role of factors other than cost in determining the access to treatment for women. For instance, health infrastructure is inadequate relative to the scale of the AIDS crisis, especially given the impact of the migration of health professionals with regard to loss of skills and quality of care (see Chapter 10 by Gerein and Green). Efforts promoting access to treatment therefore need to occur concomitantly with measures designed to improve not only the coverage but also maintain the quality of health care systems.

In conclusion, the TRIPS Agreement represents one of the most noteworthy and indeed controversial treaties within the framework of the international trade regime. Although the TRIPS provisions have not yet been fully implemented in many developing countries, the South African experience of securing access to ARV treatment in response to the AIDS crisis has served to highlight the problematic nature of pricing and the protection of patent rights. Legal provisions, such as compulsory licensing and parallel imports, have been incorporated into TRIPS, allowing countries to override drug patents and manufacture or import generic versions of drugs when confronted with health emergencies. Yet, in practice, these flexibilities have been fiercely contested and besieged by implementation problems. Policy-makers at the national level are expected to be singularly committed to reconciling obligations to international trade agreements and the progressive realization of the right to health. However, in an era of increasing morbidity and mortality, mass migration of trained medical personnel, over-stretched health care infrastructure and persisting gender inequalities, striving for such a balance may ultimately come with a high human cost.

Notes

1. Clause 15 of the Act indicated that:

   The registrar shall ensure that such an application in respect of medicine which appears on the latest Essential Drugs List or medicine which does not appear thereon but which, in the opinion of the Minister, is essential to national health is subject to such procedures as may be prescribed in order to expedite the registration ... The minister may prescribe conditions for the supply of more affordable medicines in certain circumstances so as to protect the health of the public, and in particular may ... prescribe the conditions on which any medicine which is identical in composition, meets the same quality of standard and is intended to have the same proprietary name as that of another medicine already registered in the Republic ... may be imported (Republic of South Africa 1997, cited in Bond 1999).

2. These included multinational corporations such as Merck, GlaxoSmithKline, Bristol-Myers Squib and Boehringer Ingelheim.

3. The 1996 Constitution ratifies property rights in its Bill of Rights.

4. The latter is, in effect, a list of countries against which the US government may impose trade sanctions as it deems them to be infringing drug or other patents.

5. The petition managed to secure almost 300,000 signatures from more than 130 countries.

6. The TAC has been at the forefront of the struggle for better access to affordable and quality medicines. It has done this by building alliances with a number of national and international organizations such as MSF. For a while, the TAC was able to set aside their deep divisions with the Department of Health about how to address the AIDS epidemic in South Africa. The TAC, together with the Congress of South African Trade Unions (COSATU) and international players, was a supporter of the government in the court hearing brought by the multinational pharmaceutical industry with argument based, in part, on international human rights laws and obligations (Heywood 2001).

References

Albertyn, C. (2003) 'Contesting Democracy: HIV/AIDS and the Achievement of Gender Equality in South Africa', *Feminist Studies*, vol. 29, no. 3: 595–615.

Annas, G. (2003) 'The Right to Health and the Nevirapine Case in South Africa', *New England Journal of Medicine*, vol. 348: 750–4.

Baker, B. (2002) African AIDS: Impacts of Globalisation, Pharmaceutical Apartheid, and Treatment Activism, Northeastern University School of Law, draft manuscript.

Barnett, T., and A. Whiteside (2002) *Aids in The Twenty-First Century: Disease and Globalisation*, Basingstoke: Palgrave.

Berger, J. (2001) Tripping over Patents: AIDS, Access to Treatment and the Manufacturing of Scarcity, Thesis, Faculty of Law, University of Toronto, Toronto.

Bloom, D., and River Path Associates (2000) 'Something to be Done: Treating HIV/AIDS', *Science*, vol. 288: 2171–3.

Bond, P. (1999) 'Globalization, Pharmaceutical Pricing and South African Health Policy: Managing Confrontation with U.S. Firms and Politicians', *International Journal of Health Services*, vol. 29, no. 4: 765–92.

Braveman, P., and S. Gruskin (2003) 'Poverty, Equity, Human rights and Health', *Bulletin of the World Health Organization*, vol. 81, no. 7: 539–45.

Budlender, D. (2004) *Why Should We Care about Unpaid Care Work?* Harare: UNIFEM.

Buch, E. (2001) 'The Health Sector Strategic Framework: A Review', *South African Health Review 2000*, Durban: Health Systems Trust.

Commission on Intellectual Property Rights (CIPR) (2002) *Integrating Intellectual Property Rights and Development Policy*, Report of the Commission on Intellectual Property Rights, London.

Constitution of the Republic of South Africa (adopted 8 May 1996, amended 11 October 1996).

Correa, C. (2000) *Intellectual Property Rights, the WTO, and Developing Countries*, New York: Zed Books.

Cullet, P. (2003) 'Patents and Medicines: The Relationship between TRIPS and the Human Right to Health', *International Affairs*, vol. 79, no. 1: 139–60.

Declaration of Commitment on HIV/AIDS (2001) 'Global Crisis-Global Action', United Nations, General Assembly, 26th Special Session. Available online, Joint United Nations Programme on HIV/AIDS (UNAIDS).

Department for International Development (DFID) (2004) Increasing Access to Essential Medicines in the Developing World: UK Government Policy and Plans, London: DFID.

Doherty, T., and M. Colvin (2004) 'HIV/AIDS', *South African Health Review 2003–2004*, Durban: Health Systems Trust.

Doyal, L. (2002) 'Putting Gender into Health and Globalization Debates: New Perspectives and Old Challenges', *Third World Quarterly*, vol. 23, no. 2: 233–50.

Du Guerny, J., and E. Sjoberg (1993) 'Interrelationship between Gender Relations and HIV/AIDS Epidemic: Some Possible Consideration for Policies and Programmes', *AIDS*, vol. 7: 1027–34.

Ford, N. (2003) 'Patents, Access to Medicines and the Role of Non-governmental Organisations', *Journal of Generic Medicines*, vol. 1, no. 2: 137–45.

Foreman, M. (2002) *Patents, Pills and Public Health: Can TRIPS Deliver?*, London: The Panos Institute.

Fosse, F. (2002) 'Controversy over TRIPS and the Public Health Agreement', *International Gender and Trade Network Monthly Bulletin*, vol. 2, no. 10 (December).

Gray, A., and T. Matsebula (2001) 'Drug Pricing', *South African Health Review 2000*, Durban: Health Systems Trust.

Gupta, D. (2003) 'The Neoliberal Case for South African Patent Defiance', *Law, Social Justice & Global Development Journal*, no. 2.

Hankins, C. (2000) 'Preventing Mother-to-Child Transmission of HIV in Developing Countries: Recent Developments and Ethical Implications', *Reproductive Health Matters*, vol. 8: 87–92.

Harrison, A., N. Xaba, P. Kunene, and N. Ntuli (2001) 'Understanding Young Women's Risk for HIV/AIDS: Adolescent Sexuality and Vulnerability in Rural KwaZulu/Natal', *Society in Transition*, vol. 32, no. 1: 79–82.

Hassan, F. (2004) 'Slow Road to Drugs Roll-Out', *Mail and Guardian*, July.

Heywood, M. (2001) Debunking 'Conglomo-Talk': A Case Study of the *Amicus Curiaeas*, an Instrument for Advocacy, Investigation and Mobilisation, Johannesburg, Treatment Action Campaign.

Ijumba, P., C. Poole, G. George, and A. Gray (2004) 'Access to Antiretroviral Therapy', *South African Health Review 2003/2004*, Durban: Health Systems Trust.

International Intellectual Property Institute (IIPI) (2000) *Patent Protection and Access to HIV/AIDS Pharmaceuticals in Sub-Saharan Africa*, Washington, DC: The International Intellectual Property Institute.

Joint Health and Treasury Task Team (2004) *Examining Treatment Options to Supplement Comprehensive Care for HIV/AIDS in the Public Health Sector*, August 2003.

Kasper, T. (2001) *South Africa's Victory for the Developing World*, Geneva: Médecins Sans Frontières.

Kober, K., and W. Van Damme (2004) 'Scaling Up Access to Antiretroviral Treatment in Southern Africa: Who will do the Job?', *The Lancet*, vol. 364: 103–7.

Loewenson, R., and A. Whiteside (2001) 'HIV/AIDS Implications for Poverty Reduction', background paper prepared for the United Nations

Development Programme for the UN General Assembly Special Session on HIV/AIDS, Policy Paper.

Mankahlana, P. (2000) 'Buying Anti-AIDS Drugs Benefit the Rich', *Business Day*, Johannesburg.

Martinson, N., B. Radebe, M. Mntambo, and A. Violari (2003) 'Antiretrovirals', *South African Health Review 2002*, Durban: Health Systems Trust.

Matowe, L. (2004) 'Access to Essential Drugs in Developing Countries: A Lost Battle?', *American Journal of Health-Systems Pharmacy*, vol. 718: 718–21.

McCray, T.M. (2004) 'An Issue of Culture: The Effects of Daily Activities on Prenatal Care Utilisation Patterns in Rural South Africa', *Social Science & Medicine*, vol. 59: 1843–55.

Médecins Sans Frontières (2004) *Untangling the Web of Price Reductions: A Pricing Guide for the Purchase of ARVs for Developing Countries*, 6th edn, Geneva: Médecins Sans Frontières.

Nelson Mandela (NM) and HSRC (2002) *South African National HIV Prevalence, Behavioural Risks and Mass Media Household Survey 2002*, Cape Town: Human Science Research Council.

Padarath, A., C. Chamberlain et al. (2003) 'Health Personnel in Southern Africa: Confronting Maldistribution and Brain Drain', Equinet Discussion Paper Series 3, Durban: Health Systems Trust.

Parliamentary Office of Science and Technology (POST) (2001) Access to Medicines in the Developing World, Postnote 160, London.

Petchesky, R. (2003) 'HIV/AIDS and the Human Right to Health: On a Collision Course with Global Capitalism', *Global Prescriptions: Gendering Health and Human Rights*, New York: Zed Books.

Pharmaceutical Research and Manufacturers of America (PhRMA) (2004) *Pharmaceutical Industry Profile 2004*, Washington, DC: PhRMA.

Rao Gupta, G. (2000) 'Gender, Sexuality, and HIV/AIDS: The What, the Why, and the How', Plenary address at the 12th International AIDS Conference, Durban, South Africa, 12 July.

Schneider, H. (2002). 'On the Fault Line: The Politics of AIDS policy in Contemporary South Africa', *African Studies*, vol. 61, no. 1: 145–67.

Selis, S. (2003) 'Study Calculated Outlay of Pharmaceutical Marketing', Stanford Report, May.

Shisana, O., E. Hall, K.R. Maluleke, D.J. Stoker, C. Schwabe, M. Colvin, J. Chauveau, C. Botha, T. Gumede, H. Fomundam, N. Shaikh, T. Rehle, E. Udjo, and D. Gisselquist (2003) *The Impact of HIV/AIDS on the Health Sector*, National Survey of Health Personnel, Ambulatory and Hospitalised Patients and Health Facilities, Cape Town: Human Science Research Council.

Sivard, R. (1995) *Women: A World Survey*, Washington, DC: World Priorities.

Stewart, R., A. Padarath, and L. Bamford (2004) *Providing Antiretroviral Treatment in Southern Africa*, Durban: Health Systems Trust.

T'Hoen, E. (2003) 'TRIPS, Pharmaceutical Patents and Access to Essential Medicines: Seattle, Doha and Beyond', in J. Moatti, B. Coriat and

Y. Souteyrandet et al. (eds), *Economics of AIDS and Access to HIV/AIDS Care in Developing Countries, Issues and Challenges*, Paris: Agence Nationale de Recherches sur le Sida: 39-67.

UNAIDS (2000) *Report on the Global HIV/AIDS Epidemic*, Geneva: UNAIDS.

UNAIDS (2004) *2004 Report on the Global AIDS Epidemic*, Geneva: UNAIDS.

Weissman, R. (1999) 'AIDS and Developing Countries: Democratizing Access to Essential Medicines', *Foreign Policy in Focus*, vol. 4, no. 23: 1–4.

Williams, M. (2001) 'The TRIPS and Public Health Debate: An Overview', International Gender and Trade Network (IGTN).

Wood, E., P. Braitstein, J.S. Montaner, M.T. Schechter, M.W. Tyndall, M.V. O'Shaughnessy, and R.S. Hogg (2000) 'Extent to which Low-Level Use of Antiretroviral Treatment could Curb the AIDS epidemic in Sub-Saharan Africa', *The Lancet*, vol. 355: 2095–100.

Wood, F., F. Maforah, and R. Jewkes (1998) ' "He Forced me to Love him": Putting Violence on Adolescent Sexual Health Agendas', *Social Science and Medicine*, vol. 47, no. 2: 233–42.

Woolard, I., and M. Leibbrandt (2001) 'Measuring Poverty in South Africa', in H. Bhorat, M. Leobbrandt, M. Maziya, S. Van der Berg and I. Woolard (eds), *Fighting Poverty: Labour Markets and Inequality in South Africa*, Cape Town: UCT Press.

World Trade Organization (1994) *TRIPS Agreement*, Geneva: World Trade Organization.

10

Midwifery and Nursing Migration: Implications of Trade Liberalization for Maternal Health in Low-Income Countries

Nancy Gerein and Andrew Green

Introduction

There is increasing concern in national health systems and international agencies over the growing shortage of midwives and nurses in many countries. A crisis already exists in a number of low-income countries, which is compounded by active recruitment from high-income countries, themselves facing shortages. It is likely that with various initiatives in place to increase labour movement flexibility, this crisis will increase rather than decrease for particular low-income countries.

The effects of this on the achievement of the Millennium Development Goal (MDG) of reducing maternal mortality, and achieving the wider agenda of the International Conference on Population and Development (ICPD), are likely to be significant. However, there is little reliable information regarding the numbers of midwives and nurses migrating, and even less on the implications of shortages for maternal service delivery and health status.

A number of issues for national and international policy development are highlighted, including: more effective planning and management of human resources in the health sectors of all countries; coordination between ministries of health and other government departments, including those dealing with trade, to protect maternal health; active management of migration through national policy development and regional and international cooperation; and research and information systems to illuminate the size, causes and effects of migration, and to develop the policies around migration, which will protect the health of women in low- and middle-income countries.

Background

Maternal and reproductive health is a key policy area for many low-income countries. This is spelt out in the MDGs[1] and in the ICPD, which stressed a rights-based approach to reproductive health (Family Care International 1999). Midwives and nurses play a critical role in this area. However, there is a sense of crisis in many countries as a result of a growing shortage of this key professional group. While there are various reasons for this shortfall including, most critically, general under-funding of the health sector in many countries, migration is an increasingly important factor. Trade liberalization, while not a significant determinant of migration currently, offers both constraints and opportunities in managing these flows in the future. Trade liberalization could constrain management of migration and the associated benefit to public health systems by limiting the capacity of the state to manage out-migration. It also may offer opportunities to the extent that it may enable regulation at a multilateral level.

This chapter provides an overview of maternal health and health services in low- and middle-income countries, followed by an analysis of the size and effects of the migration of midwives and nurses on health services and ultimately on maternal health. The final section outlines key policy issues for stakeholders concerned with health and trade agendas.

Current State of Maternal Health

Maternal health and well-being is a profoundly important part of the health of populations in all countries. Each year about 210 million women become pregnant, and about twenty million experience pregnancy-related illness. Over 500,000 of these women die from complications of pregnancy or childbirth, complications that are mostly avoidable. Annually, there are an estimated twenty million unsafe abortions, and an associated 70,000 deaths – 95 per cent of them in developing countries (WHO 2004a). In addition to maternal health,

Table 10.1   Regional estimates of maternal mortality

UN region	Maternal mortality ratio (maternal deaths per 100,000 live births)	No. of maternal deaths	Lifetime risk of maternal deaths
World total	400	529,000	74
Industrialized countries	13	1,300	4,000
Developing countries (not including least developed countries)	440	291,700	61
Least developed countries	890	236,000	17

Source: WHO (2004c).

on which this chapter focuses, there are wider implications of the migration of health professionals for reproductive health including family planning, STIs and most importantly AIDS, as well as sexual rights.

Table 10.1 sets out indicators of maternal mortality for regions of the world and shows the particular burden carried by the least developed countries (mainly sub-Saharan Africa and Southeast Asia). The table, of course, masks further inequities within regions and countries.

The importance of these issues is directly reflected in two MDG targets:

- reduce the maternal mortality ratios (MMRs) by three quarters by 2015;
- increase the percentage of births attended by a skilled birth attendant (SBA)[2] from 40 per cent in 2005 to 60 per cent in 2015.

The Importance of Midwives and Nurses for Maternal Health

While poverty, education and culture all have a significant effect on maternal health, one of the most critical and directly related factors is the availability of appropriate quality health care for pregnancy and delivery. The global initiative to reduce maternal mortality is centred on the need for all women to have access to an SBA for delivery (WHO 2005).

Numerous studies on patterns of maternity care and mortality under-lie this focus. A global overview of different models of maternity services shows that where non-professionals (usually traditional birth attendants – TBA) carry out home deliveries, MMR is extremely high, and never falls below 100. Where midwives and nurse-midwives carry out deliveries, MMR can be reduced to 50 or lower. Where most deliveries take place by professionals in a well-equipped hospital, the lowest mortality rates of all can be achieved, although it is not a guarantee, since poor quality of care can cause mortality (Koblinsky et al. 1999). A global study has shown clear correlations between the density of health workers per population and mortality rates; the strongest impact is shown on maternal mortality, where it is estimated that a 10 per cent increase in health worker density is correlated with a 5 per cent decline in maternal mortality (Joint Learning Initiative 2004). It is not surprising, therefore, that the director general of WHO referred to the availability of nurses and midwives as 'among the most pressing concerns' for countries as they try to deliver key health interventions (WHO 2002).

The Size and Causes of Migration

In the past decade, sharp increases in demands for health professionals in industrialized countries and the Gulf States, coupled with stagnating and worsening economic development in poorer countries, have led to increased migration pressures and renewed attention to this issue. The globalization of markets and the development of free trade agree-ments, through regional and international agreements, such as the General Agreement on Trade in Services (GATS), have facilitated the mobility of people.

There are severe problems with the data on migration of health per-sonnel. The main sources of information are from professional registra-tion bodies in both source and recipient countries. Individual countries have some, but incomplete, information on migration, but global fig-ures are only indicative. Figures for midwives are rarely separated from those for nurses. There is little information concerning the length of stay of migrants, whether migration is permanent or temporary, or on return flows. The picture is further complicated by migration in and out of the same country, for example, South Africa and the Caribbean lose personnel to countries such as the United Kingdom, but they also attract professionals from elsewhere in the region. However, it is clear

Table 10.2   Overseas trained nurses and midwives registering in the United Kingdom, by year, from main source developing countries

Country	1999/2000	2001/02	2003/04
India	96	994	3,073
Philippines	1,052	7,235	4,338
South Africa	1,460	2,114	1,689
Nigeria	208	432	511
West Indies	425	248	397
Zimbabwe	221	473	391
Ghana	74	195	354
Kenya	29	155	146
Total (from overseas)	5,945	15,064	14,122

Source: UK Nursing and Midwifery Council.

that the rate of international migration overall is increasing. Table 10.2 provides evidence from one country, the United Kingdom.

Global figures show nurses coming to the United Kingdom mainly from three countries: India, the Philippines and South Africa. More than 150,000 Filipino nurses, representing 85 per cent of the total employed Filipino nurses, work internationally (Pang et al. 2002). In the Americas, large numbers of migrants are from the Caribbean: Jamaica lost 95 per cent of its output of nurses between 1978 and 1985 to international migration (Kingma 2001).

In Africa, around 23,000 professionals in various occupations emigrate annually (WHO 2004b). The public health sector is one of the most seriously affected sectors. Approximately 18,000 Zimbabwean nurses have left the country since 1982, leaving a total of only 22,483 in the country by 1999 (Chikanda 2005). Of the 1,200 physicians trained in Zimbabwe during the 1990s, only 360 were practising in 2001 (Pang et al. 2002; WHO 2005). More than 500 nurses left Ghana in 2000, representing more than double the number of graduates produced in Ghana that year (Kingma 2001). Between one-third and one-half of health profession graduates each year emigrate from South Africa (Chanda 2002). Malawi has a vacancy rate overall for nurses of 53 per cent; in the Caribbean the vacancy rate is about 35 per cent (Deyal 2003; Stillwell et al. 2003). The significance of these figures on outflow must be seen in relation to the total stock of nurses and midwives in the country, the ratio of health professionals to population and the ability of the educational institutions to produce graduates

Table 10.3 Factors influencing health care professionals' intent to migrate, reason for migrating and willingness to remain in their home country

Country	For what reasons do you intend to leave your home country?	For what reasons did you leave your home country?	What would make you remain in your home country?
Cameroon	Upgrade qualifications (85 per cent)	Recruited (29 per cent)	Salary (68 per cent)
	Gain experience (80 per cent)	Gain experience (28 per cent)	Continuing education (67 per cent)
	Lack of promotion (80 per cent)	Better pay(27 per cent)	Working environment (64 per cent)
	Living conditions (80per cent)	Living conditions (19 per cent)	Health care system management (55 per cent)
Ghana		Gain experience (86 per cent)	Salary (81 per cent)
		Lack of promotion (86 per cent)	Work environment (64 per cent)
		Despondency (86 per cent)	Fringe benefits (77 per cent)
		Living conditions, economic decline (71 per cent)	Resources in the health sector (70 per cent)

Country			
Senegal	Salary (89 per cent) N/a N/a N/a		Work environment (n/a) Salary (n/a) Better career path (n/a) Benefits (n/a)
South Africa	Gain experience (43 per cent) Violence and crime (38 per cent) Heavy workload (41 per cent) Declining health service (38 per cent)		Salary (78 per cent) Work environment (68 per cent) Fringe benefits (66 per cent) Workload (59 per cent)
Uganda	Salary (72 per cent) Living conditions (41 per cent) Upgrade qualifications (38 per cent) Gain experience (24 per cent)	Salary (55 per cent) Economic decline (55 per cent) Save money (54 per cent) Declining health service (53 per cent)	Salary (84 per cent) Fringe benefits (54 per cent) Work environment (36 per cent) Workload (30 per cent)
Zimbabwe	All factors	All factors	All factors

Source: Vujicic et al. (2004).

(Buchan et al. 2003). For example, a Malawi teaching hospital lost 114 nurses between 1999 and 2001 (mostly to migration), but this represented 60 per cent of the 190 nurses in the hospital (Martineau et al. 2002).

Data from receiving countries show an upward trend in the number of nurses from developing countries registering to migrate: about 4,500 nurses left the Philippines in 1996, compared with over 12,000 in 2001. There were 511 requests for verification of nursing qualifications (an indicator of intent to move) in South Africa in 1995, but over 2,500 in 2000, a fivefold increase (Vujicic et al. 2004).

Understanding and mapping migration patterns is made more complex by the fact that a number of migrants will return to their home country after a temporary period abroad, yet data on return flows is very limited.

A report by the WHO Africa region in 2004 describing the results of interviews in six countries with 2,364 health professionals, mainly nurses, indicated that the 'push' factors leading to migration were broadly similar to factors reported from the Caribbean and Philippines, although there are some country variations (Buchan et al. 2003; Vujicic et al. 2004). These include low salaries and poor working environments, encompassing a number of issues: inadequate resources to perform their functions, heavy workloads and high stress levels from lack of security or having to cope with many HIV/AIDS patients, inflexible management styles, lack of opportunities for professional development and promotion, economic instability, and, for midwives and nurses especially, poor relationships with physicians, lack of involvement in management and the low status of the profession (WHO 2001; Buchan et al. 2003). Table 10.3 shows the main factors which influence professionals' intentions to migrate as well as willingness to remain at home.

The current global shortage of nurses and midwives is unlikely to be lessened in the short term. A number of health systems will continue to pursue international recruitment, at least as a short- to medium-term option. A variety of strategies exist ranging from special visa arrangements for health professionals to in-country recruitment campaigns. The ability of richer health systems to fund increasing numbers of health care workers, coupled with increasing professional mobility, suggests that the impact of this is most likely to fall on those health systems least able to absorb them – the low- and middle-income countries.

The Effects of Midwife and Nurse Migration

Given the strong relationship between maternal mortality and the utilization of SBAs[3] for pregnancy and delivery care, what can we infer about the effects on health of migration-related shortages of midwives and nurses? What are the costs and potential benefits of migration to the health system? The general lack of research[4] on these questions makes it difficult to differentiate between the effects caused by migration and those caused by a general under-investment in the health sector, but the following suggests some potential effects of migration.

The effects on health can be broadly related to:

- direct effects of reduced quality, and/or restricted availability of and equitable access to services, and
- indirect effects arising from the extra workload caused by migration, which leads to further staff losses through further migration.

Quality, availability and equity of access to services

At the workplace there are always staff shortages. This hospital is very busy. We have about 80 deliveries in 24 hours. So you can imagine how I manage with my skeleton staff. It has not been very easy. You cannot satisfy your clients. Because if there are long queues, you are trying to fight to finish the long queue and you don't have time to talk to your client to counsel her ... So you don't satisfy the client and you don't satisfy yourself. You are also frustrated. The queue is too long. You become so irritable. You don't even want to hear anybody talking. Then you frustrate the employer since you are not giving quality services.

Nurse, urban hospital in Kenya, quoted in Van Eyck (2004)

The quality of care has really suffered. I have only 300 nurses, for 450 posts.
Mam Jagne, chief nurse of the national teaching hospital, the Gambia, personal communication (2003)

There is overwhelming evidence that as levels of nurse staffing rise, the quality of care improves, because nurses can monitor patients more closely and quickly detect changes in their condition. A strong and consistent relationship exists between high nurse staffing levels and reduced medical and surgical complications, with lowered overall mortality rates (ICN 2004). One recent study in the United Kingdom of the relationship between levels of staffing in midwifery and outcomes of care found that midwifery shortages led to some adverse events[5] and frequent 'near misses',[6] which were unreported, and to midwives not taking up opportunities for training or updating (Ashcroft et al. 2003).

No similar research was found from low- and middle-income countries. However, since ratios of staff to patients in poor countries are up to 100 times lower than those in developed countries, any further reductions in staffing could have a disproportionate effect on service quality and outcomes, or result in the service being completely unavailable. A WHO study in six African countries with over 10,000 health personnel and service users provides considerable evidence of worsening quality of care, as a result, in part, of loss of professionals. For example, in Cameroon, 25 per cent of health workers agreed that quality of care had deteriorated due to long queues and lack of mutual respect between the users of services and the health professionals. Over 80 per cent of those interviewed believed that the increasing workload of service providers was one of the factors related to a decline in quality of care (WHO 2004b).

Figure 10.1 shows the wide variations in the availability of nurses and midwives in a number of different countries. Of these, the Gambia, Malawi, India, Ghana and the Philippines are primarily exporting/sending, United Sates is primarily importing/receiving, and South Africa is both a receiver and sender of health professionals. It is important to recognize that many nurses are also midwives, but migration statistics do not often record this.

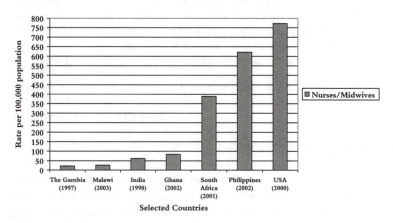

Figure 10.1   Estimates of nurses/midwives supply.
Source: Joint Learning Initiative (2004).

The United States, with one of the highest ratios of nurses to population ratios in the world (nearly 800 per 100,000 population) recruits from Jamaica, where the ratio is 165 nurses per 100,000 population, and from India, with a ratio of 62 nurses per 100,000 (Joint Learning Initiative 2004). India produces a 'surplus' of nurses in order to export to richer countries, even though it has one of the lowest ratios of nurses to population in the world. This is because the ratios reflect the number of nurses who are employed by the health system, and poorer countries tend to employ fewer nurses per patient.

As we have suggested, it is not easy to differentiate between the effects of globalization and domestic policies. The latter clearly remain a major influence on the availability of nurses in the health sector. This is for a variety of reasons and in particular under-investment in the health sector[7] – often the result, of course, of the general economic status of the country. Trade liberalization may, however, in the long-term, affect the willingness or capacity of domestic policy-makers to address nursing shortages.

Health care is a labour-intensive sector. The World Health Report (WHO 2005) estimates that to provide about 75 per cent of the world's mothers with professional delivery care by 2015, there will need to be huge increases in personnel: an additional 334,000 midwives need to be produced, 140,000 midwives need upgrading, and 27,000 doctors and technicians need training to provide back-up care. A recent review of migration found that in Caribbean countries there were insufficient nurses to support the delivery of essential health services, compromises in the quality of care occurred and consumers were dissatisfied (Buchan et al. 2003). In South Africa, nurses commented on the loss of skills and lowered quality of services, and 60 per cent of institutions surveyed reported that it was difficult to replace nurses who had left (ibid.). Migration also has important negative effects on the accessibility and equitable distribution of health care. The rural-to-urban migration of health professionals, and from the public to the private sector, is a longstanding phenomenon in many countries, leaving public health institutions in rural areas poorly staffed and the staff who work there affected by heavy workloads and poor morale (WHO 2004b; Chikanda 2005). Poor and rural women are disproportionately affected, since they are left to receive services from overstretched, younger staff with less professional qualifications, or to rely on traditional, unqualified health practitioners or private, expensive facilities (Chikanda 2005). The ICPD placed considerable

emphasis on people's rights in health care, which implies more attention to good quality in the process of providing care, and not just the
amount of care provided; however, the implications of migration for
women's reproductive and health rights have not been explored in
detail in published literature.

Effects on the working environment

> Many basic health facilities do not even have a midwife so patients all come
> to the [national] hospital and the workload has increased in the past years.
> You see the midwives sweating away, they cannot even have a cup of tea.
>
> Mam Jagne, chief nurse of the national hospital, the Gambia, personal
> communication (2003)
>
> There is no respect for nurses who stay and make the sacrifices.
>
> Glenda Caesar, Trinidadian returned migrant nurse, in Deyal (2003)

Low staffing levels cause increased workload and job stress; long hours
cause fatigue and reduce productivity (IOM 2003). Midwives and
nurses place considerable importance on the satisfaction they derive
from providing good quality care. A continued inability to provide
such care leads to high levels of stress and dissatisfaction, burnout, and
plans to leave the profession (Baumann and O'Brien-Pallas 2001). In
one study of migration, the staff that remained noted that resulting
staff shortages led to frustration, demotivation and lowered morale of
nurses (Buchan et al. 2003). These 'results' of migration then become
'push' factors, which lead to more emigration.

Costs of migration

The costs to sending countries are significant, including both the
investment costs of training professionals and the loss of their services.
The United Nations Commission for Trade and Development has estimated that each migrating African professional represents a loss of
$184,000 to the country of origin. This contrasts starkly with the levels
of expenditure on the health sector in such countries that were as low
as $7 per capita in Liberia and $20 per capita in Malawi in 2002[8] (WHO
2005). The educational cycle to prepare health workers is long and it is
difficult to respond quickly or flexibly to losses of staff (Stillwell et al.
2003). The high vacancy rates created by migration may have to be offset by costly recruitment of expatriate professionals, leading to a
dependence on donors. For example, Africa spends $4 billion a year on

the salaries of 100,000 foreign experts (in all sectors, including health), representing one-third of rich countries' official development assistance to Africa (Pang et al. 2002; Marchal and Kegels 2003). Foreign staff have variable education, backgrounds, language skills and clinical standards, which has administrative and other costs (WHO 2002). The African Union has said that 'low-income countries subsidize high-income countries with $500 million a year through the movement of health workers' (Joint Learning Initiative 2004: 102).

Because the most mobile nurses and midwives are likely to be younger and better qualified, their permanent migration means a great loss of potential future contributions and of the next generation of potential leaders (Buchan et al. 2003). The effects of shortages on the education and research systems may be even more pointed, since it takes longer to replace these personnel.

Many midwives and nurses who migrate experience downward occupational mobility, partly because of problems of recognition of their qualifications: for example, professional nurses working as auxiliary nurses in the recipient countries (Hardill and Macdonald 2000). As a result, the home country loses the services of an SBA and/or a professional nurse, while the receiving country may gain a health worker who is treated as having lower skill levels. This phenomenon has been termed 'brain waste'; at a global level, it is an inefficient use of resources.

Potential benefits of migration to low-income countries

Although there are overwhelming concerns for the negative impacts of migration on low-income countries, there are potential benefits. Exported labour of all forms provides significant financial resources: in 1996, India received US$7.6 billion in remittances (Martineau et al. 2002). This compares with a GNP of US$357.8 billion (World Bank 1998). Remittances now exceed official development assistance and are the second largest source of external funding for developing countries (Stillwell et al. 2003). However, remittances do not flow directly to the public sector, unlike the direct benefits of retaining domestic health professionals.

The education and practice experiences gained by the individual migrants is a benefit, but only if the individual returns and the skills are relevant to the health system – a so-called 'brain exchange'. The new skills might be most relevant for private sector facilities, or middle-income countries where similar health problems and levels of technology exist (Martineau et al. 2002). Migration can also act as a safety valve, when the economy is unable to provide employment for all the available health professionals.

The continued loss of human resources and increased competition for workers may stimulate governments to reduce the 'push' factors that lead to migration or to leaving the profession. For example, as a reaction to migration losses in Botswana, the conditions of service for nurses have recently been greatly improved, offering overtime allowance, part-time employment of nurses to reduce high nurse–patient ratios, flexi-time and housing (SEW 2002; South Africa Migration Project 2002). Such desirable human resource policies might act as a model for dealing with other health workers, and hopefully result in improvements in the quality and quantity of health care for the population.

Free Trade and Migration

Globalization appears to be having an effect on the mobility of health professionals (WHO 2002) in several ways. Widespread access to the Internet allows greater spread of information about employment opportunities in other countries, and active international recruitment from developed countries and greater international recognition of national qualifications are contributing to a more global labour market generally.[9] Negotiations in the WTO over GATS are likely to lead to further increases in the mobility of professionals, through, for example, development of international norms for working (through ILO), recognition of qualifications and developments in managed migration, such as has occurred in the Caribbean, where people are trained for export on a rotational basis, in order to regulate the export of labour and limit negative effects of losses (Buchan et al. 2003).

For receiving countries, reliance on migration can be criticized as a way to avoid paying the true social costs of care. These costs include the costs of producing health care professionals that are avoided by the receiving country. However, it can also be argued that developing countries may be competitive suppliers in this area, and their economies will benefit from trade liberalization. Although migrants tend to be better educated than the average workforce left behind, not all migration implies significant economic losses – it depends on whether migrants have left permanently and whether they would have found employment matching their qualifications in their home country. In the long-term, free trade may reduce the 'push' factors in migration, in part by creating more local opportunities for employment of health professionals.

There is also a delicate balance to consider between the human and the labour rights of individuals, including the right to migrate, and a concern for the health of a population. The effects of trade liberalization may be both beneficial and harmful to working environments in source countries, both decreasing and increasing the force of the 'push' factors for migration, depending on governments' responses. For example, a positive effect could be an improvement in staff salaries and benefits due to competition among an increased number of private hospitals; a negative effect might be pressure on staff to implement suboptimal quality control practices, if a large increase in private medical industries and hospitals meant that the government was unable to regulate them adequately. The impact of globalization and free trade on equity, access, costs and quality of health services is largely dependent on the policies and safeguards that national governments put in place, including on migration.

Global migration flows are fundamentally a result of push–pull imbalances in labour markets worldwide, and immigration to recipient countries is determined mainly by factors other than trade issues: for example, countries' concerns about security, the state of the economy, political factors, the domestic birth rate, humanitarian concerns and other issues (Vujicic et al. 2004). Given the many technical, institutional and economic barriers – for example, government monopolies and free or subsidized services – the role of trade will probably be more limited in health than the overall share of services trade in world production. However, increasingly free global trade in professionals will become more prominent, as more countries make commitments in new sectors, including the health sector, under the GATS Agreement. Globalization must be managed to maximize its economic and social benefits, by designing international rules and institutions that can be activated to deal with the downsides of globalization, and support national policies to optimize health outcomes (Bhagwati 2004).

Free trade is intended to lead to a situation globally in which all resources are used to their optimum, and all countries benefit from being exposed to market forces. In this schema, the free migration of people is a part of free trade, and short-term imbalances are seen to eventually balance out so that all benefit. However, assuming the presumption is correct, 'eventually' can be a very long time; during the transition period to a global liberalized economy, the costs can be much higher in some countries than in others. For countries such as India, China and the Philippines, which have large populations and a substantial capacity to generate health professionals, migration may be seen as an opportunity at both the individual and national levels. For small countries, especially in Africa where training institutions are relatively few and where losses may both form a high percentage of total numbers and fluctuate significantly, out-migration of their few health professionals is a threat (Bhagwati 2004). Even countries that champion free trade do not consider that their health sector should be a freely marketable good. Should health be seen in the same way internationally as it is nationally? Those in government and civil society concerned with health, economic development and trade should consider whether sufficiently diverse voices and perspectives are taking part in the debate.

Policy Issues for Key Stakeholders

This final section outlines a number of policy issues for key stakeholders who see midwifery and nursing roles as essential to achieving the MDGs in maternal health, within a context of continuing strong pressures for international migration and trade liberalization.

National policy development

There are three critical issues that need greater attention in policy formation in both source and recipient countries. First, greater emphasis needs to be placed on the broad area of human resource planning, production and management and its links into wider programme policies – such as trade liberalization (Egger and Adams 1999). Second is the related issue of international recruitment and migration. Last, there are wider questions that national policy needs to consider concerning the rights of individual professionals to use migration as a means of furthering their careers and raising their economic status.

It is inevitable that international and regional migration pressures will continue. As such it is imperative that it is managed. An example of this is a region-wide strategy in the Caribbean that has been implemented to improve retention and succession planning in all the countries involved. Good human resource policies will reduce the push factors in sending countries and help achieve self-sufficiency in nurses and midwives in all countries, including destination countries. Strategies to improve working conditions and the status of nursing and midwifery are needed in order to improve recruitment and retention of these professionals, and to reattract professionals back to the sector (Buchan 2002). Special programmes are needed to facilitate the return to work of staff who have had a career break and returned migrants. Emphasis on reducing 'push' factors in the workplace can be more cost-effective than increasing recruiting, since this will not only reduce migration but can have complementary effects on improving the quality of health services.

WHO (2005) estimates that doubling or trebling salaries would be the minimum necessary to recruit and retain necessary staff for maternal and child health programmes. However, some recent research on the importance of wage differentials between source and receiving countries was not optimistic that wage increases in source countries would decrease migration, but emphasized that much more research was needed on the effect of policies to reduce the 'push' factors in migration (Vujicic et al. 2004).

Policy in professional education needs to address the issues of international qualifications and postgraduate programmes that facilitate migration. These are undoubtedly attractive to the workforce, but their cost and potential effects need to be weighed against alternative options, such as preparing health workers whose qualifications are not recognized internationally, or making investments in improved working conditions (such as salaries and pensions), which are also desired by staff but do not facilitate migration. Other strategies being pursued by source countries include requiring graduates to work a certain period of time in less-favoured parts of the country before allowing emigration, or requiring migrants to reimburse the government for their education, although these have been found difficult to enforce in some countries (Kingma 2001).

Alternatively, rather than constraining demand for migration, source countries could enhance the outflow of and benefits from migrants, through, for example, having a policy of dual citizenship, which allows taxation of citizens abroad. This could be a substantial benefit: the aggregate income of Indian-born residents in the United States is 10 per cent of India's national income (Bhagwati 2004). Indeed, India is proposing 'GATS' visas, to enable its citizens to work internationally for specific periods of time. Some countries encourage continued contacts with their expatriates, through direct investments, collaborative education and research activities, and incentives to work in the home country. The enhanced diplomatic and economic relationships that could result from migrants are a benefit to both source and receiving countries (Bhagwati 2004).

Finally, there are various issues concerning the development of national policies related to the rights of individuals to further their own professional and economic position through migration. These are of particular interest and indeed are difficult issues for national professional bodies that have to balance their responsibilities to their own members with the needs of the national health system. There are potentially particular gender issues also within this area given that nursing may be one of the few areas in which women are given opportunities to migrate.

Bilateral, regional and international policies

'The economy is becoming increasingly global, while social and political institutions remain largely local, national or regional' (ILO 2004). By its very nature, international migration cannot be dealt with by national governments alone – intergovernmental and wider international processes are necessary. Many international agencies (WHO, ILO, International Organization for Migration, WTO) and health professional organizations have an interest in international recruitment and migration issues. Their role is critical to help understand the trends and impacts of migration through support to data collection, and to establish an 'international benchmark for effective and ethical practice in recruitment', as well as to monitor countries' (importers and exporters) practices (Buchan et al. 2003).

Ethical recruitment and employment policies need to be developed by recipient countries and enforced for both the public and private sectors. These can include a simple ban on recruitment activities from countries experiencing severe shortfalls (as between the United Kingdom and South Africa, Ghana and other countries), a limitation in the numbers that can be recruited overall (as in Norway), limited time period contracts (although these are difficult to enforce) and employment in specialized areas needed by developing countries. Reimbursement to receiving countries, including investment in training programmes, is also a possibility, but this will raise the costs of recruitment in receiving countries.

These codes of practice would have international legal status under GATS, and it has been suggested that GATS should have a code of conduct on recruitment that would be enforceable (Martineau et al. 2002). Although the section of GATS dealing with the movement of professionals has not been used extensively to date, this is open to change. The fit of ethical recruitment codes with overall trade liberalization policies, and the possibility of their enforcement through GATS are key issues for clarification.

Coordinated support for maternal health

One of the more strategic tasks of the Ministry of Health is to learn the language of the Ministry of Finance, of trade commissions and GATS. The health department must learn to champion the causes of sound health policy considerations in trade negotiations by preparing an overall departmental health and trade policy strategy and coordinating the health inputs to trade policy initiatives. It also needs to develop an outreach strategy to influence the government trade policy agenda and ensure that health is considered in decision-making at an early stage (Vellinga 2002). Development partners could support Ministries of Health to undertake trade negotiations.

Development partners are committed to supporting programmes for maternal health worldwide. A central element in these programmes is the frontline role of midwives and nurses, who often take the brunt of the frustrations caused by lack of resources for care and lack of training for new roles. An innovative approach to help countries to minimize external pull factors in migration was seen in Zambia where financial support provided by donors enabled the government to more than double nurse salaries in 2001 in a bid to retain the country's nurses (SEW 2002). Development partners need to work with their own country health systems, including through lobbying the relevant ministry, to examine recruitment issues – a country's development assistance agency could easily be spending millions on developing health professionals in a country such as India, while at the same time the health department is busy recruiting trained, experienced health personnel from the same country.

National midwifery and nursing professional organizations could be key to the achievement of MDGs for maternal health. Governments and development assistance agencies need to support them to collect and disseminate information on migration (numbers, push and pull factors, the activities of recruiting agencies), to help develop policies to recruit, retain and reattract midwives and nurses, and contribute at a policy level in discussions on migration and health (WHO 2001).

Opportunities for development partners to advocate the importance of midwifery and nursing at national levels arise in their policy dialogues with governments concerning reproductive health programmes, health reforms, human resource development and resource allocations to health service programmes. Opportunities also arise when dealing with global and international policy about development and labour through forums such as the WHO, the WTO, the ILO, the World Bank, the International Confederation of Midwives (ICM), the European Union and Commonwealth Ministers' meetings. Work with GATS to develop an enforceable code of conduct would underpin such efforts in an important way.

Knowledge management

All these goals would be supported by developing our understanding and monitoring of the situation. One useful initiative is seen in South Africa, where the University of the Witwatersrand is offering a course on migration policy and management for government and civil society managers (South Africa Migration Project 2003).

While there are initiatives within international organizations, such as WHO and the ICM, to map migration patterns (WHO 2002), country-level initiatives are needed to improve human resource information systems and to collect data to understand the specific national characteristics of migration – for example, on the economic, social and cultural influences on migration, age and seniority of migrants, and their previous places of employment – to illuminate the effects of migration on workplaces and on health care. In addition, countries aiming for managed programmes of migration need a well-developed system of information exchange among the network of countries involved. This would help to illuminate to what extent brain drain and brain exchange are occurring, and to define the requisite policy responses.

Conclusions

The connections between globalization and free trade, on the one hand, and migration and maternal health, on the other, need to be made clearer and more explicit. A fundamental problem is that there are few reliable data on the size of migration, its characteristics and the effects on health systems. Global programmes for health must integrate workforce issues into their strategies if they are to succeed. If national governments and international development partners are serious about reaching the MDGs for maternal health, and about protecting the reproductive rights of women, more attention must be paid to the issue of migration of midwives and nurses from developing countries, and the potential role of free trade in this. Policies are beginning to be developed to deal with the issue of migration, but they are fragmentary and non-cohesive.

Notes

The authors would like to acknowledge the helpful insights provided by Professor Mary Renfrew of the Mother and Infant Research Unit, University of Leeds, UK and Dr Stephen Pearson, Nuffield Centre for International Health and Development , University of Leeds.

1. The MDGs are a set of targets for the implementation of the Millennium Declaration agreed by the UN General Assembly in September 2000. There are eight goals, of which three are directly related to health; one deals with maternal health.

2. Skilled birth attendants are defined by WHO as 'people with midwifery skills who have been trained to proficiency in the skills necessary to manage normal deliveries and diagnose, manage or refer complications'. This includes professional midwives, nurse-midwives and those doctors who have the appropriate training. The definition excludes traditional birth attendants (TBAs), whether trained or untrained (WHO/UNFPA/UNICEF/World Bank 1999.

3. Although doctors are also critical for reducing maternal mortality, this chapter focuses on the movement of one key group: midwives and nurses.

4. Most research has looked at the issue of migration in terms of numbers and motivating factors, without attempting to examine the direct effects on the health systems.

5. Adverse events are those events that have given or may give rise to actual or possible personal injury.

6. Near misses are events that under slightly different circumstances could have been an accident.

7. For example, total spending on health in India is 6.1 per cent of gross domestic product in 2002, but government expenditure accounts for only 21 per cent of spending (WHO 2005).

8. For comparison: per capita spending, in international dollar rates, on health in 2002 in the United Kingdom and United States was $801 and $2,368, respectively (WHO 2005).

9. For example, in response to medical and nursing shortages in developed countries, some governments have fast-tracked foreign-trained professionals through domestic licensing procedures, and maintain lists of countries where training is thought to be equivalent (Vujicic et al. 2004). Both public and private agencies from these countries recruit abroad actively; in the United Kingdom, an outcry about the effect on developing countries has led to the development of an ethical recruitment code governing recruitment of health professionals from specific developing countries to the United Kingdom (DoH 2001).

References

Ashcroft, B., M. Elstein, N. Boreham and S. Holm. (2003) 'Prospective Semistructured Observational Study to Identify Risk Attributable to Staff Deployment, Training and Updating Opportunities for Midwives', *British Medical Journal*, vol. 327: 1–4.

Baumann, A., and L. O'Brien-Pallas. (2001) *Commitment and Care: The Benefits of a Healthy Workplace for Nurses, their Patients and the System: Final Report*, Ottawa: Canadian Health Service Research Foundation.

Bhagwati, J. (2004) *In Defence of Globalization*, New York: Oxford University Press.

Buchan, J. (2002) 'Nursing Shortages and Evidence-Based Interventions: A Case Study from Scotland', *International Nursing Review*, vol. 49: 209–18.

Buchan, J., T. Parkin and J. Sochalski. (2003) International Nurse Mobility: Trends and Policy Implications, WHO/EIP/OSD/2003.3, Geneva: WHO.

Chanda, R. (2002) 'Trade in Health Services', in N. Drager and C. Vieira (eds), *Trade in Health Services: Global, Regional and Country Perspectives*, Washington, DC: PAHO/WHO.

Chikanda, A. (2005) *Medical Leave: The Exods of Health Professionals from Zimbabwe*, in J. Crush (ed.), South African Migration Project, Capetown: Idasa.

Department of Health (DoH), UK (2001) Code of Practice for NHS Employers Involved in International Recruitment of Health Care Professionals, London: DoH.

Deyal, T. (2003) 'Hasta la vista, paradise', *Perspectives in Health Magazine* (of PAHO), vol. 8, no. 2. Available from: www.ops-oms.org/English/DD/PIN/Number17_article5_1.htm, accessed 21 February 2004.

Egger, D., and O. Adams (1999) 'Imbalances in Human Resources for Health: Can Policy Formulation and Planning Make a Difference?' *Human Resources for Health Journal*, vol. 3, no. 1: 52–63.

Family Care International (1999) *Meeting the Cairo Challenge: Progress in Sexual and Reproductive Health*, New York: FCI

Hardill, I., and S. Macdonald (2000) 'Skilled International Migration: The Experience in the UK', *Regional Studies*, vol. 34, no. 7: 681–92.

International Council of Nurses (2004) *The Global Shortage of Registered Nurses: An Overview of Issues and Actions*, Geneva: ICN.

International Labour Organization (2004) *A Fair Globalization: Creating Opportunities for All*, Final report of the World Commission on the Social Dimensions of Globalization, Geneva: ILO.

Institute of Medicine (IoM) of the National Academies, USA (2003) *Keeping Patients Safe: Transforming the Work Environment of Nurses*. Available from: www.iom.edu/report.asp?id=16173, accessed 10 March 2004.

Joint Learning Initiative (2004) *Human Resources for Health: Overcoming the Crisis*, Global Equity Initiative, Boston: Harvard University.

Kingma, M. (2001) 'Nursing Migration: Global Treasure Hunt or Disaster-in-the-Making?', *Nursing Inquiry*, vol. 8, no. 4: 205–12.

Koblinsky, M.A., O. Campbell and J. Heichelheim (1999) 'Organizing Delivery Care: What Works for Safe Motherhood?', *Bulletin of the World Health Organization*, vol. 77, no. 5: 399–405.

Marchal, B., and G. Kegels (2003) 'Health Workforce Imbalances in Times of Globalization: Brain Drain or Professional Mobility?', *International Journal of Health Planning and Management*, vol. 18: S89–101.

Martineau, T., K. Decker and P. Bundred (2002) 'Briefing Note on International Migration of Health Professionals: Levelling the Playing Field for Developing Country Health Systems', Liverpool School of Tropical Medicine.

Pang, T., M.A. Langsang and A. Haines (2002) 'Brain Drain and Health Professionals: A Global Problem Needs Global Solutions', *British Medical Journal*, vol. 324, no. 2 (March): 499–500.

Socio-Economic Welfare (SEW) (2002) *Newsletter of the International Council of Nurses*, January–March 2002. Available from: www.icn.ch/sewjan-mar02.htm, accessed 30 January 2003.

South Africa Migration Project (2002) Available from: www.queensu.ca/samp, accessed 31 January 2003.

South Africa Migration Project (2003) Migration Training, Available from: www.queensu.ca/samp/Training.htm, accessed 27 January 2003.

Stillwell, B., K. Diallo, P. Zurn, M.R. Dal Poz, O. Adams and J. Buchan (2003) 'Developing Evidence-Based Ethical Policies on the Migration of Health Workers: Conceptual and Practical Challenges', *Human Resources for Health*, vol. 1, no. 8, 28 October. Available from: www.human-resources-health.com/content/1/1/8, accessed 10 March 2004.

UK Nursing and Midwifery Council (2005) Statistical Analysis of the Register, 1 April 2004–31 March 2005, London: NMC.

Van Eyck, K. (2004) *Women and International Migration in the Health Sector*, Ferney-Voltaire Cedex: Public Services International. Available from: http://www.world-psi.org/Content/ContentGroups/English7/Publica-tions1/Final_Report_Migration.pdf, accessed 6 March 2005.

Vellinga, J. (2002) 'An Approach to Trade and Health at Health Canada', in N. Drager and C. Veira (eds), *Trade in Health Services: Global, Regional and Country Perspectives*, Washington, DC: PAHO.

Vujicic, M., P. Zurn, K. Diallo, O. Adams, M.R. Dal Poz (2004) 'The Role of Wages in the Migration of Health Care Professionals from Developing Countries', *Human Resources for Health*, vol. 2, no. 3: 1–13. Available from: www.human-resources-health.com/content/2/1/3, accessed 20 May 2004.

World Bank (1998) *World Development Indicators*, World Bank. Available from: www.worldbank.org/data/archive/wdi, accessed 20 May 2004.

World Health Organization (1999) Reduction of maternal mortality: a joint WHO/UNFPA/UNICEF/World Bank statement. Geneva: WHO.

World Health Organization (2001) Strengthening Nursing and Midwifery: Progress and Future Directions, Summary Document 1996–2000, WHO/EIP/OSD/2001.6.

World Health Organization (2002) Global Advisory Group on Midwifery and Nursing, Report of the Seventh meeting, Geneva 27–29 November 2001, WHO/EIP/OSD/2002.1.

World Health Organization (2004a) Making Pregnancy Safer, Fact Sheet No. 276, February 2004. Available from: www.who.int/mediacentre/factsheets/fs276/en/, accessed 21 May 2004.

World Health Organization (2004b) Migration of Health Professionals in Six Countries: A Synthesis Report. WHO AFRO, July 2004.

World Health Organization (2004c) Maternal mortality in 2000: Estimates developed by WHO, UNICEF, UNFPA, Geneva: WHO.

World Health Organization (2005) World Health Report: Making every mother and child count, Geneva: WHO.

PART IV

Policy and Advocacy

Trade Agreements and Reproductive Health and Rights: An Agenda for Analysis and Advocacy

Marceline White

Introduction

The International Conference on Population and Development (ICPD) held in Cairo, Egypt, in 1994 represented a milestone in the history of population and development and women's rights. At the conference, 179 countries adopted, by consensus, a Programme of Action that shifted the focus of population and development policies and programmes from demographic change to empowering women and ensuring women's reproductive rights. The ICPD platform defined reproductive rights as: the right of couples to decide freely the number, spacing and timing of their children; the right to affordable and accessible reproductive health services including information about pregnancy, breast-feeding, family planning and STDs. Reproductive rights include the right to a variety of high-quality contraceptive and abortion options. Freedom from sexual violence, coercion or discrimination is integral to the reproductive rights agenda. In addition, the ICPD programme detailed a set of concomitant rights that create an enabling environment for women to exercise their reproductive rights. These include: universal education; a reduction of infant and child mortality; a reduction of maternal mortality; and more sustainable consumption patterns, particularly in wealthy, developed nations. Conceptually, the ICPD agenda places women and their empowerment at the centre of population and development strategies – both as an end in itself and as a strategy for improving the ability of couples to plan the size of their families and spacing of their children.

Yet, since the historic achievement of the ICPD agenda, new challenges have emerged for reproductive rights and health advocates. One challenge has been the emergence of international, regional and bilateral trade agreements. Trade agreements have moved beyond the negotiation of tariffs and quotas on manufactured goods, and now extend to agricultural products, services and 'trade-related' areas such as intellectual property rights and foreign investment. At the same time, more detailed rules are being developed to reduce perceived structural and institutional impediments to trade, including a wide range of domestic laws and regulations. Over the past two decades, there has also been a parallel trend in many countries to privatize industries and services formally owned or provided by governments. One result is that many goods and services that have traditionally been provided by the public sector are now increasingly subject to competition from foreign companies. Moreover, national and local laws that have been enacted to promote economic development, human and labour rights, environmental protection and the empowerment of women and other disadvantaged groups may now be challenged as barriers to trade.

As the free-trade paradigm ascends, there has been a concomitant erosion of gains for reproductive rights and health advocates. Since 1994, there has been a marked decline in both policy achievements and funding for the ICPD agenda. Under President George W. Bush, the United States decreased its funding for reproductive rights and health and imposed restrictions on that funding. The shift to a more conservative ideological approach to reproductive rights was recently exemplified at a meeting to affirm the ICPD platform in which the US government attempted to excise references to 'reproductive health', 'family planning services', 'sexual health' and 'condoms' and include references to abstinence.

While embattled advocates for reproductive rights and health fight to protect previously won gains, issues such as global trade have emerged with repercussions for their work. Trade agreements may include new rules and commitments that affect access to and quality of reproductive health care, as well as lead to changes in the costs and availability of reproductive pharmaceuticals, services and technology. Because the effects of trade agreements may enhance or erode the gains of the ICPD platform, it is important for reproductive rights advocates to understand trade policies and advocate for those that support reproductive rights and health.

The purpose of this chapter is to suggest specific and strategic entry points for advocacy by reproductive rights and health supporters. This chapter suggests entry points for narrowly targeted, as well as broader, advocacy strategies, discusses the relative advantage of national and international level advocacy and finally suggests some routes for strategic alliances for effective advocacy.

Entry Points for an Effective Advocacy Strategy

Advocacy on reproductive rights and trade is essential to ensure that trade agreements enhance the ability of countries to achieve their ICPD commitments on reproductive rights and health as well as to mitigate any adverse effects. To date, there have been few advocacy initiatives that specifically link the trade and reproductive rights agendas.

For reproductive rights advocates to influence trade negotiations effectively, they will have to overcome several challenges. The first is to define their advocacy goals and target agreements. Advocacy on trade issues can resemble Hercules battling the many-headed Hydra – once an advocacy goal is achieved within one agreement, a new trade agreement is introduced with many of the same issues and challenges present as in the prior trade pact.

A second challenge is to define at what level they want to try to influence the negotiations. Trade-policy advocacy takes place at local, national and international levels, and reproductive rights advocates must decide where they have the best potential to achieve their aims.

A third challenge is to surmount the steep learning curve of trade analysis. There are many technical aspects of trade policy that reproductive rights advocates may have to master in order to influence the negotiations.

While the ultimate aim may be to create a global trade system of agreements and enforcement that is rights-based, gender-sensitive and development-centred, a short-term, feasible goal might be to support facets of trade agreements that lead to increased access for women and enable them the better to exercise their reproductive rights and secure high-quality reproductive health care, while minimizing or thwarting aspects of trade agreements that would undermine the ICPD platform.

Strategically, it makes sense for advocates to focus on the TRIPS (intellectual property rights) and GATS (services) Agreements. These agreements have the most immediate implications for the ICPD platform, continue to be negotiated in subsequent two-year 'rounds', which means that advocacy can be ongoing, and include more than 140 countries, which are members of the WTO, enabling advocates to collaborate with many civil society groups, academics and policy-makers.

Specifically, reproductive rights and health advocates may want to develop two to four concrete policy recommendations that would enhance women's reproductive rights and health outcomes as well as two to four policy recommendations that would thwart trade commitments that might undermine the ICPD platform. These recommendations may require different advocacy strategies and may attract different partners, alliances and targets to influence.

There are several advantages in pressing for specific policy recommendations. One is that it provides reproductive rights advocates with a focused, achievable policy agenda. A second is that the very specificity of the recommendations increases advocates' credibility among policy-makers, in contrast to NGOs calling for wholesale changes or eradication of the WTO agreements. Moreover, a focused advocacy agenda can also help reproductive rights activists to define and develop the necessary research, communications and organizing strategies that will enable them to influence the policy agenda. Another advantage is that many of the aforementioned proposals work within the existing WTO framework, rather than calling for a wholesale systemic change of the institution. This incrementalist approach may generate more support among policy-makers than other, more radical advocacy initiatives. Finally, policy-makers may find it politically difficult to oppose measures like those proposed for TRIPS that could prevent HIV/AIDS transmission, particularly mother-to-child transmissions.

Specific, targeted goals

Some specific suggestions for reproductive rights advocates to consider are detailed below.

In the GATS negotiations, reproductive rights advocates may want to do any of the following:

- Identify areas that could enhance reproductive rights, such as the use of telemedicine, the Internet and other services supplied across borders, which could increase access to reproductive health information, testing or contraceptives and press for the inclusion of these methods within the country's commitments. Within the GATS Agreement, countries negotiate what areas they will open to foreign providers and what areas they would like other countries to open. Reproductive rights advocates should determine what types of services would enhance reproductive rights and health in their country (such as the illustrative list above) and lobby developing country trade negotiators to include these sectors in their negotiations with wealthy nations.

- Seek to persuade trade negotiators, given that countries can place limits or conditions on how services are delivered, to require that foreign service providers also transfer new technology to the country, collaborate with local suppliers and/or use local employees in the delivery of the service in order to spur national economic development.

- Call on governments to allow greater flexibility for countries to exempt basic public services such as health from the legal requirement that the sector is progressively liberalized. The GATS Agreement mandates that the goal is progressive liberalization of services, which means that there should be continuous efforts to open areas such as health care to market forces. Reproductive rights advocates may want to press their trade negotiators to press for an exemption of basic public services such as health care from this requirement.

- Call on governments to issue a declaration on GATS clarifying that governments have the right to regulate and develop new domestic regulations and policies that are in the public interest. The current language in the GATS Agreement states that governments have the right to regulate, but is unclear as to whether governments could develop new legislation that is in the public interest but may conflict with the GATS Agreement.

- Call on governments to include in a GATS declaration a clarification that the right to health takes precedence over GATS obligations. The current trade text is unclear about whether a country's GATS obligations would supersede national health priorities.

In the TRIPS negotiations, reproductive rights advocates may want to:

- Urge their trade negotiators to press the WTO to comply with the WHO's 'revised drug strategy', which states that public health concerns are paramount during international trade disputes.

Currently, the WTO TRIPS text is unclear about whether health or trade concerns would be paramount regarding access to medicines.

• Press for the Doha Declaration to be interpreted to support reproductive rights and health. The Doha Declaration of 2001 reaffirmed that countries can and should implement the TRIPS Agreement in a manner that promotes public health and access to medicines for all.

• Invoke the Doha Declaration to enable advocates and/or governments to negotiate parallel imports or compulsory licenses in order to procure generic or lower-cost purchases of female-controlled contraceptives or microbicides. Reproductive rights advocates should press their trade negotiators to use the Doha Declaration to purchase generic or lower-cost bulk purchases of contraceptives and medicines, such as HIV/AIDS medicines.

Broader goals

In addition to these specific goals, advocates may want to press for a broader goal to 'engender' trade policy-making and trade analysis. Many civil society organizations are pressing for various social impact assessments. Reproductive rights and health advocates could ally with different NGOs to press for these assessments and ensure that the assessments include a strong reproductive rights and health component. Reproductive rights advocates could take advantage of already existing frameworks to incorporate reproductive rights into the assessments and ally with groups already engaged in advocacy for assessments.

Public health assessments

For example, the WHO developed an analytical framework to evaluate the interaction between global trade and global health (Woodward et al. 2001). The conceptual framework traces the direct and indirect effects of globalization on health systems, populations and individual households. The framework implicitly includes reproductive rights but the relationship is not explored in detail. Reproductive rights and health advocates could press WHO to use the framework explicitly to pursue the links between reproductive health and rights and global trade. Moreover, advocates could use this framework as a launching point for developing their own research and analysis of the linkages.

Public health advocates, associations and trade unions representing health care workers have called on governments to assess the impacts of trade liberalization on public health outcomes. Working in coalition with public health allies, reproductive rights advocates could press for such an assessment and ensure that the ICPD agenda is incorporated into any such assessment.

Gender and social impact assessments

Similarly, gender and trade advocates have called for gender and social impact assessments of trade agreements for the past seven years. Therefore, including reproductive rights and health within the gender and social impact assessment campaigns would be an important and logical step in securing reproductive rights.

To date, there is little coordination between reproductive rights advocates and gender and trade activists. While both are important facets of the global women's movement, these actors often have different advocacy agendas, targets and priorities. For example, much of the advocacy around reproductive rights may focus on parliamentarians or ministries of health, while trade advocacy focuses on trade or economic ministries and often a different set of parliamentarians. Moreover, many reproductive rights advocates are struggling to maintain freedom of choice in their countries, increase funding for reproductive health programmes, and ensure service delivery; few organizations may have the time and resources to develop a new programme area on reproductive rights and trade. Similarly, gender and trade advocates are besieged with the number of trade and investment agreements being brokered globally, and are often ill-equipped to take on a new area of research or policy advocacy. Finally, because the reproductive rights and health agenda is so politically contentious, some gender and trade advocates may be reluctant to associate themselves with the movement.

Despite these challenges, there are many reasons why this collaboration is a natural and strategic one. Many gender and trade advocates have been part of the activism around reproductive rights and health; many are broadly concerned with women's rights rather than just interested in gender and trade, and there are clear synergies between the issues, constituencies and advocacy. Closer collaboration between reproductive rights advocates and gender and trade advocates to hone these indicators, participate in the research and advocate for the adoption of these assessment tools would be an important first step to more firmly integrating reproductive rights concerns into the trade debate.

In recent years, at least two organizations moved beyond calling for gender and social impact assessments to actually developing indicators and frameworks, which can be used to ascertain the potential benefits and drawbacks that trade agreements may have for women.

Women in Development Europe (WIDE), a coalition of European and Southern gender and development groups, developed a set of indicators to assess trade's effect on women. These indicators include separate sections on women's labour and earnings, on political participation and decision-making, and on trade tariff reductions, trading volumes, trade direction (export surplus or import surplus), and also include a sectoral breakdown of trade (over agriculture, industry and services and sectors within industry, such as textile production or automobile assembly). WIDE developed the indicators to be simple, easily accessible tools for policy-makers, rather than creating a complex framework for analysis, which they believe is not necessary to influence EU policy-makers. WIDE partnered with organizations in Latin America to use these indicators to assess the gender-differentiated effects of EU–Latin American trade agreements on women in both regions. They published papers using their indicators and presented their work before members of the European Parliament.

Women's Edge Coalition, a US-based coalition of women's groups and development groups, developed a Trade Impact Review (TIR) for assessing the gender and social effects of trade agreements on women and the poor. The TIR differs from other gender assessments in that it includes both economic and legal/regulatory analysis. In laying out a framework to model the differential impact of trade and investment agreements on women, the authors develop a 'feedback loop' that describes how a change in trade policy may affect relative prices – which, in turn, could affect labour demand in the public and private sectors, bring about a change in real wages and affect consumption. Finally, the implementation of trade agreements can also affect the receipt of taxes by governments as tariffs are reduced, and may bring about a change in the provision of public sector services if they are privatized or revenues are insufficient to sustain current levels of service delivery. The economic framework clearly illustrates that a policy change can set into motion a series of other economic changes that directly affect the livelihoods and well-being of women and men in the Global South and the United States.

The legal and regulatory section of the framework employs both a content and conflict analysis to ascertain possible gender-differentiated effects of trade and investment agreements. Policy-makers should consider whether the content of a trade or investment commitment contains any overtly gender-biased provisions. Another way to analyse the content of a commitment is to consider whether gender-neutral provisions might affect women differently. Finally, the analysis should consider whether the implementation or enforcement mechanisms of the agreement could disadvantage women.

A conflict analysis would consider the possible interactions between proposed trade or investment commitments and the laws relevant to women in a particular country, including the array of formal and informal laws and norms that determine women's status and rights.

The TIR is the centrepiece of the Look FIRST (Full Impact Review and Screening of Trade) campaign. The Look FIRST campaign combines research, policy advocacy, grassroots organizing and media to press the US government to conduct a TIR on how trade affects the poor, particularly poor women, prior to completing each bilateral, regional and multilateral trade agreement. The campaign is described in more detail below.

National Level Advocacy

Since many of the specific policy recommendations identified above are related to the WTO, it would be natural to assume that the WTO is a critical site for advocacy. However, the WTO has been somewhat impervious to international advocacy efforts and it is unlikely that WTO staff will be the ones to secure reproductive rights as they relate to trade agreements.

Member countries of the WTO are responsible for negotiating and adhering to the WTO agreements. Each country assigns a ministry or several ministries to coordinate and negotiate trade policy on behalf of the nation. Trade negotiators and trade ministers deliberate different positions among WTO members and try to reach a consensus. Therefore, a national-level advocacy strategy is likely to be most effective for guaranteeing that trade liberalization enhances reproductive rights and health.

A national-level advocacy approach would enable reproductive rights and health advocates to use their prior experience in trying to influence national leaders to inform their political strategies on trade and reproductive rights and health. Moreover, organizations with an active citizens' lobby can mobilize their base to influence parliamentarians and members of the administration. Presumably, parliamentarians and national leaders are somewhat more responsive to constituent pressure than, say, a civil servant at the WTO. In addition, many reproductive rights advocates are already familiar with effective national media strategies that they can adapt to influence national trade positions.

National level campaigns that combine research, advocacy, media and citizen mobilization have had some success influencing policy-makers in state, foreign affairs or development posts. For example, the Women's Edge Coalition's Look FIRST campaign included collabo-rative research with Mexican and Caribbean women's groups to develop case studies using the TIR to examine the effect of trade on women in Mexico and Jamaica. Although research efforts were con-strained by the lack of data for a comprehensive review, nevertheless the case studies uncovered new information illustrating why women and men are differentially affected by trade, generated pragmatic policy recommendations and put a 'woman's face' on the impact of global-ization. The research has led to some media interest in the subject of women and trade. Women's Edge Coalition has presented this research to US policy-makers including Members of Congress, staff at the Department of State, the US Agency for International Development, the US Trade Representative's Office and the Department of Labor.

As a result, for the first time, the United States included a gender-specific section in their labour–employment analysis of a bilateral trade agreement with Chile. Unfortunately, other administration offi-cials deleted the majority of the gender-specific findings, leaving intact only a few paragraphs on how trade liberalization affects women's employment and earnings.

However, after the case studies were presented to the Members of Congress, congressional leaders called on the US Trade Representative's Office and the Department of Labor to include a gender section in the labour analysis of the regional US–Central America Free Trade Agreement (CAFTA), which has been completed but not yet ratified. The Department of Labor has agreed to disaggregate employment analysis by gender and to include a discussion of gender-related labour rights issues in workplaces. Whether or not this analysis is more sub-stantive than the US–Chile one remains to be seen.

Similarly, WIDE has been able to leverage their gender and social impact assessments to present the case for gender and social impact assessments to EU ministers. WIDE has presented their analysis and advocacy platform before EU ministers during the WTO meetings in September 2003 and in other venues.

In addition to trying to influence trade negotiators and parliamentarians, reproductive health and rights advocates in donor countries could focus on national development agencies. Many development agencies contribute to national policy-making deliberations regarding a country's trade negotiating positions. In addition to pressing for development funds, reproductive rights activists could work to ensure that newer reproductive health commodities under patent and HIV/AIDS drugs can be procured cheaply by developing country governments. This may mean, for example, pressing for a broad interpretation of the TRIPS Agreement and the Doha Declaration on TRIPS.

Strategic Alliances

As previously noted, there is a steep learning curve on trade issues for reproductive health and rights advocates to master to effectively lobby on these issues. This may be particularly challenging for small organizations that are already engaged with pressing reproductive rights and health challenges. Rather than spending time becoming 'experts' on this issue, it may behove reproductive rights and health advocates to engage in strategic alliances with organizations working on these issues where there may be shared interests. Several categories of candidates for strategic alliances emerge: gender and trade advocates, public health advocates, development organizations as well as GATS and TRIPS advocates.

Gender and trade advocates present an obvious ally for reproductive rights and health advocates. As mentioned previously, groups could engage in joint advocacy on gender and social impact assessments as well as on several of the key policy recommendations on GATS and TRIPS. One challenge working with gender and trade advocates is that many are calling for systemic changes within the WTO and are unlikely to support policy recommendations that encourage the WTO to play a role in public health. However, gender and trade groups would be strong allies in any aspect of the reproductive rights and health agenda that seeks to curtail or minimize the role of trade in relation to public health.

In addition to working with the WHO, public health organizations have emerged as strong critics of trade policies that they believe may lead to negative outcomes for public health. Public health advocates include public health associations, such as the American Public Health Association, labour unions, such as Service Employees International

Union, Public Services International and the American Nurses Association, all of which represent nurses and other health care employees, and public health and trade advocacy groups, such as the Center for Policy on Health and Trade. Reproductive rights and health groups could partner with these organizations and similar organizations in refining a public health agenda on trade which includes reproductive rights and would be supportive of specific policy recommendations as well as a public health assessment of trade policies.

Development organizations represent another potential ally for reproductive health and rights advocates. In Europe, the Trade Justice Movement (TJM) is a coalition of development organizations, including Oxfam International, Save the Children UK and Christian Aid, which seeks to influence EU trade policy from a development perspective. Several members of TJM are engaged in advocacy on TRIPS and GATS. Reproductive rights and health advocates could work with these organizations to develop a reproductive rights component for advocacy and research by emphasizing the linkages between reproductive rights and sustainable development.

In the United States and Canada, international development coalitions such as InterAction and the Canadian Council for International Cooperation are also increasingly engaged in trade analysis and advocacy, as international relief and development staff in developing countries begin to see first-hand how macroeconomic policies affect development initiatives.

Other potential allies include coalitions devoted to influencing TRIPS and GATS negotiations. For example, the Global Treatment Action Campaign (GTAC) focuses on ensuring access to essential medications. Reproductive rights and health advocates could partner with GTAC to influence the TRIPS agenda from a feminist, rights-based perspective. In the United States, HIV/AIDS activists have achieved some success in advocating that the United States stop challenging developing countries' efforts to import generic HIV/AIDS medications. Reproductive rights advocates could collaborate with HIV/AIDS activist organizations to promote female-controlled methods of HIV/AIDS prevention and to broaden the TRIPS advocacy agenda to encompass an affirmative definition of reproductive rights and health. In the same way, many coalitions have surfaced which focus exclusively on the GATS negotiations. Advocates could collaborate with these organizations and bring a reproductive health perspective to the table.

Conclusion

There is little empirical research to date on the nexus between reproductive rights, health and trade agreements. Current analyses suggest that trade in services and intellectual property will most likely directly affect access to and the affordability of reproductive health care.

Reproductive rights and health advocates need to develop specific policy recommendations for the WTO TRIPS and GATS Agreements, create national campaigns to influence policy-makers and press for specific impact assessments on gender and social issues as well as on public health. To do all of this, reproductive rights and health groups should develop strategic alliances to increase the collective weight of their advocacy initiatives, minimize the time and expertise required to engage on the issues and broaden the number of constituencies that can be engaged in lobbying national policy-makers to assert and expand the scope of women's reproductive rights and mitigate any adverse effects of trade on these rights.

Reference

Woodward, D., N. Drager, R. Beaglehole and D. Lipson (2001) 'Globalization and Health: A Framework for Analysis and Action', *Bulletin of the World Health Organization*, vol. 79, no. 9: 875–81.

Reproductive Health Advocacy

Alaka Malwade Basu

Introduction

Let me step right into this chapter with a framework for describing, very roughly, the road from economic globalization to reproductive health (RH), as illustrated in Figure 12.1. In this figure, the dotted lines represent positive, negative and/or ambiguous effects – that is, it is debatable, as many of the chapters in this book testify, 'exactly' what one can say about the relationship without reference to the larger context and without several caveats. This is so, notwithstanding the extreme polarization on these matters that the pro- and anti-globalization positions have brought about. The bold lines represent more definite and more direct effects.

There are two related propositions in this chapter, one indirect and the other direct, but both are of strategic importance for successful advocacy. The first, and relatively tangential, proposition is that the current extreme polarization of views in the debate on globalization and gender is unfortunate and self-defeating. This polarization means that while the globalizers and economic liberalizers can see only the benefits of economic restructuring, their opponents are completely absorbed in demonstrating the many ways in which it is bad for society and especially for women.

This is not the place to comment on the first pole, which sees economic globalization as only positive. But from the standpoint of the gender and RH lobby, it is worth reflecting upon the disadvantages of the opposite stance too. This is the stance that is focused solely on identifying the *negative* fallout of globalization (and indeed development

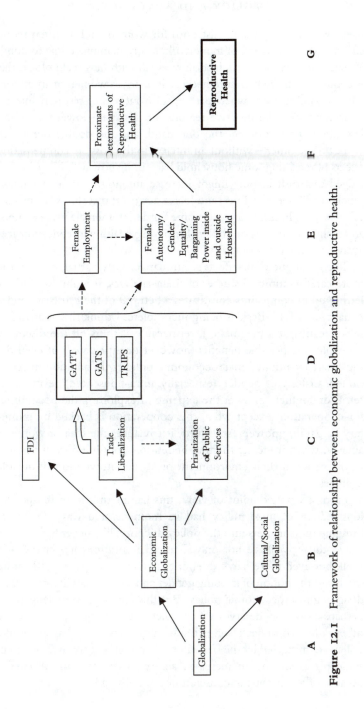

Figure 12.1 Framework of relationship between economic globalization and reproductive health.

itself, as defined by the mainstream) for women, and on interpreting all evidence in this kind of framework. Many examples come to mind. When female labour participation rates fall with new technology, this is bemoaned in the literature because it deprives women of an important bargaining tool; when participation rates rise, research interest concentrates on the negative reasons for this rise – lower wages and less labour protection on the one hand, and the double burden of work on the other – without an interest in the possible compensating effects of regaining some household bargaining power. If it is acknowledged that cash income might increase autonomy, the researcher is quick to add (see, e.g. Evers and Juarez 2003: 13) that this is 'at the cost of worsening health and greater time burdens for female wage earners' and a shift in the responsibility 'for paying health and education fees away from men to women'.

The catalogue of ill-effects seems dangerously partial, even in the more careful empirical studies or meta-analyses. It is almost as if any letting up in complaints constitutes a betrayal of the cause of gender equality and RH. Besides being incomplete, I think this approach is self-defeating at a pragmatic level because it shuts off the discourse on exploiting possible benefits (however unanticipated) of even the most narrow-minded macroeconomic policies. In addition, its continued analysis of gender (especially intra-household) relations in terms of conflict comes at the expense of exploiting the possibilities for cooperation, except when this cooperation is backed by monetary bargaining power. And third, it trivializes the idea of women's agency, when it locates them as benefiting from life only at the will of the males in their environment or at the intervention of outside agencies.

From a strategic point of view, this hammering in of the gender lopsidedness of most policy had its moments and was effective at bringing these matters into the policy discourse like never before. As a result, today we have not only financial institutions like the World Bank but even more hawkish entities like the IMF paying at least lip service to the notion of keeping gender and social issues in mind while designing macroeconomic policy. But this kind of acknowledgement perhaps now also deserves the parallel acknowledgement from the other side that at least some of the ill-effects of global economic policy are mitigated by the benefits of such policy at some time and in some places and by an increased ability to confront the ill-effects, because of greater public consciousness if nothing else.

From a practical point of view, just as we now have many case studies and statistical analyses (see, e.g. the extremely one-sided catalogue in Shah et al. 1999) about the negative impact of economic globalization processes, it would be useful to have detailed case studies of situations in which the poor (and especially women) have actually benefited from globalization. At the very least, we need to explore the ways in which women can potentially benefit from globalization (as discussed, e.g. in Hensman 1996, in the context of globalization and technological change).[1] This kind of literature could provide more concrete ideas for replication and expansion into communities/groups in which the relationship has been largely adverse.

For example, quite apart from the access to health services that directly impact on both preventive and curative RH outcomes, there are indirect pathways to RH that lie in more 'biodemographic' factors. Of particular importance here is the nature and extent of a woman's fertility; one way to explore the implications of globalization for RH might be to look at its implications for fertility. More importantly, one needs to be able to do this without simultaneously assuming that any declines in fertility associated with the new marketplace are involuntary and undesirable. Such a tack again denies the very real possibility that economic opportunity might now make it both less necessary to maintain high fertility and easier to achieve lower fertility goals through heightened household autonomy.

The second (and central) proposition of this chapter is that advocacy is best served by efforts to address interventions as close to the final outcome of interest as possible. In the case of Figure 12.1, therefore, the most effective and perhaps the most strongly evidence-based RH advocacy would be that which tries to affect the 'proximate determinants' of RH. This proximate determinants approach is directly lifted from fertility and mortality studies in demography (see Davis and Blake 1956: 211–35; Mosley and Chen 1984, for the first descriptions of the proximate determinants of fertility and child mortality, respectively) and gives us an analytical handle on the means through which larger socioeconomic forces like female employment or trade liberalization (TL) can have an ultimate effect on RH outcomes.

I discuss these proximate determinants of RH later in the chapter. But first, I want to make the case that advocacy efforts are best directed at the direct influences on these proximate determinants rather than at points further removed from RH in Figure 12.1. That is, advocacy on A, B, C, D and E in Figure 12.1 stands the risk of being both less successful to achieve at a policy level as well as less obviously useful for improving women's RH if it is successful, than advocacy aimed at the proximate determinants of RH.

Of course, it is a different matter if the outcome measures sought to be changed are those represented by A, B, C, D or E, for themselves rather than for their presumed instrumental relationship with RH. This is not the focus of this chapter, even if a case can be made for limiting the scope of, say, TL in developing countries for ideological reasons or because of its possible influence on the next link in the chain in Figure 12.1, female employment. And there is certainly a case to be made, at least in principle, as has been made, for example, in the Canadian Alternative Federal Budget (see Elson and Cagatay 2000) for increasing the social justice principles inherent in macroeconomic policies. In the context of gender justice, there is also a strong case for reducing the 'male breadwinner' bias in most macroeconomic policies today. But once more, I would tie this case to the inherent value of gender justice per se, not to its role in RH.

That is, I would be wary of using a TL–RH or female employment–RH argument to advocate for or against TL or female employment, because that can be counterproductive. If the presumed TL–RH link can be demonstrated to be weak (as it well could be, at least in specific cases, given the many intermediate variables involved), that would demolish the pro- or anti-TL positions in a way that cannot happen if TL is opposed or supported for itself (or for its immediate consequences) rather than for its more distant instrumental properties.

My point here is better illustrated by the value of advocacy for gender equality as a desirable goal in itself, rather than for its impact on reduced fertility. In the short term, the ability to tie up with more powerful population control lobbies to push for gender equality (or girls' education) might make strategic sense; in the long term, it is best to jettison these justifications and use more absolute standards of norms and ethics.

The RH goal does not need any larger justification; it is legitimate and desirable in itself, so a focus on its proximate determinants stands less chance of being derailed by attacks on the instrumental role of RH.[2] In addition, this approach allows advocacy to press for the protection and enhancement of RH through programmes that are permanent[3] and non-negotiable because they are not tied to any instrumental properties of RH or to other macroeconomic polices that can change and vary in so many unplanned and contextual ways.

Nevertheless, it is a large and cumbersome animal; RH is not *one* thing, and towards the end of the chapter I also call for more effective disaggregation of the idea of RH and better prioritization of its many components from a policy point of view.

I have already made the general point that the further back on the chain in Figure 12.1 efforts at reform are directed, the greater the strategic and operational risks of the enterprise. The various chapters in this volume also make the same point often enough, sometimes directly, sometimes incidentally or even inadvertently. In the following sections, I want to pull out a few specific reasons for reinforcing this call to focus on the proximate rather than the distal determinants of RH in the chain linking globalization and RH. Where possible, I use specific examples from this book to illustrate my points.

In the process of elaborating this in the next section, I am also making a case for greater subtlety and less polarization in drawing conclusions about the positive and negative effects of globalization. In the section 'A Framework for Effective Advocacy', I go on to describe the proximate determinants of RH and the possible advocacy strategies to improve RH through these proximate determinants.

The Difficulties with General Advocacy

The inevitability of globalization

The kind of selective advocacy that I suggest in this chapter is important because globalization, economic globalization and versions of TL are here to stay and fighting for their wholesale elimination might be a futile dissipation of energy. In any case, what are the alternatives to TL: national self-sufficiency or bilateral trade agreements (see Hensman 2004)? The former, besides being economically inefficient, is capable of constraining individual rights and opportunities as often as it promotes them. And in bilateral agreements, inequalities in power can have even more hazardous consequences for the weaker partner than truly international trade agreements in which the weak can at least collectively influence some of the rules of the game.

Of course, it is true that while globalization and TL may be inevitable, the forms they take are not immutable and TL, for example, can mean many things, some of which are less desirable than others. In particular, TL is more complex than merely the opening up of markets, and much of the political opposition is not to free trade per se as much as to the undue advantage that free trade as currently practised gives to multinational corporations and to industrialized countries to decide the rules of the game. But it is precisely the international, as opposed to bilateral, nature of trade agreements today that can also allow some of these rules to be changed though encouraging partnerships among the weak. If this collective strength were not at least partially real, we would not today have a situation in which the economic superpowers are among the most vociferous opponents of international treaties and anti-protectionism.[4]

A hydra-headed creature

If TL takes many forms, 'globalization' is even more difficult to pin down with a definition. Besides, from the standpoint of its effects, the central point is that, like TL, it is a double-edged sword. If it does harm through the spread of neo-liberal capitalism, by its very nature it also facilitates the potentially more effective global opposition to such capitalism. If I were to choose, on the grounds of potential effectiveness, between local resistance to local exploitation and global resistance to global exploitation, I am not sure that the former would necessarily win. The strength in numbers that the latter confers is precisely analogous to the strength of collective bargaining that TL is supposed to weaken through its scattering of the workforce into the informal sectors of the economy.

Indeed, by insisting on the sacrosanct nature of national boundaries, one is in danger of playing into the hands of a kind of domestic fundamentalism that might be even worse for marginalized populations, given contemporary right-wing tendencies in nationalistic politics that are every bit as poisonous as the imperialism being demonstrated in international politics.

The double edgedness of the sword remains even when one looks at a narrowly defined form of economic globalization like the TL that has been imposed on the developing world since the 1990s. This is so even if the case can be made that the underlying objectives of such TL are the further enrichment of the developed countries and of the multinational corporations. Fortunately for us, 'any' opening of doors and windows (the doors and windows of national borders in this case) carries the risk of subversive[5] winds blowing in together with the winds of unequal trade.

The box of cultural/social globalization in Figure 12.1 can therefore, in principle, be incorporated into the larger framework of globalization–RH relationships in greater detail. One could, for example, include the spread of an ideology of gender equality or the ideology of RH rights as mediators between cultural globalization and RH. I have not followed these leads here simply because this volume focuses on TL and RH. But Third World (or feminist or socialist) policy and advocacy may be more useful if it recognizes and exploits these avenues for subversion rather than seeking an unconditional closing of doors and windows.[6]

Such a strategy of protecting the positive and subverting or rejecting the negative possibilities in globalization makes even more sense when one is interested in the specific relationships between TL and RH, which is what the present volume is about. This is because both TL and RH are multi-tentacled creatures, whose various arms often do not work in unison, and so that the relationship between the two also operates at several levels, not all of them detrimental to RH. Indeed, not only can some aspects of this relationship be neutral, some might even be positive, and using the negative potential effect of TL on RH to advocate the elimination of TL might be a case of cutting off the nose to spite the face.

The distinction made by Elson and Cagatay (2000) between the social *impact* of macroeconomic policy and the social *content* of such policy is extremely appealing in this context, and in this chapter that is the approach I take – that macroeconomic policies must incorporate a social (in this case the social refers to the RH) component. However, I depart from Elson and Cagatay by not tying this need for a social content to the potential impact of policy. I do this partly because, as the following sections discuss, it is so difficult to delineate this impact in a policy relevant way and because, as already stated, so many impacts are unanticipated, contextual and often positive. The more useful form of advocacy in my formulation, therefore, is one which persists in asking for all macroeconomic policies to include or make room for an RH component for all women in need, instead of relating RH needs to specific aspects of macroeconomic policy like GATS or TRIPS or GATT.

In the next two subsections, I use specific examples from the real world to illustrate some of the pitfalls of using the rhetoric of pro- and anti-globalization to make demands for policy on RH matters.

Example 1: Globalization and 'feminization'

'Feminization' is an extremely popular word in the literature on TL and the economic reforms of the 1980s and 1990s.[7] It is also a frequently misused word that needs to be repeatedly clarified conceptually if it is to provide any real wisdom on its larger implications. As far as I can make out from the literature, the word is applied interchangeably to more than one economic process.

When the impact of TL and economic globalization is discussed, two terms that come up repeatedly are 'the feminization of poverty' and 'the feminization of the labour force'. The reader of this stream of literature is struck by the way in which the two terms are used interchangeably as if they mean the same thing. Of course, at a definitional level, the academic literature is aware that the two terms have precise meanings, but for all practical purposes as well as to attach a normative (usually negative) significance to them, they are assumed to be the same thing.

But this need not be the case at all and while one might rightly bemoan any feminization of *poverty* that accompanies the process of economic globalization, a feminization of *the labour force* may have both positive and negative implications; hopefully, empirical studies of the social impact of globalization processes like TL will focus on some of these. In particular, there is a need to look at positive trade-offs associated with feminization, not because economic reform is such a good thing but because it is inevitable and because positive trade-offs need to be exploited. Moreover, a focus on positive trade-offs will also acknowledge the notion of 'agency', the idea that women in a country experiencing economic reform are not merely passive victims of globalization. But to know when this is the case, one needs to disaggregate the notion of the feminization of the labour force a little more carefully than is done in the activist literature.

A careful reading of the literature reveals that the concept of the feminization of the labour force has two meanings – to refer to the rise of female labour force participation rates, and to refer to the rise of traditionally female kinds of work and work contracts whether done by women or by men. In principle, both these processes have more neutral implications for social welfare than is automatically assumed. I discuss some of these possibilities shortly; here I want to urge a renewed emphasis to contextualize for clues as to whether they represent positive or negative possibilities for society and women.

To return to the first definition of feminization of the labour force, this can be an increase in the absolute levels of female labour force participation, or only in relative levels. The second of these more readily suggests negative consequences, for it implies that women's representation in the labour force is rising only because male participation rates have fallen. Indeed, falling male employment may also lead to a rise in the absolute levels of female participation, as more women enter the market to make up for lost male incomes. Given universally worse wage and work conditions for women, this second development implies a fall in household incomes and a possible rise in poverty, neither of which can have good social consequences in general, nor on RH in particular.

The trouble is that even the academic/technical discourse on the subject is sometimes difficult to unravel on this kind of detail. For example, Cagatay and Ozler (1995: 1883–94) in their macroanalysis seem to use women's share of the labour force as their measure of feminization; however, the accompanying text seems to be talking of feminization as an absolute increase in female labour force participation rates. While it is true that the latter will also lead to the former, it is not clear that the latter has the same kind of negative implication as the former. Indeed, some of these implications may well be positive.[8]

In any case, many data sets do also suggest that the feminization of the labour force is caused by a rise in absolute levels of female labour force participation, independently of male participation rates (for a recent empirical review, see Swamy 2004, which reiterates however that an increase in female employment does not necessarily mean an improvement in gender equality). This can occur because there are now new opportunities for female employment or/and because women need to make up for lowered family incomes arising out of male incomes falling as they move into worse-paying occupations owing to economic reform. Once again, the second of these effects has some (but not all, as I discuss soon) negative implications for different aspects of social welfare. But if it is largely a case of women responding to new opportunities for work, then, besides family incomes rising, one must in fairness acknowledge the possibility of positive trade-offs.

These positive trade-offs might occur even if these new job opportunities are nothing to crow about. As the literature makes clear, most of the new jobs for women are concentrated in the feminized sector of the labour market – lower wages than for men, unsatisfactory work conditions, lower job security, short-term and flexible work contracts, piece-meal rather than time-based wage rates.

While these are all conditions to fight to change, they are not necessarily reasons to abolish these new work opportunities altogether, by clamping down on TL, for example. What they mean for women and therefore also for social welfare is heavily context-dependent.

As Amin (Chapter 6), for example, describes, new factory jobs for women in Bangladesh have had the positive effect of delaying marriage, increasing women's economic and household autonomy and improving overall demographic outcomes, because until these new jobs beckoned, women were either unemployed or working as unpaid family labour. In Pakistan too, Sathar (2002) reports the new respect conferred on women who have entered some of the high 'status' professions associated with TL; these women might still work out of the home, have temporary and piece-rate contracts, but they bring in a tangible income and this is seen as contributing to their elevated position at home and in society. In Egypt or Vietnam on the other hand, which have a history of women's education and employment in the public sector, the withdrawal of this old job security and the push into more stringent and unpleasant factory work can mean a loss of status and autonomy (Amin, Chapter 6).

In countries like India, there has also been a rise in rural female labour force participation rates, at least some of which may be an outcome of women taking on the responsibilities of men who have left for other (sometimes more attractive) jobs outside. Once again, one can view this development as positive if one looks at the entry of women into traditionally 'male' occupations, such as farm management and ploughing. Or one can perceive its negative implications if one considers that public services provide so little support to these women workers that they are now in effect doing a double shift of work, with all the implications of this for their own and household health and welfare (see the discussions on this theme in Singh and Meenakshi 2004).

All this means that we should aim for much greater clarity before making generalizations on the impact of reform on feminization and (especially) of feminization on RH. A research project on the relationship between different kinds of 'feminization' and social outcomes has much to recommend itself.

If I am beginning to sound like a stuck record in my repeated reference to the need for more research, this is not just a form of advocacy for more resources for such research (though it is that too). Instead, it is to bolster the second proposition of this chapter – that if we are interested in improving RH, it makes more general sense to focus on the proximate determinants of RH and on the influences on these proximate determinants, including female employment. There can also be a case for more direct interventions in work

conditions, of course, from the RH perspective, but a more genera-
lized advocacy about TL itself cannot be made on RH grounds. For
that, the case is best addressed at point F in Figure 12.1.

Example 2: Globalization, marginalization and the Peter versus Paul effect

The process of globalization, even when it helps overall growth,[9] could
marginalize and impoverish some groups. This can of course have huge
negative social and political fallouts. Before discussing how this can happen, I want to add a note of caution about not misreading this analysis.
Champions of globalization and economic reform or TL often deny
that these processes can cause poverty to increase or any group to be
marginalized. On the other hand, critics of globalization and reform
often point to the fact that some groups are hurt by these processes to
argue against such changes. I wish to resist both these points of view.
As I try to demonstrate, negative fallouts are very likely during such
economic reforms. On the other hand, it should be stressed that the fact
that individual groups may have a tendency to be marginalized must not
be taken as axiomatic for abandoning reform. Such a position is essentially reactionary since it amounts to resisting all economic change,
because there are hardly any major changes that help everybody.

Instead, one needs ways to assess realistically who becomes marginalized because of TL and then devise corrective policies to offset
these effects. Such offsetting is best done at the level of providing
social welfare nets, rather than being stridently anti-TL. It is the job
of a socially friendly policy to identify the groups that are vulnerable
to such marginalization and to protect their interests and social well-
being. The academic literature has been very good at identifying
some of these groups – women in general, women-headed households in particular, large families, the lower castes, the least educated,
the landless, workers in traditional occupations like weaving and
handicraft production, and so on.

But it is easy to criticize economic globalization (or any other kind
of economic policy change) when the winners and losers are so obviously the rich and the poor. The righteousness of the protest is also
shored up when one looks at individual vulnerable groups in isolation
and does not look at what I call positive trade-offs. In particular, there
is an aspect of economic reform here that I call the 'Peter and Paul
Principle' that is largely overlooked in the literature. By this I mean that

even as some disadvantaged groups lose out in the reform process, others stand to gain much. Are the gains of the latter to be discounted even though, prior to reform, the positions of the two groups were reversed?

Does one need a more ambiguous critical position on policy when certain groups worsen their circumstances if other, equally disadvantaged, groups are now better off? The trouble is that there are too few intra-poor studies that allow us to face this problem head-on. Let me give two examples here. First, traditional textiles and handlooms have been crippled by the advent of cheap imports in many of the trade liberalizing countries. This has also meant a marginalization of those traditional weavers who have not been absorbed by the modern textile sector and do not have the highly specialized traditional skills that would assure them of a market among the rich. But we know too little about the village poor who can now afford a little more clothing because the imported fabrics are cheaper and longer lasting and easier to care for, freeing some of the time and money of poorer women for more food and child schooling perhaps.

Similarly, traditional midwives have lost income and clients as rural fertility falls and as more and more women prefer to use a medical centre for their deliveries. But the lower fertility of these poor clients of the traditional midwife means all kinds of benefits to these clients themselves (in addition to being convenient for the national population goals of the developing countries). The midwife situation hardly calls for a halt to the new female employment opportunities that may be causing (as well as resulting in) this low fertility and increased hospital use.

This kind of Peter and Paul Principle might explain the Poverty Assessment Project's finding in Pakistan (World Bank 2004) that even though poverty levels of the population have continued to hover around 30 per cent (this steady figure is of course bad in itself, given that economic reform and TL are also supposed to be about eradicating poverty), the vulnerability of the lower socio-economic groups to falling into poverty has increased (Basu and Nolen 2004). What this combination of unchanged poverty and increased vulnerability means is that just as groups are now prone to become poor more easily than before, there are also groups that are enabled to lift themselves out of poverty more easily than before. If this were not the case, overall poverty levels too would increase with increased vulnerability. This implication surely deserves some further analysis, so that it can be exploited.

A Framework for Effective Advocacy

From a strategic point of view it is immaterial what the motives of the most ardent proponents of TL are. If the ethics of the TL pushers are troubling (as they most certainly are in many cases), it is a matter between them and God. For the activist interested in women's RH as fallout of TL, it is more important to try to analyse the various links in the relationship and then to push for policy that maximizes the positive links and weakens or even completely destroys the negative ones. As I have already tried to justify, policy efforts must be directed to the extent possible to the immediate/proximate determinants of RH rather than to more diffuse and more ambiguous influences on these proximate determinants.

First, a definition of RH. According to the WHO,

> Reproductive health is a state of physical, mental, and social well-being in all matters relating to the reproductive system at all stages of life. Reproductive health implies that people are able to have a satisfying and safe sex life and that they have the capability to reproduce and the freedom to decide if, when, and how often to do so. Implicit in this are the right of men and women to be informed and to have access to safe, effective, affordable, and acceptable methods of family planning of their choice, and the right to appropriate health-care services that enable women to safely go through pregnancy and childbirth. (WHO 1998)

The right-hand box in Figure 12.2 lays out the salient components of RH thus defined and the left-hand box lists the proximate determinants of these components. These proximate determinants are both biological and social, because the definition of RH goes beyond medical well-being. At the same time, they are the mediating variables through which larger processes like TL and women's employment and the restructuring of health programmes must operate.

If one were to collapse these proximate–proximate determinants, one might classify them into three groups:

1. user-friendly contraceptive services and advice, including abortion services and post-abortion care;
2. user-friendly health services for preventive and curative reproductive tract health and for safe pregnancy and delivery;
3. intra-household (and workplace) bargaining power to ensure non-coercive sexual relations and voluntary contraception and childbearing.

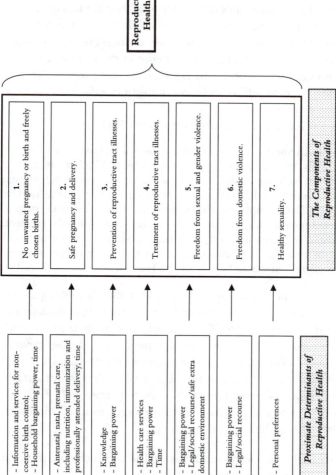

Figure 12.2 The components of reproductive health and their proximate determinants.

This classification might be considered to leave out one component of RH – that of healthy sexuality. I do this because it is partly captured by the notion of non-coercive and risk-free sexual relations and because the rest of what goes to define it is often a matter of personal preference – one man's poison is indeed another man's meat in this case.

It is to categories 1 and 2 that a state that determines macro-economic policy must be held directly responsible; state responsibility for 3 is likely to be more indirect – through the provision of legal and social safety provisions that accentuate or mitigate respectively the positive or negative implications of TL for women. There is a large (and sometimes contentious) literature on issues of female empower-ment, the determinants of intra-household bargaining power, the role of the state in these matters and so on, and I will not go into it here, except to add to RH advocacy efforts the effort to impose 'safer' con-ditions in the workplace as well as on the commute that frequently accompanies entry into the labour force. This question of 'safety' is integral to all provisions of RH care, even when it affects gender vio-lence rather than sexual violence. Indeed, it makes sense to substitute the idea of gender violence for sexual violence in our definitions of RH, because violence can be directed at women that is not overtly sexual but nevertheless harms RH.

One other role for the state and for the society that will never be pushed enough is the need to develop and promote more labour-saving domestic technology. So much of the literature on the possible adverse effects of economic restructuring focuses on the increased demands on women's time – for both paid and unpaid labour (see, e.g. Floro 1995 and the references within). At least some of the disappoint-ment about the 'double shift' of work that in effect working women are doing could be mitigated by cheap and safe technology to cut down the time spent on household maintenance tasks. And yet, except for much hyped occasional attempts to develop smokeless chullahs (stoves) or cheap pressure cookers (see Basu 2000), the need to save labour seems to be restricted to the wealthy in technology develop-ment. In any case, it is usually not even a matter of technology devel-opment, but of technology access – even something as non-technical as safe piped water could make enormous cuts in women's time and energy on household tasks, with implications for health in general as well as RH in particular.

Indeed, much more could be explored in the relationship between women's time use and their RH, including more research on the beneficial effects of time unproductively spent (i.e. on leisure activities) for reproductive and sexual health. These are not esoteric subjects of enquiry: they carry real implications for public services.

To move on, advocacy in the areas of categories 1 and 2 above is a full plate of work for anyone interested in promoting and protecting RH and reproductive rights as inalienable regardless of larger macroeconomic policies. But this is not to say that macroeconomic policy is not implicated. I would distinguish between two kinds of advocacy here, one of which is indeed intimately tied up with larger economic policy, although, as I now discuss, it need not be.

The two kinds of advocacy needed to press for RH as a right revolve around advocacy to put RH back in the middle of social policy and advocacy to make RH care 'access' a matter of economic policy. The two are not quite the same thing.

Advocacy for keeping RH in social policy

I refer here to the need to emphasize to the state and to the public that the work of guaranteeing reproductive health and reproductive rights is far from done. Just because the majority of states signed the Cairo document on Population and Development, it does not follow that they are now doing what needs to be done. It is not simply a matter of allocating resources for RH. It is a matter of ideology at a very basic level.

What is interesting is the common partial interpretation of the new paradigm of RH that the Cairo conference created. An important feature of that paradigm is the woman's (or couple's) right to decide freely on the number and timing of children. This right is now enshrined in all definitions of RH and is a call for the removal of state attempts to influence childbearing decisions and contraceptive use; that is, it is a call for childbearing decisions to be a matter of individual choice. But it is not a call for childbearing behaviors (by this I mean the accessing of resources to prevent births as well as go through safe pregnancies and deliveries) to become a matter of private responsibility alone.

And yet this is how many states seem to be interpreting the idea of reproductive freedom and rights – by washing their hands of the whole business. Thus, we have several reports of the Indian government, for example, giving up not only its old attachment to demographic and contraceptive use targets (although there is some disturbing evidence that there is some political rethinking on this issue now) but also its responsibility for providing safe and effective family planning services altogether. Women who need birth control information and services now either have to go to a private practitioner or seek the attention of family planning workers who are being increasingly diverted to other duties, if they are not being removed from their posts altogether. But reproductive freedom surely means the right not to have more than the desired number of births as much as the right not to have less than the number wanted.

Nowhere is this new climate of abdicating responsibility for RH better reflected than in the fact that RH does not even find a mention in the Millennium Development Goals that national governments agreed to work towards in 2000 (UNDP 2003; see Gillespie 2004). This does not bode well for family planning of course; in addition it has drastic implications for what states now feel obliged to do even in the matter of maternal and child health services and in the matter of diseases of the reproductive tract, including sexually transmitted diseases. This last seems to be significant now more and more only in the context of HIV/AIDS; but the fact that a range of debilitating and demeaning sexually transmitted infections do not result in certain death seems to be less important in any list of health priorities.

Advocacy for free and accessible RH services

This is certainly an area of macroeconomic policy, but it is not clear that this macroeconomic policy is necessarily tied up with issues of TL. If nothing else, the various trade agreements that members of the WTO have signed have nothing explicitly to say on the privatization of the health sector[10] (or any social sectors for that matter).

However, as several of the chapters in this volume document, the privatization of public services has been an important concomitant of economic liberalization in many countries. In the area of health care, the notion of user fees (a term that I had not heard of until some years ago and is now a part of social science vocabulary) seems to be debated only at the level of detail, not much in the context of whether user fees should exist at all. What Elson and Cagatay (2000) call the 'commodification bias' in macroeconomic policy seems to have infiltrated the social services with a vengeance. As Sen (1998) notes, a more legitimate economic ideology of 'financial conservatism' seems to have given way to a much less justifiable one of 'anti-deficit radicalism,' whereby an unmitigated and narrow-minded focus on zero inflation and zero budget deficits has come at the expense of major cutbacks in public services, and especially in public services that are provided without cost to the population.

Sen (1998) makes the necessary economic arguments against this trend. But there is nevertheless an advocacy role here that focuses not so much on the instrumental economic rationality of this new macro-economics but on the need for free and good RH services as an inalienable component of economic development success.

The question of whether the state increases its income through TL, given that it loses income through the lowering of tariffs and such, has been discussed in Grown, this volume; see also Winters et al. (2004). To the extent that it does, at least eventually (especially if TL spurs economic growth), it makes more sense to advocate that the extra national income that accrues through TL is allocated to support the new women workers as well as cushion those women/workers who lose out in the process. In the context of RH, this would mean advocacy for more and better RH services for all women, regardless of their changing fortunes with TL.

Such across-the-board access to good and free (or virtually free) state-provided RH care for all women also makes more operational sense than policy that passes on the liability for such health care to individual employers. This is so because so much of the new employment created by TL has no clear individual employer; it has been amply demonstrated that the increased employment of women that TL has spawned has tended to be contractual, home-based and irregular. While these are all conditions that need amelioration, that is a long-term goal and one which might in any case not do as much for RH as good and cheap state-provided health care services.

Finally, given the importance for RH of knowledge, and of bargaining power both within the household and in the workplace, it is worth adding that this description of the rationale for free and good-quality public health services also extends to the provision of free and good-quality services in education, both primary and secondary. There is probably no better guarantor of rights than a consciousness of rights and the political confidence to demand these rights. Besides economic power, the two contemporary influences on such consciousness seem to be education, and local and global consciousness raising efforts outside and inside the formal state system. Saying this of course brings me back to the point made towards the beginning of this chapter that it would be a mistake to underestimate the power of

REPRODUCTIVE HEALTH ADVOCACY 293

global interactions and alliances to foster human welfare and gender equality just as often as they can do the very opposite.

Conclusion

This chapter has tried to translate the difficult enterprise of advocacy into words. It is well aware that words are always easier than action and that it is all very well to suggest the kind of ground rules that have been suggested here. Actually putting these ideas into practice comes up against such formidable barriers of vested interests and resource constraints and real disagreement about priorities and means, that real-world advocacy is often finally left to be played by ear. The assumption in this chapter is that even the playing-it-by-ear role has something to gain by trying to keep a few rules of thumb in the background and so it has tried to formulate some such possible rules of thumb.

Notes

I am extremely grateful to the anonymous reviewers of this chapter for several useful suggestions. I wish to thank Deladem Kusi-Appouh for help with discussions and research, and Kaushik Basu and Arvind Panagariya for their help in clarifying some of my thoughts. I also learnt a lot from the other chapters of this book.

1. Some of these potential benefits need a different time perspective to be visible, especially if they are benefits related to ideology and attitudes, rather than immediate economic gain. Kelkar et al. (2004), for example, discuss the drastically changed meaning of female respectability or *samman* in Bangladesh today. Whereas in the past being respectable meant being economically unproductive and physically indoors, a decade and more of access to microcredit and employment in export industries has now made it legitimate and honourable for women to be mobile and to even own and buy land and gold in their own names.

2. The well-intentioned and scholarly Alan Guttmacher Institute–UNFPA report (Singh et al. 2004) on the non-medical benefits of investing in RH is an example of the efforts to focus on the instrumental value of RH. To my mind, such efforts have to contend with the possibility that more conservative viewpoints could choose either to play down these benefits or else discover some non-medical 'costs' to investments in RH services – safer access to sexual promiscuity, for instance. It makes much more strategic sense to treat RH as a non-negotiable right, regardless of its positive or negative instrumental value.

3. Such a stance also enables one to confront IMF statements (see Gupta et al. 1998, cited in Elson and Cagatay 2000) that the negative consequences of economic reform can be cushioned 'by "temporary" social safety nets to transfer income or protect consumption'.

4. Even in the specific context of women and structural adjustment, representatives of First World women have expressed as much concern as those from the developing countries (see, e.g. OECD 1994), once again suggesting that these are not merely North–South issues – the battle lines are much more ambiguous.

5. Even if the winds are not subversive, they can be refreshing and invigorating. I am tempted to quote on this matter the views of two of the otherwise vastly different leaders of modern India, Gandhi and Tagore.

   Gandhi: I do not want my house to be walled in on all sides and my windows to be stuffed. I want the cultures of all the lands to be blown about my house as freely as possible.

   Tagore: Where the world has not been broken up into fragments by narrow domestic walls; ... Into that heaven of freedom, my Father, let my country awake.

6. At least partly, this is because 'economic' globalization comes with baggage, however unwanted on all sides. This baggage is made up of the cultural, social and political globalization that economic globalization cannot shake off, and that have often very different implications for social and political change from the implications for direct economic policy.

7. 'Reform' is another example of the way language is co-opted in the marketplace of ideology. The positive connotations of the word make it popular both among proponents of open trade accompanied by regulation in other parts of the economy, such as in China and Vietnam, and among defenders of open trade with structural adjustment programmes involving privatization, fiscal restraint and tight monetary policy.

8. For example, they might be positive for the converse reasons for which the falling part of the U-shaped curve of women's share of the labour market with economic development was a cause of genuine concern in the literature of the 1960s and 1970s (which Cagatay and Ozler also refer to). I am particularly struck by the way in which Cagatay and Ozler's (1995) analysis interprets the positive relation between feminization and TL and between feminization and increasing income disparity with the same critical lens. While the latter (but even here, a distinction needs to be made between increasing disparity through increasing poverty and increasing disparity through different levels of income growth in different classes) is likely to represent greater female labour force participation for negative reasons, the same cannot be assumed about the former.

9. Whether globalization does indeed foster economic growth is of course also a matter for debate. See, for example, Rodrik (2001).

10. I make this assertion with some trepidation however. Given that the WTO is already prominent in non-trade areas like TRIPS, I may be

misjudging the future even if I am right about the present. I am also hesitant to comment on the present because, as the WTO web page informs one, the WTO rulebook 'runs to some 30,000 pages consisting of about 30 agreements and separate commitments (called schedules)' – I cannot think of a better example of hiding something in plain sight.

References

Basu, A.M. (2000) 'Women, Poverty and Demographic Change: Some Possible Interrelationships over Time and Space', in B. Garcia (ed.), *Women, Poverty and Demographic Change in Developing Countries*, Oxford: Clarendon Press.

Basu, K., and P. Nolen (2004) 'Vulnerability, Unemployment and Poverty: A New Class of Measures, its Axiomatic Properties and Applications', BREAD Working Paper No. 069, Cornell University, Department of Economics.

Cagatay, N., and S. Ozler (1995) 'Feminization of the Labor force: The Effects of Long-Term Development and Structural Adjustment', *World Development*, vol. 23, no. 11: 1883–94.

Davis, K., and J. Blake (1956) 'Social Structure and Fertility: An Analytic Framework', *Economic Development and Cultural Change*, vol. 9, no. 4: 211–35.

Elson, D., and N. Cagatay (2000) 'The Social Content of Macroeconomic Policies', *World Development*, vol. 28, no. 7: 1347–64.

Evers, B., and M. Juarez (2003) 'Understanding the Links: Globalization, Health Sector Reform, Gender and Reproductive Health', Women's Development – Reviews, A set of papers commissioned by the Ford Foundation's Reproductive Health Affinity Group (RHAG).

Floro, M.S. (1995) 'Economic Restructuring, Gender and the Allocation of Time', *World Development*, vol. 23, no. 11: 1913–29.

Gillespie, D.G. (2004) 'Whatever Happened to Family Planning and, for that Matter, Reproductive Health?', *International Family Planning Perspectives*, vol. 30, no. 1: 34–8.

Gupta, S., B. Clements, C. McDonald and C. Schiller (1998) The IMF and the Poor, Pamphlet Series No. 52, Washington, DC: Fiscal Affairs Department, IMF.

Hensman, R. (1996) 'Impact of Technological Change on Industrial Women Workers', Human Development Report, New York: UNDP.

Hensman, R. (2004) 'Globalization, Women and Work: What are we Talking About?', *Economic and Political Weekly*, vol. 39, no. 10: 1030–4.

Kelkar, G., D. Nathan and R. Jahan (2004) 'Redefining Women's "Samman": Microcredit and Gender Relations in Rural Bangladesh', *Economic and Political Weekly*, vol. 39, no. 32: 3627–40.

Mosley, W.H., and L.C. Chen (1984) 'An Analytical Framework for the Study of Child Survival in Developing Countries', *Population and Development Review*, vol. 10 (Suppl.): 25–48.

OECD (1994) *Women and Structural Change: New Perspectives*, Paris: OECD.

Rodrik, D. (2001) 'The Global Governance of Trade as if Development Really Mattered', New York: UNDP.

Sathar, Z. (2002) 'Trade Liberalization Impacts on Gender and Reproduction in Pakistan', Paper presented at the workshop on Trade Liberalization and Reproductive Health, Washington, DC: ICRW.

Sen, G. (1998) 'Human Development and Financial Conservatism', *World Development*, vol. 26, no. 4: 742–73.

Shah, N., S. Gothoskar, N. Gandhi and A. Chhachhi (1999) 'Structural Adjustment, Feminization of the Labor Force and Organizational Strategies', in N. Menon (ed.), *Gender and Politics in India*, 145–93, New Delhi: Oxford University Press.

Singh, J., and J.V. Meenakshi (2004) 'Understanding the Feminization of Agricultural Labor', Women in Agriculture and Rural Development, *Indian Journal of Agricultural Economics*, Supplement to vol. 59, no. 1: 1–17.

Singh, S., J.E. Darroch, M. Vlassoff and J. Nadaeu (2004) *Adding it Up: The Benefits of Investing in Sexual and Reproductive Health Care*, Washington, DC: The Alan Guttmachjer Institute and New York: UNFPA.

Swamy, G. (2004) 'International Trade and Women', *Economic and Political Weekly*, vol. 36, no. 45.

UNDP (2003) *Human Development Report 2003*, New York: Oxford University Press.

Winters, A., N. McCullogh and A. McKay (2004) 'Trade Liberalization and Poverty: The Evidence So Far', *Journal of Economic Literature*, vol. 42: 72–115.

World Bank (2004) *World Development Report 2004: Making Services Work for Poor People*. Available from: http://econ.worldbank.org/wdr/.

World Health Organization (1998) *Progress in Reproductive Health Research*, no. 45, Geneva: WHO.

About the Contributors

Sajeda Amin is a senior associate in the Policy Research Division of the Population Council. She works on family and gender issues in population and is currently involved in a multi-country study on adolescent livelihoods. She received a PhD in Demography and Sociology from Princeton University in 1988.

Alaka Malwade Basu is an associate professor in the Sociology Department and the director of the South Asia Program at Cornell University. She specializes in population studies, child health and mortality, reproductive health, women's studies, and culture and behaviour.

Elissa Braunstein is an assistant professor of economics at Colorado State University in Fort Collins. Her current research focuses on the relationship between foreign direct investment and gender inequality in China. She received her PhD from the Department of Economics at the University of Massachusetts in 2000.

Catalina A. Denman is an anthropologist, senior professor–researcher and current president, El Colegio de Sonora. She conducts research on working women, border health collaboration and reproductive health. She is the country editor for Mexico of *Medical Anthropology Quarterly*, Co-director of the Transborder Consortium for Research and Action in Gender and Health on the US Mexico Border and founding member of the NGO Red Fronteriza de Salud y Ambiente (Border Health and Environment Network). She holds a PhD in Social Sciences from El Colegio de Michoacan.

Nancy Gerein manages the research programme in reproductive health, and does teaching and consultancy in the areas of reproductive health, health systems development, and monitoring and evaluation at the Nuffield Center for International Health and Development. She holds a PhD in Health Care Epidemiology from the London School of Hygiene and Tropical Medicine and an MSc in Health Policy and Planning from the University of British Columbia in Canada.

Andrew Green is professor of international health planning and Head of the Nuffield Centre for International Health and Development. His primary research interests lie in health planning, health systems, health economics and non-government organizations. He holds a social sciences degree from Oxford University, an MA in Development Economics from the University of Sussex, and a PhD from Leeds University.

Caren Grown is co-director of the Gender Equality and the Economy Program at the Levy Economics Institute of Bard College and former director of the Poverty Reduction and Economic Governance Team at the International Center for Research on Women (ICRW). She has guest co-edited three special issues of *World Development* on macroeconomics, international trade and gender inequality, and has written widely on gender and development issues. Grown holds MA and PhD degrees in Economics from the New School University.

Sandya Hewamanne is an assistant professor of anthropology at Drake University, Des Moines, Iowa. Her work has been published in journals such as *Cultural Dynamics, Anthropology of Work Review* and *Feminist Studies*. She received her BA in Sociology from the University of Colombo, Sri Lanka, and her MA and PhD in Anthropology from the University of Texas at Austin.

Debra J. Lipson is a senior health researcher at Mathematica Policy Research, Inc., which conducts research to support decisions about current health and social policy problems. She specializes in studies on the financing and delivery of health care, health insurance and long-term care for vulnerable populations. She received her Masters in Health Services Administration (MHSA) from the University of Michigan School of Public Health.

Pranitha Maharaj is a research fellow at the School of Development Studies at the University of KwaZulu-Natal, Durban. Her main area of interest is reproductive health with specific focus on gender dynamics. She holds a PhD from the London School of Hygiene and Tropical Medicine and a Masters of Social Science in Sociology from the University of Natal, Pietermaritzburg.

Anju Malhotra is group director of Social and Economic Development at the ICRW. She leads ICRW's research in the areas of women's empowerment, adolescence, reproductive health and rights, migration, and programme evaluation. She holds a PhD in Sociology and Demography from the University of Michigan.

Priya Nanda is the director of Research at the Center for Health and Gender Equity (CHANGE), where she has developed a body of research on health sector reforms and reproductive health and rights. Her research focuses on globalization, health equity, and women's reproductive health and rights. She has a PhD in Public Health Economics from the School of Hygiene and Public Health, Johns Hopkins University, and MA degrees in International Affairs from the School of International and Public Affairs, Columbia University, and in Economics from the Delhi School of Economics.

Benjamin Roberts is a research specialist in the Human Sciences Research Council's Integrated Rural and Regional Development (IRRD) research programme and the Southern African Regional Poverty Network (SARPN) His research focuses on poverty and economic policy. He holds an MSc in Urban and Regional Planning from the University of Natal, Durban.

Yueping Song is a PhD candidate in Demography in the Sociology Department, Nankai University in China. Her interests are in gender, health and stratification studies. She holds an MA in economics from Nankai University.

Lin Tan is director and professor of the Women and Development Research Center at Nankai University. Tan has combined her academic work with research on women's employment, women's reproductive health and family planning. She received her PhD in Population Studies at Xian Jiaotong University in 1990.

Marceline White is deputy director of the Greater Access to Trade Expansion (GATE) project at Development & Training Services (DTS) in Washington, DC, and former director of the Global Trade Program at Women's Edge Coalition. She has written about many aspects of women and trade. White received her Master's in Public and International Affairs at the University of Pittsburgh's Graduate School of Public and International Affairs.

Zhenzhen Zheng is a research fellow at the Institute of Population and Labour Economics at the Chinese Academy of Social Sciences in Beijing. Currently, she is involved in research on youth, reproductive health and educational attainment. After receiving two MSc degrees, one in Medical Informatics from the University of Utah and another in Statistics from Brigham Young University, she completed a PhD in Demography at Beijing University in 2000.

Index